TENNIS
A PICTORIAL HISTORY
by Lance Tingay

Foreword by Jack Kramer

HASTINGS HOUSE

First published in U.S.A. in 1977 by
HASTINGS HOUSE, PUBLISHERS, INC.

First published 1973 under the title
History of Lawn Tennis in Pictures
Reprinted and updated 1977

This book was produced in Great Britain by
London Editions Ltd, 30 Uxbridge Road, London W12 8ND

Library of Congress Cataloging in Publication Data

Tingay, Lance, 1917–
    Tennis: a pictorial history.

    1. Tennis–History–Pictorial works. I. Title.
GV993.T55   796.34'2'09   76-51842
ISBN 0-8038-7167-8

Printed in Great Britain
by Chromoworks, Nottingham

Picture Credits   Mansell Collection pages 14 (top), 19, 20-21, 22, 23, 25 (top), 28 (top), 34, 40; Mary Evans Picture Library 14 (bottom), 15, 16, 17 (top), 24, 25 (bottom), 26, 27, 28 (bottom), 33; Freelance Photographers Guild 17 (bottom), 37, 56, 59 (bottom), 62 (left), 74 (top), 76 (top), 81 (bottom), 82 (bottom), 83; Radio Times Hulton Picture Library 32, 35, 47, 50, 51, 52, 60 (top right and bottom right), 62 (top right), 64, 65 (bottom), 70, 71 (centre and bottom), 72 (top), 76 (centre and bottom), 81 (top), 82 (top), 84 (top and bottom left), 90 (bottom), 91 (bottom), 93 (bottom), 96 (bottom left); Central Press 38, 58, 72 (bottom); H. Roger-Viollet 41, 73; Sport and General 46, 60 (left), 63 (left), 85 (right); Studio Editoriale 49, 80 (top); Culver Pictures Inc. 53, 59 (top), 61, 68, 79, 85 (bottom left), 98 (left); Syndication International 57 (top), 95 (bottom), 97 (bottom left), 99 (bottom left), 102 (right), 111 (left), 116, 117 (top), 120, 121, 124-5; Press Association 57 (bottom), 62 (bottom right), 65 (left), 71 (top), 93 (top); Topix 63 (right), 74 (bottom right), 75 (bottom), 77, 78, 80 (centre), 84 (bottom right), 85 (top left), 86, 87 (top), 92, 94 (top), 96 (top and bottom right), 97 (top and bottom right), 99 (top left), 102 (top left and bottom left), 103 (top), 104 (left), 109, 130; Tennis de France 65 (top right), 72 (bottom), 104 (top right), 105, 111 (right); Keystone 75 (top), 94 (bottom), 95 (top), 99 (top right), 107 (top), 110; Corriera dello Sport 87 (bottom); Fox Photos 98 (right); Camera Press 99 (bottom right), 104 (bottom right), Rivo Tournassi Tennis Club 106 (top); Signor Candi, Italian Federation of Tennis 106 (bottom); United Press 107 (bottom), 128; Coloursport 115, 126, 131, 132 (top right and bottom); Gerry Cranham 118, 119, 123, 127, 132 (top left), 134, 135, 137, 138, 139, 141, 142, 143; London Express News and Feature Service 129.

Contents

Foreword by Jack Kramer

One of the pleasures of having been so closely involved with the game of tennis over nearly half a century is the memories. Like all memories, the pleasanter predominate. The British think nostalgically of vicarage tennis parties, with graceful young girls in long skirts and young men in white flannels and blazers mouthing sweet nothings over cucumber sandwiches under the shade of great cedars on cloudless summer days. My memories are not quite like that. The world of first-class tennis and especially of professional tennis is a harder one. And in the United States I don't think we ever quite fell for that British dream.

But the memories are still sweet — of great matches and great players; of friends I have made and of travels all over the world; of triumphs and of surprises; and of the spectators, so varied in their reactions and their enthusiasm.

This is why I was so pleased to be asked to write this Foreword to Lance Tingay's book. Some of the players he writes about were legends before my time. But many have been at their peak during my lifetime, and most of these I have been lucky enough to watch, and many to know.

Reading his text and turning the pages of fine photographs, I have been struck by how much I have half-forgotten. Now, with this book, those memories are revived.

I wish it the success it deserves.

Key to Table of Results

showing their order on pages 145-168

WIMBLEDON CHAMPIONSHIPS
Men's Singles
Women's Singles
Men's Doubles
Women's Doubles
Mixed Doubles

Junior International Tournament
All England Plate
Veterans' Event

Major Events at Wimbledon (other than the
Championships)
Wimbledon Referees
Wimbledon Secretaries
Long Matches
Championships won from Match Point Down
Triple Wimbledon Champions
Singles Winners at their First Attempt

UNITED STATES CHAMPIONSHIPS
Men's Singles
U.S. Open Championships – Men's Singles
Women's Singles
U.S. Open Championships – Women's Singles
Men's Doubles
U.S. Open Championships – Men's Doubles
Women's Doubles
U.S. Open Championships – Women's Doubles
Mixed Doubles
U.S. Open Championships – Mixed Doubles

U.S. Championships won from Match Point Down

AUSTRALIAN CHAMPIONSHIPS
Men's Singles
Women's Singles
Men's Doubles
Women's Doubles
Mixed Doubles

Australian Championships won from Match Point
Down

FRENCH CHAMPIONSHIPS
Men's Singles
Women's Singles
Men's Doubles
Women's Doubles
Mixed Doubles

French Championships won from Match Point Down

ITALIAN CHAMPIONSHIPS
Men's Singles
Women's Singles
Men's Doubles
Women's Doubles
Mixed Doubles

OTHER CHAMPIONSHIPS
Davis Cup
Federation Cup
Galea Cup
Annie Soisbault Cup
King of Sweden's Cup
Virginia Slims Champions
Wightman Cup
W.C.T. Champions

An A–Z of Players Mentioned

The Genesis of a Sport—

Le chasteau du Louvre

Life for many people in the England of 1873 was still easy and spacious, with income tax a few pence in the pound, the purchase of army commissions not long abolished, and on £500 a year a man could live like a gentleman.

In December of that year a country gentleman drove along a lonely road in Wales towards Oswestry. Major Walter Clopton Wingfield was forty-years old, a former captain in the First Dragoon Guards, a magistrate for the county of Montgomeryshire and one of the honourable corps of Gentlemen-at-Arms at the court of Queen Victoria. He had come from his seat at Rhysnant Hall, a few miles from Llandysilio, and was bound for a house party at Nantclwyd Hall in Denbighshire. His luggage was particularly bulky, for as well as the usual trunk there was also a curious wooden box.

A few days later, in the morning room at Nantclwyd Hall, it was obvious that the house party was beginning to drag. The hostess was becoming decidedly anxious, for her satiated guests would not respond to her bright suggestions of a ride on a beautiful morning, or a game of charades. Desperately she asked them if any of them had any ideas and at that moment, so the story has it, Major Wingfield suggested a new game called Sphairistike which he described as a kind of tennis played out of doors.

Fascinated out of their weary sophistication the guests demanded to know how to play, Major Wingfield, by a happy coincidence, was able to find exactly what they all needed: the rackets and balls were in his car, and a little booklet, which he had just happened to have printed, was in his trunk. Moreover he had noticed the day before a bit of ground near the stables which would do very well. This is one story of how lawn tennis began its life in the private

left *A game of La Paume. This medieval woodcut shows a game similar to tennis before the invention of the racket. The balls were made of wool or animal hair and covered in sheepskin.*

below left *Le Château du Louvre, Paris, in the fourteenth century. The two Emplacements des Jeux de Paume are marked 0.*

right *A section of an early seventeenth-century drawing of Windsor Castle, which shows the tennis court in the moat below the Round Tower.*

THE HIGH BORNE PRINCE IAMES DVKE OF YORKE.

borne October = the 13. 1633.

M.Merian.1

above *At the age of two, in 1552, Charles IX of France was probably the youngest junior champion in history.*

left *James, Duke of York, the future James II of England, playing tennis in 1641 at the age of eight. The court was probably in Whitehall, London.*

right *The tennis court and tennis racket in use in 1659. With a change to the net, these players might be anticipating the modern training method of three-somes.*

below right *A tennis match in France in the seventeenth century. Both the court and the galleries seem crowded by modern standards.*

gardens and vicarage lawns in the England of the 1870s.

Major Wingfield was awarded the M.V.O. in 1902 and he died in April 1912 in his eightieth year. During his lifetime a public subscription was made in his honour, and he was presented with £200 and a gold watch in recognition of his pioneer efforts for lawn tennis. His bust may be seen in the council chamber of the Lawn Tennis Association in London.

However, having paid one's respects to Major Wingfield, one must now take away some of the glory. For lawn tennis, like cricket and football and golf, was less of an invention than an evolution. Edgbaston, a suburb of Birmingham, is seen by many people as the birth-place of lawn tennis, and in fact the people of Edgbaston see the major as something of an upstart. They worship different gods: Major T. H. Gem and Mr J. B. Perera. These gentlemen were cradling lawn tennis while the then Captain Walter Clopton Wingfield was dragooning his guards on Wimbledon common.

In 1858, indeed, Major Gem and Mr Perera had marked an Edgbaston lawn as a tennis court. Many of the adjuncts to the venerable game of tennis (now often referred to as real tennis, royal tennis or court tennis to distinguish it from its monstrously grown child properly to be called lawn tennis on whatever surface it is played) had necessarily to be discarded. Penthouses, dedans, sidewalls, tambour and such like cannot be transferred to a lawn. The floor chases, those markings across the real tennis court so puzzling to the uninitiated, could be and were abandoned.

For twelve months this game thrived on Edgbaston turf until 1870, when a move was made to Leamington and the lawns of the Manor House Hotel. There, to this day, a plaque records that 'On this lawn in 1872 the first lawn tennis club in the world was founded.'

The name lawn tennis to some degree explains itself. It is tennis played on a lawn. Originally it was played on nothing else. It is, of course, also played on many other surfaces including clay, wood, cement and synthetic carpet, both in and out of doors, but the game is strictly 'lawn tennis' no matter what the surface. Again 'tennis', in strict usage, can only refer to the venerable game from which lawn tennis was derived.

King Henry VIII was tennis champion of England – who would have dared beat him? – and it was an old game even then. It was played by hitting a ball over a net inside an enclosed stone courtyard and is still played today, though

far left *A racket-maker of the seventeenth century. This French print shows a member of the Guild of Racket and Brushmakers.*

above *Raymond Masson, a famous French professional who was acknowledged champion from about 1765 to 1785. His wife was notorious for her bad court behaviour.*

left *A French gentleman of the eighteenth century, with one of the early rackets.*

below *Jacques Edmund Barre, another famous Frenchman. He was world tennis champion from 1829 to 1862.*

An open rackets court of the mid-nineteenth century. It would have been about 60 foot long and 40 foot wide with a front wall of about 45 foot high. Open courts for rackets were popular in Ireland, but the game never seriously rivalled the enclosed court. The open rackets court, however, clearly influenced those nineteenth-century pioneers who took tennis out of doors. The front wall need only be replaced by a net and the court extended on the other side in order to become a (lawn) tennis court.

as a minor sport, and often called 'court tennis', 'real tennis', or 'royal tennis'.

Tennis enthusiasts often played their game out of doors. Yet their efforts to do so on the fine green turf of England must have been far from satisfactory, for it happens that the real tennis ball, made of tightly compressed rags within a woollen cover, is singularly inelastic. Its bounce is sufficient on a stone floor but on grass it will hardly come up at all.

The adaptation of tennis to grass was not a practicality until the rubber ball came into use in the Victorian era. Then, as tennis was taken out of doors, it took its ancient scoring with it.

The terms 'fifteen' for one point, 'thirty' for two and 'forty' for three, puzzle the uninitiated. It seems likely that this came about by recording the progress of the rallies (called 'rests' in real tennis) on a simple clock face by the court. On winning a rally a player would have his pointer moved through one quarter, that is to the fifteenth minute division. The second point would take him another quarter, that is on to thirty. Then it moved to the three-quarter mark, or forty-five and it was only during the eighteenth century that the convention arose of abbreviating 'forty-five' to 'forty'. The full circle of the pointer marked the end of the game. The contest was 'set' to comprise so many games.

Pioneering honours in lawn tennis belong to two men: Major Harry Gem and Major Walter Clopton Wingfield. They were the enthusiasts whose initial efforts wooed the bright young things of Victorian days from croquet on the vicarage lawn to the more strenuous lawn tennis. It was Wimbledon that transformed a social pastime into a major international sport.

A roller, designed to be drawn by horse or pony, stands behind the stop netting on the north side of the Centre Court at Wimbledon, its long,

An Australian family group of the late nineteenth century illustrates the early popularity of the game. The oldest championship in Australia is that of the State of Victoria, which was first held in 1879, only two years after the first meeting at Wimbledon.

*Women's Lib on the
vicarage lawn. As a social
pastime lawn tennis soon
rivalled croquet in the 1870s.
Despite the more strenuous
nature of the game, women
made their mark from the
very beginning.*

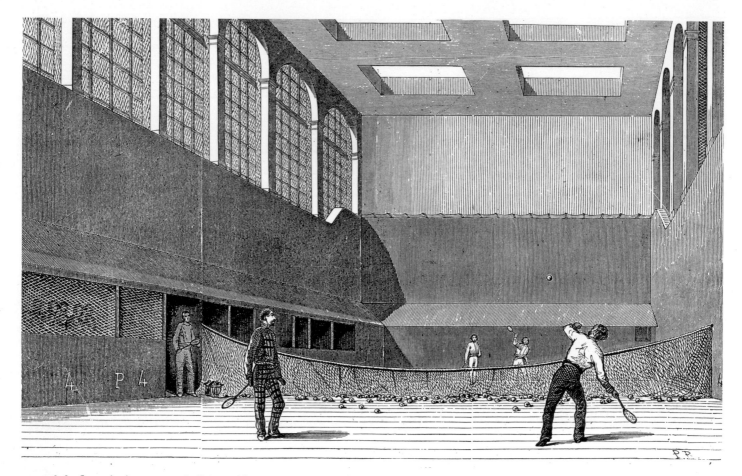

The last game of real tennis played at the Passage Cendrier, Paris. The court was demolished in 1861.

curved shafts pointing upwards. It is a wide roller, so wide indeed, that having been used to level the immaculate turf while the new All England Club was being built in 1922, there is now no way of taking it out of the arena. All the exits are too narrow. In pictures of the old Centre Court at Worple Road, Wimbledon, the same roller may be seen in the corner. It first appeared in 1869 when Mr J. W. Walsh, one of the founders of the All England Club, presented it on the understanding that his daughter would be made an honorary life member.

Had it not been for this pony roller there would probably not have been the Wimbledon Lawn Tennis Championships, and without Wimbledon, the first tournament in the world, the sport of lawn tennis would almost certainly have been different from what it is today.

For it happened that in 1877 the All England Club, founded as a croquet club, was short of money. One major need was to repair that very same pony roller and it was suggested that funds could be raised by staging a lawn tennis championship. With a profit of ten pounds the

above *Tennis on ice in 1876,
as illustrated by Du Maurier
in* Punch.

right *Tennis at sea played
on board the* Serapis.

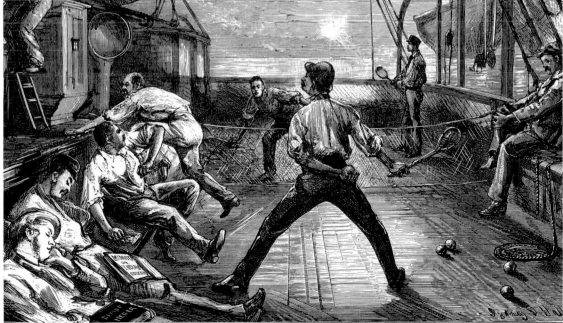

A match at the New Lawn Tennis Club. This drawing of the 1880s emphasizes the family nature of the sport.

pony roller was repaired and Wimbledon never looked back.

The All England Club itself was born on 24 July 1868, when Whitmore Jones, his cousin Henry Jones and two other croquet enthusiasts met in the office of J. W. Walsh, editor of *The Field,* to explore the possibility of starting a croquet club. Five pounds was raised to finance the search for a suitable ground.

The search took more than a year. The Crystal Palace at Sydenham was approached, but the proprietors of the great showpiece of the age were not interested. Nor was the Princes Club in Hans Place, Knightsbridge. In Regent's Park, the Royal Toxopholites spurned the notion that their archery should be mixed with croquet. Six acres were available in Holland Park, but the rent of £500 per annum caused the five-man committee to shudder.

At Wimbledon there was a site of four acres

By the end of the nineteenth century lawn tennis was being taken seriously by the fashion designers. Both pictures are taken from La Mode Illustrée *of 1899. One can see how the hats inhibited an overhead service.*

left *L'embarras de richesses: Young Robinson (mentally):*
'O would I were a ball
That I might fly – to all.'

below left *Trials of an umpire at a ladies' doubles (1884):*
Lilian and Claribel: 'It was out, wasn't it, Captain Standish?'
Adeline and Eleanor: 'Oh, it wasn't out, Captain Standish, was it?'

right *Major Walter Clopton Wingfield, MVO. He was not the first to take real tennis out of doors, but he was the first to sell it to the general public.*

just off Worple Road, adjacent to the London and South Western Railway. The rent was £50 a year, which would increase to £100. The five men raised £600 between them, closed the deal and arranged for laying out the ground at a cost of £425. By the end of the year a pavilion had been built and the All England Croquet Club was in being. In 1870 a croquet championship was staged.

Henry Jones was a popular sports writer of his day under the pen name of 'Cavendish' and Walsh, in fact, was one of his editors. Always a keen innovator, Henry Jones proposed in 1875 that part of the grounds should be devoted to the new fangled game of lawn tennis and £25 was allocated for the necessary equipment. It rapidly began to supplant croquet as the main interest of the members.

Expanding activities brought some financial strain. It seemed a good idea then, when at a committee meeting in the spring of 1877, Mr Walsh proposed holding a Lawn Tennis Championship open to all comers. Mr B. C. Evelegh, one of the most prominent croquet players in the club, seconded the motion, and Mr Walsh persuaded the proprietors of *The Field* to present a silver challenge cup worth twenty-five guineas.

There was much spade work to be done before the first Lawn Tennis Championship could take place. The first task was to settle the rules of the game, and a committee comprising Henry Jones, Julian Marshall and C. G. Heathcote were deputed to do so. Both Marshall and Heathcote were 'real tennis' enthusiasts, and their joint work was to shape the game as we know it today.

At that time there were almost as many codes as there were players. Major Gem at the Leamington Club used tennis scoring, but Major Wingfield preferred a method derived from rackets, each game consisting of fifteen points up with only the 'hand in' server being able to score. Major Gem favoured a rectangular court. Major Wingfield's patent had court boundaries in the shape of an hourglass.

An effort to bring order out of chaos had been made in 1875, when the Marylebone Cricket Club, by virtue of its authority as the governing body of real tennis and rackets, convened a public meeting to try to settle standard rules for lawn tennis. But these M.C.C. rules were devised in a spirit of British compromise. They were not binding and could be altered in accordance with the capabilities of the players. The court was shaped as an hourglass: 78 feet long, 30 feet wide

at the base, 24 feet in the middle. The net was a formidable 5 feet at the sides, 4 feet at the centre. The service line was 26 feet from the net, delivery being made with one foot outside the baseline according to the rules of Mr J. H. Hales. His further suggestion that the ball must bounce twice within the court, for the sake of the fair sex whose dress prevented them running backwards and forwards, was rejected. Scoring was as in rackets, with deuce at fourteen points each. By and large the efforts of the M.C.C. to standardise the game failed.

It mattered little while lawn tennis remained a friendly game and club visitors merely had to enquire about the local variations of the rules. But a cup worth twenty-five guineas altered matters, for competitors paying one guinea entry fee had a right to know exactly what to expect.

Messrs Jones, Marshall and Heathcote laid down the rules that have held, except for minor changes, ever since. They decreed that the court should be rectangular: 78 feet by 27 feet. Tennis scoring was adopted. But for this last decision it is doubtful whether the game would have grown into the major spectator sport it is now. There is nothing logical about tennis scoring and presumably no-one could have invented it out of the blue. It is the division into points, games and sets which means that every match is full of recurring crises, all adding to the dramatic element in the conflict.

The Championship meeting of 1877 differed from its modern counterpart in that the net was 5 feet at the post and 3 feet 3 inches at the centre. The service line was 26 feet from the net. What is now a let ball on service was considered good, though two deliveries were allowed and a fault could not be taken. The dimensions of the ball were much the same as today but it was lighter, the limits being set between one and a quarter and one and a half ounces.

There was only one event, the men's singles. The winner was awarded the Gold Champion prize, value twelve guineas, together with the Silver Challenge Cup presented by *The Field*. There was a second prize of silver worth seven guineas, a third prize worth three guineas. It was open to all amateurs and scheduled to take place from Monday 9 July to Thursday 12 July, with play adjourned over Friday and Saturday in order not to conflict with the important social occasion of the Eton and Harrow cricket match at Lord's. In the event, the timetable did not work out, and the final was rescheduled for Monday

16 July. That did not go to plan either and the final was actually played on Thursday 19 July starting at 4.30 p.m. Over the years Wimbledon has not done badly for weather but it did not promise well in 1877.

Despite the bad weather there were enough spectators, at one shilling a head, to ensure the success the promoters had hoped for. The profit of ten pounds was held to be satisfactory enough to allow them to look ahead to 1878; though hardly to the 1960's when £50,000 was the sort of figure taken for granted. The gate for the final day was 200, and they were thrilled by Spencer W. Gore's heavily spliced underarm service which drew his opponent out of position before he closed up to the middle of the net. Gore was twenty-seven when he beat twenty-two competitors to become Wimbledon champion in 1877, and he died in 1906. He beat H. T. Gillson 6–2 6–0 6–3 in the first round, Montague Hankey 6–4 6–4 6–2 6–1 in the third. In the semi-final he beat C. G. Heathcote 6–2 6–3 6–2, and in the final W. Marshall by 6–1 6–2 6–4.

A total of 601 games were played at this first Wimbledon championship, the exact figure was noted down because a topic that has echoed over the years, the undue preponderance of service, occupied the attention of enthusiasts even then. Henry Jones worked out that of these 601 games, 376 were won by the server and 225 by the receiver, a proportion of five to three. When the most closely contested sets were compared the proportion was nine to five. The server at that date had an obvious advantage, but a comparable modern figure would be nine to one.

Tennis Grows Up–

The name of Spencer W. Gore will endure as the first champion of Wimbledon and one would like to picture him as a whole-hearted enthusiast for the game in which he played so famous a role. He was nothing of the sort. In 1890 he wrote:

'. . . it is its want of variety that will prevent lawn tennis in its present form from taking rank among our great games. . . . That anyone who has played really well at cricket, tennis or even rackets, will ever seriously give his attention to lawn tennis, beyond showing himself to be a promising player, is extremely doubtful: for in all probability the monotony of the game as compared with the others would choke him off before he had time to excel in it.'

Spencer Gore was an old Harrovian, a rackets player and devotee of real tennis. P. F. Hadow, the winner of Wimbledon's second meeting in 1878, was also an old Harrovian, a rackets man and a good cricketer besides. His outlook towards lawn tennis was not basically different from that of Gore. In 1878 he was on leave from the coffee plantations of Ceylon and apparently he took up lawn tennis in much the same way as an adult might take up tiddley-winks with children. Having won the championship he returned to Ceylon, never played lawn tennis again and never even witnessed a first class match until he

The first important championship in which two women took part was the Irish meeting in Dublin in 1879 which was won by May Langrishe. The women's singles at Wimbledon in 1884, depicted here, was played after the men's events had finished.

The twenty-year-old William Renshaw (right) playing against the thirty-year-old Herbert Lawford in the Wimbledon semi-final of 1881. Renshaw won 1–6 6–3 6–2 5–6 6–3 and went on to take the first of his record seven singles titles.

came back to Wimbledon in 1926 for the jubilee celebrations.

Despite the iconoclastic attitude of Gore and Hadow, those early meetings now have much fascination. There was a touch of ruthlessness about Gore. He won because he came up to the net and volleyed, even to the extent of reaching over the net. Since the net was five feet high at the sides and only three feet three inches at the centre, fast passing shots down the lines were out of the question and Gore had everything his own way. In 1877 lobbing was unheard of and Gore's net rushing technique provoked criticism.

Lobbing was the inspiration of Hadow. In the challenge round against Gore he was at first nonplussed by this opponent who was darting about at the net. To add to his troubles he was

beset by some oriental fever and had a raging headache. Whether despite or because of this he had the brainwave of tossing the ball over Gore's head. No-one had done it before and there was no smash in Gore's repertoire. Hadow won 7–5 6–1 9–7, advantage sets being played in the challenge match.

A. T. Myers played at Wimbledon in 1878, and his name should be written in gold. Whether he was the first to serve overhead I know not, but he was the first to do so at Wimbledon. Previously all services were either underarm or played like a drive from the level of the waist. The example of Myers changed this pattern within a few years, and when one considers the sharp shooters of the game such as W. T. Tilden, Maurice McLoughlin, Ellsworth Vines and Geoff Brown,

left *The youngest ever Wimbledon champion: Lottie Dod. She was only fifteen years and ten months when she took the first of her five singles titles in 1887, and was never beaten at Wimbledon. She was also an international golf and hockey player.*

right *The most famous lawn tennis twins playing against each other: William versus Ernest Renshaw in the Wimbledon challenge round of 1882. William won 6–1 2–6 4–6 6–2 6–2. The artist claimed that this scene depicted the final set; it appears to have been a singularly awkward rally.*

Myers must be awarded the laurels of the pioneer.

The Harrovian tradition continued. The 1879 winner, Canon J. T. Hartley, also came from that school and, as befitted his cloth and the association of the game with the vicarage lawn, he was more enthusiastic than his predecessors. Since Hadow was tending his coffee plants there was no challenge round and Hartley gained the title by winning the all-comers' singles. Before doing so, he had to return to his Yorkshire living, perform his Sunday duties and depart before breakfast the next day in order to be at Wimbledon by two o'clock on the Monday.

Hartley won the final against 'St Leger' scoring 6–2 6–4 6–2, the loser having won his native Irish title in Dublin not long before. Here one must record the facts in the tragic case of 'St Leger', the only notable player, certainly the only Wimbledon finalist convicted for murder.

'St Leger' was Vere Thomas St Leger Goold, born in 1853. His elder brother inherited a baronetcy, though the family seems to have come down in the world for at the time of Vere's trial he was reported to be working as a railway ganger in Australia. It seems that in August 1907 Vere Goold and his French wife, formerly Mlle

Violet Girodin, were out of money and out of luck in Monte Carlo. Precisely what occurred was never made clear, but it is certain that the jewels owned by a Danish widow, Mme Emma Levin, offered to the Goolds a way of getting out of their monetary difficulties and that in the endeavour to bring about this desirable state of affairs they found themselves with a body on their hands. On 6 August they arrived at Nice railway station and asked for their two trunks to be sent to England, but the condition of the trunks was such that railway officials had no hesitation in detaining them and calling the police. When the trunks were opened the dismembered and decaying remains of the unfortunate Mme Levin were disclosed.

Goold and his wife were tried in Monte Carlo and the erstwhile Wimbledon finalist made a brave attempt to shoulder all the blame; but his viewpoint was not shared by the court. Mrs Goold was sentenced to death, Goold to life imprisonment. The death sentence was subsequently remitted to penal servitude for life and Mrs Goold was sent to prison at Montpellier where she died in 1914. Goold was sent to Devil's Island in April 1908 and died there in September 1909.

The Wimbledon Championships of 1880 were again won by Hartley when he beat the challenger H. F. Lawford. One of the early writers on lawn tennis, Lieutenant Colonel R. D. Osborne, recorded the match. Lawford had an impressive topspin forehand, whipping the ball with an exaggerated action that began with the racquet hanging almost vertically from his hand. Standing in the left court he hit obliquely across the net while Hartley stood his ground, holding the onslaught on his backhand with a cut return. Defence prevailed over attack.

Modern lawn tennis had been born the year before when the twins William and Ernest Renshaw played in their local tournament at Cheltenham, William beating the unfortunate St. Leger in the final. In 1880 William won the Irish title, then as hard a tournament as Wimbledon. In the same year he and his brother won the All England Doubles championship at Oxford which had been founded twelve months before.

At Wimbledon in 1880 both Renshaws, competing there for the first time, lost to O. E. Woodhouse, of whom more will be said when dealing with the early game in America. The Renshaws were then kindling the flame that has

The US Championship at the Newport Casino, Rhode Island, in 1896. Robert D. Wrenn won the third of his four titles when he avenged his defeat of the previous year by beating Fred H. Hovey 7–5 3–6 6–0 1–6 6–1 in the challenge round. Wrenn was more renowned for his athleticism than for his finesse, and at Harvard he shone at football, hockey and baseball.

not since been extinguished. Until they came lawn tennis was a pastime. They made it a sport.

The next decade was dominated by these two brilliant and spectacular players, both perfect sportsmen. The era of pat ball was over. The Renshaw smash was famous throughout their lifetime and beyond. The late H. S. Scrivener, one of the greatest critics of the game, still spoke with awe of the Renshaw smash in the late 1930s. Renshaw volleying was equally famous. They volleyed, not like Spencer Gore with racquet poised half way over the net, but from near the service line. They volleyed deep and hard and were invulnerable to lobbing.

The last resistance to the old style crumbled to the Renshaw attack in 1881. At Oxford they won the doubles for the second time. At Wimbledon, William Renshaw, after five sets against Lawford in the semi-final and three sets against R. T. Richardson in the final, burst into the challenge round and blasted through the vicarage lawn defence of Hartley with the loss of only three games. Such an annihilating victory in the last match was not recorded again for fifty-five years.

Colonel Osborne compiled what was probably the first ranking list in the autumn of 1881. It ran:

1 W. Renshaw
2 H. F. Lawford and R. T. Richardson
4 O. E. Woodhouse
5 E. Renshaw
6 E. Lubbock
7 J. T. Hartley

All seven, he stated, were well ahead of any rivals.

The Renshaws taught Britain, and eventually the world, to play modern lawn tennis. The records show that William was probably a greater player than Ernest. Having won the Wimbledon singles in 1881, William kept the title for six years until 1887 when an injured arm kept him out. His record was unsullied by defeat in that period, for when the doubles championship moved to Wimbledon in 1884, he and Ernest collected that title as well.

William, incidentally, was 20 years 6 months old when he won his first Wimbledon championship, the third youngest to have done so. Wilfred Baddeley was younger than he at 19 years and 5 months when he won in 1891, and Sidney B. Wood, 19 years and 8 months, won in 1931.

Most of the older writers' who knew the brothers personally, agree that Ernest could have been the better player had he had the ambition. When he did play his brother, which was rarely and then reluctantly, he never gave of his best.

Both were fine stylists, easy and graceful, but William darted about the court like a terrier. By contrast Ernest was restrained, even lethargic, but his manner belied his real quality for he was a superb retriever and, when pressed, had the quick and effortless movement of a panther.

Ernest won the Wimbledon singles only once, in 1888. That year William, after his absence the year before, lost to W. J. Hamilton, an Irishman with a fine running forehand who was known, because of his frail appearance, as 'The Ghost'. Ernest, provoked by this slight to the family honour, promptly demolished Hamilton in the semi-final and went on to win in the challenge round against Lawford, his conqueror twelve months before in the all-comers' final. Renshaw domination was thus resumed and in 1889 William won the title from his twin. The swan-song of Renshaw greatness came in 1890. Hamilton took the championship from William, who, having led two sets to one, tired and was overwhelmed.

The 1880s were halcyon years for lawn tennis and for Wimbledon in particular. At a cost of half-a-crown big crowds flocked to see the Renshaws, both charming personalities, and the crowd at Worple Road almost rivalled Lord's as an attraction for the fashion and society of those palmy days.

The game flourished throughout the country. The Scottish championships had started in 1878, the Irish meeting in 1879 and the Cheltenham tournament in the same year. The Northern Lawn Tennis Association was formed in 1880. In 1881 the Oxford and Cambridge match began, the Midland counties championships at Edgbaston and tournaments at Bath and Exmouth. The North of England championships started in 1884, the Welsh championships, the covered court championships and the Buxton tournament in 1885. The Kent championships at Beckenham started in 1886.

During these years the All England Club was the game's authority, and though nominally the rules were the joint concern of the club and the M.C.C. the latter body had, inevitably, less and less to do with a sport in which it had no direct concern. In 1883 a club conference was instituted by the All England Club, in 1888 legislative functions were gracefully relinquished to the newly formed Lawn Tennis Association, a democratic body that has flourished over the years. The prime movers in the founding of the L.T.A. were H. S. Scrivener and G. W. Hillyard and the inaugural meeting of what was then

above *May Sutton of California, the first overseas player to win Wimbledon. In 1905, at the age of eighteen, she exploited her topped forehand drive to win the women's singles at her first attempt. It was the first of three successive challenge rounds against the British player Dorothea Douglass, who had her revenge in 1908, but who was again beaten by Miss Sutton in 1907.*

right *Norman E. Brookes of Australia, the first man from overseas to win at Wimbledon, and one of the 'greats' of the game. He was twenty-nine when he won the first of his two singles titles, in 1907. He used the same grip for both his forehand and backhand.*

called the National Lawn Tennis Association was held on 28 January at the Freemasons' Tavern in London. The first president was William Renshaw. The total income for the first year was forty-five pounds seven shillings, a hundredth of what is now spent on postage, telegrams and telephones.

There were three landmarks between the birth of lawn tennis and 1890. The first two have already been dealt with, the Renshaws and the foundation of the L.T.A. The third was – women. They had played from the very beginning but were not allowed, at first, to take part in the Championships.

The Fitzwilliam Club, Dublin, was the first to give women the honours which were their due, and the Irish Championships had its women's singles event from the start in 1879. The first winner was May Langrishe, a pioneer whose name should be honoured. It is difficult to know now how good she was or what style she affected, but she gained her native title three times in all and partnered Lottie Dod for the hat trick in the All England women's doubles at Buxton.

The first woman champion at Wimbledon was Maud Watson in 1884 when, in the final, she beat her sister Lilian 6–8 6–3 6–3. She was one of the first women players to create a tradition of invincibility. Her initial adventure into an open tournament was at Edgbaston in 1881 and, between that time and June 1886 when at Bath she lost to the prodigious Miss Dod, she was undefeated. She had an easy stylish game, could volley well and in six years as queen of the game she played fifty-five matches and yielded only eleven sets.

Miss Dod was more than a fine lawn tennis player. She was probably the outstanding woman athlete of the nineteenth century. She was only fourteen when she checked the unbeaten record of Maud Watson and she won at Dublin and at Wimbledon the next year. She was never defeated at Wimbledon, winning in 1887, 1888, 1891, 1892 and 1893, and was hard pressed only once during the challenge round of her last year by Mrs Hillyard.

She was nimble, graceful and with that knack of easy timing which gives a deceptive pace of shot. Her forehand drive was a terror to all opponents as were her volleying and smashing, rare strokes then in a woman's repertoire. She enjoyed aggressive play and when, in 1939, she saw Alice Marble she did not hesitate to declare her the greatest woman player of all time, rating

left *The Doherty brothers: Reggie on the left, Laurie on the right. They dominated lawn tennis for a decade from 1897 to 1906, during which time Reggie won the Wimbledon singles four times and Laurie five. Laurie was the first overseas victor in the US singles in 1903 and was never beaten in the Davis Cup. Their skill and personality revived the game which had begun to lose some of its initial popularity.*

The courts in Hamburg in the early 1900s. The first German championships were staged in 1892, and until World War I overseas players dominated the meeting. Clarence Hobart was the men's singles champion in 1899, but no other American won the men's singles again until Budge Patty in 1953.

her above Helen Wills and Suzanne Lenglen.

It is a source of pride to Britain that the first lawn tennis champion of America was an Englishman, O. E. Woodhouse. This statement is made in spite of the fact that the records show Richard Sears as the first title holder in 1881.

The game came to the United States via Bermuda. In the early spring of 1874 the British garrison in Bermuda had equipped itself with Major Wingfield's patent. May Ewing Outerbridge played enthusiastically and when she returned to New York she carried a set of 'Sticky' with her. Her brother A. Emilius Outerbridge helped her set up a court in the grounds of the Staten Island Cricket and Baseball Club.

A court was also laid down at the home of William Appleton at Nahant, a suburb of Boston in August 1874. Dr James Dwight and F. R. Sears, elder brother of Richard Sears, played there, to the reputed amazement of the local inhabitants who, hearing of the new British game, watched it under the impression it was cricket. For the next few years lawn tennis was played sporadically in New England with balls and equipment differing from one place to another. A club tournament was held at Nahant in August 1876. It was a handicap event and both finalists, Dr Dwight and F. R. Sears, were on the scratch mark. Dwight won 12–15 15–7 15–13.

The first open meeting was staged at the Staten Island Club in September 1880. It was advertised and a letter was received from O. E. Woodhouse in Chicago saying he was a member of the West Middlesex Club in England and could he please take part? Woodhouse was no tyro. Only two months before at Wimbledon he had beaten both William and Ernest Renshaw, each by three sets to one, before losing to Lawford in the all-comers final. He is believed to be the originator of the smash.

The event for which Woodhouse was accepted was the Championship of America. His debut was sensational. He served overhead, a method not seen before in the United States, and though James Rankine held this phenomenal performer to a close match in the opening round all further opposition crumpled until the final. In that match Woodhouse was hard pressed by the Canadian J. F. Helmuth. At the end the score, in terms of

Arthur Wentworth Gore in action in 1908. A steady baseliner, Gore was not only the oldest Wimbledon singles champion – he was forty-one when he won it for the third time in 1909 – but also one of the game's most zealous proponents. He first played at Wimbledon in 1888 and competed every year until 1927. He died at the age of sixty in 1928.

Woodhouse, was 15–11 14–15 15–9 10–15, two all in terms of sets, but a winning margin for the Englishman on the tally of 54 games to 50.

So Woodhouse was the first Champion of America and nothing can gainsay the fact. The assumption of the title by the Staten Island Tournament was perfectly reasonable. There was then no national association and, as the first open tournament in the field, it was logical to hold the winner as the best in the country.

There is no suggestion that this overseas victory rankled with the American pioneers, though after the first official national championship under the sponsorship of the U.S.L.T.A. in 1881 the entry was restricted to American citizens, a ban lasting until 1885. Incidentally, after Richard Sears had won the first official title he played an Englishman J. J. Cairns, for a special trophy. Cairns, about whom it would be interesting to know more, was the winner.

The United States Lawn Tennis Association was formed early in 1881 and is thus seven years senior to its English counterpart. Its first move was to standardise the rules and to initiate the official national championships, men's singles and doubles at Newport, Rhode Island. The All England Club rules were adopted *in toto*.

There are some curious similarities between the Newport meeting of 1881 and the Wimbledon tournament of 1877. Spencer Gore won because he volleyed through all the defences, Richard Sears won for the same reason. The Wimbledon entry was twenty-two and the same number challenged each other for the American title. At Wimbledon in 1878 Hadow exploited the lob in reply to the volleyer. At Newport in 1882 the opponents of Sears (he played throughout the first three meetings since the challenge round system did not start until 1884) tried to do the same. Unlike the first English champion, Sears was prepared and had learned to smash.

Richard Sears was a giant of the American game and as dominant in the United States as the Renshaws in Europe. Like W. A. Larned and W. T. Tilden after him, he won the American singles seven times, but Sears was unique in winning for seven successive years. He was, in fact, unbeaten in championship singles and, except for the first year, in doubles also. He won five times with James Dwight and once with J. S. Clark.

Clark played in the first contest between the United States and Great Britain in 1883, seventeen years before the first Davis Cup match. Before leaving the U.S., the brothers C. M. and J. S. Clark got the consent of the American doubles champions Dwight and Sears, with whom they were fairly evenly matched, to act as a representative American side. Two doubles matches were played at Wimbledon on 18 and 23 July 1883 against William and Ernest Renshaw.

British superiority, first illustrated by Woodhouse in 1880 and then by Cairns, was clearly illustrated. The Renshaws won the first match 6–4 8–6 3–6 6–1 and the second by 6–3 6–2 6–3 showing they had a greater mastery of strokes and overall strategy of the game. The Renshaws played two up or two back, the Clark brothers one up and one back and the Americans immediately adopted the British technique on their return home. In this day and age it seems odd, but one can detect a slight American inferiority complex in doubles games against British players which persisted right through to the 1930s.

Sears and Dwight came to Europe after the American championships of 1883. When they returned in the late summer of 1884 Sears brought back three notable acquisitions. One was a pair of spiked shoes, not hitherto used in America, secondly a top spin forehand, the famous 'Lawford Stroke' named after H. F. Lawford from whom he learned it, and finally a racquet made by Thomas J. Tate, the most famous craftsman of his kind in the late nineteenth century. This racquet was used by William Renshaw when he won the singles and doubles championships of both England and Ireland, and he then gave it to Sears. Sears, in turn, used it to win the American singles and doubles titles in 1884 and 1885.

Sears and Dwight were the first Americans to play at Wimbledon. This was in 1884 and they had some success in doubles initially. They beat the 1882 winners, Hartley and Richardson, but were routed by the Renshaws 6–0 6–1 6–2, a worse defeat than that suffered by the Clark brothers the year before. The performance of Sears and Dwight indicates that the American standard of that time was on a par with the top British players but below the skill of the prodigious Renshaws.

The U.S.L.T.A. was asked in 1888 to authorise a women's championship. It replied frostily that it had no power to do so, but twelve months later it officially recognised women players and the championships were established at the Philadelphia Cricket Club.

This was no more than recognition of a *fait accompli* since the club had organised the first women's championship in 1887. The winner was Ellen Hansell, afterwards Mrs Allerdice, who beat Mrs J. Willis Martin in the final. It does not do to underestimate the pioneers of the women's game. Not until 1902 was the championship reduced from the best of five to the best of three sets, a reform doubtless hastened by the tremendous match played in 1901. In that year Elizabeth Moore, winner in 1896, gained her second title when, in the challenge round, she beat Myrtle McAteer 6–4 3–6 7–5 2–6 6–2. The previous day, in the all-comers' final, she beat Marion Jones, the 1899 winner, by 4–6 1–6 9–7 9–7 6–3 after saving match point in the third set. There is no record of a longer women's singles than this affair of fifty-eight games. Miss Moore was a hardy creature, even by modern standards of athletic performance. She won her fourth and last national singles in 1905 and was indoor doubles champion in 1909, seventeen years after reaching the final at Philadelphia for the first time.

Lawn tennis today, at the top level, is thoroughly international and a world class performer may spend little time in his own country. The urge to carry a racquet abroad was by no means lacking at the turn of the century and the first Englishman to take part in the official American championships in 1889 was E. G. Meers, one of the top ten men in Britain. He lost in five sets to Oliver S. Campbell, who became the title winner a year later.

Campbell returned the compliment by coming to Britain in 1892, a time when the game was languishing between the fame of the Renshaws and the might of the Dohertys. Campbell partnered G. W. Hillyard to reach the doubles semi-final at Wimbledon, but since this entailed no more than winning one match it is not easy to assess the merits of the performance. Campbell won both American singles and doubles titles on his return and then retired from championship play.

M. F. Goodbody was, in 1894, the first British player to come within striking distance of the official American title. At that time his best performance at Wimbledon was to reach the semi-final of the doubles with H. S. Scrivener in 1893, but at Newport he reached the all comers' singles final and beat W. A. Larned, but he failed in the challenge round to R. D. Wrenn.

The first representative contest in the United States between America and Britain took place in 1895 when Dr Joshua Pim and H. S. Mahony were invited to play against Larned, C. H. Hovey, M. G. Chase and C. Hobart. Pim had been Wimbledon singles champion in 1893 and 1894 and Mahony was to win the title in 1896. Of the Americans, Hobart and Hovey had won the doubles for the last two years and Hovey was to take the singles that year. Chase was destined for the doubles championship and only Larned had not then come to his best.

All played all – in the system still known as an 'American tournament' – and the British emerged with the honours since each lost only one out of five matches. Pim's only loss was to Hobart, and Mahony, unbeaten by the Americans, yielded only to Pim. Neither British player was able to take part in the national meeting. Larned came to Wimbledon the following year but did not reach the later rounds.

Anglo-American relations prospered in 1897. Mahony returned accompanied by Dr W. V. Eaves, a notable pioneer of the game, and by H. A. Nisbet, and the three played in tournaments at Hoboken and Chicago as well as at Newport. Their visit caused much excitement and did much to boost the game in the United States, while not the least of its results was the start of the Davis Cup competition. The British dominated the singles and Eaves defeated Nisbet in the all-comers final, but American prestige was saved by Wrenn. As in 1894, he held off the overseas challenge and Eaves could no more cope with his famous lobbing than could Goodbody three years earlier.

The Davis Cup competition started in 1900 and the interchange between the United States and Britain ceased to be conducted by individual enterprise.

Australia readily took to lawn tennis. When or by whom sets of Sphairistike were first imported is not known, but the game quickly took root in an organised way, more speedily, in fact, than in the United States. The oldest of the state championships, those of Victoria, were first held in 1880. New South Wales followed in 1885, New Zealand in 1886, Queensland in 1889, South Australia in 1890, Tasmania in 1893, and Western Australia in 1895. The outstanding players of the new game were Dudley Webb and Ben Green. Webb, a crafty baseliner, came originally from Victoria, but he switched to New South Wales where he was champion in 1888, 1890, 1892, 1893 and 1894. Green was champion of Victoria for the last three years of the century.

Dr Eaves, ubiquitous apostle of international play who later took his racquet to America, played in Australia in 1891. He was, in fact, Australian by birth but had settled in England where he learned the game. His playing standard was better than that of the best Australians, and in both that year and in 1902, when he came again, he won the New South Wales title. In addition he did much to standardise the game, for he was not slow to criticize the lack of co-operation between states when he discovered that a covered ball was standard in New South Wales and a coverless one standard in Victoria.

The most far reaching effect of his visits derived from his trip in 1902. A keen young Australian sat at his feet and absorbed all he could. The youngster was a left hander called Norman Brookes destined to become one of the greatest players of all time.

In the early days of the century the finest woman exponent in Australia was Rose Payten. She was reckoned as good as, if not better than, Mrs Lambert Chambers or May Sutton, though such opinion was never put to the test. She dominated the game between 1900 and 1904, and her closest rivals thought themselves fortunate to win two games in any set. Miss Payten, predecessor of Nancy Bolton and Margaret Court, served strongly and came up to the net behind her delivery. She was New South Wales singles champion in 1900, triple champion in 1901, 1902, 1903, 1904, doubles champion in 1905 and 1906, and triple champion again in 1907.

In New Zealand at that time the women's game was dominated to an even greater degree by Miss K. M. Nunneley. She was unbeaten in the national championships from 1895 to 1902 and was singles champion thirteen years running between 1895 and 1907. She was New South Wales champion in 1896 but her prowess was never pitted against that of Miss Payten.

That fine Australian player and critic the late Stanley Doust maintained that after playing with and against Miss Payten, Mrs Lambert Chambers and Miss Sutton he was of the opinion that the Australian was best of all. Miss Payten learned the game by making a fourth with three brothers. Her name, hardly known today, deserves to be resuscitated from the past.

And so to Reggie and Laurie Doherty. The greatest of all time? Men who saw both them and Donald Budge say that such was the case. Take what standards you will, their achievements were terrific.

They reigned supreme for ten years, from 1897 to 1906. Reggie won the Wimbledon singles four times, Laurie five times as well as acquiring the American singles title. They won the Wimbledon doubles eight times, the American twice. In the Davis Cup Reggie played eight matches for Britain and lost only one, having won a singles match the same morning. Laurie's record is unlikely to be equalled. He played twelve matches and was never beaten; out of forty-nine sets, all in the challenge round, he dropped only thirteen.

When youngsters are given their first lawn tennis lessons they are shown how to hold the racquet. Unless they show a marked individual preference they are taught the 'standard' grip and as they advance in technique they learn that this is the 'eastern' grip as opposed to the 'western' or 'continental' grip. It leads to ease of stroke, to purity of style, to control of shot and accuracy of placement. With such natural foundation the lawn tennis genius may build a game of fluent artistry and rhythm, those attributes that make the game such a happy combination of beauty, movement and athletic skill.

It used to be known as the 'Doherty' grip and it is sad that the name is no longer used. It would help keep alive one of the greatest names in the game, a name one rarely hears on the lips of the post-war generation. How many people, one wonders, who pass through the south-east entrance to the All England Club realise that those are the 'Doherty Gates', erected in memory of two of the finest players of all time.

Despite their Irish names the Dohertys were Londoners, born at Clapham Park. They went to Westminster school and Trinity Hall, Cambridge. Neither was robust in the sense of being burly, muscular and athletic and Reggie was plagued by indifferent health all his life; it was said that days when he felt really well were the red letter ones. Reggie usually beat Laurie when they played each other, as they did a good deal on private courts.

Reggie, six feet one inch but weighing only 140 pounds, had grace and ease of style, superb control and was a consummate lawn tennis artist. Laurie was a master overhead, where he had unique skill until the advent of Maurice McLoughlin, the 'Californian Comet', just before the first world war. He had exceptionally long arms and could smash with consistent effect from the baseline. A third Doherty, 'W.V.' the eldest, was responsible for introducing the

left *The Centre Court at Wimbledon in 1910. This match, played in the rain, was the quarter-final of the men's doubles in which J. C. Parke and W. C. Crawley (GB), seen here on the far side of the court, beat the left-handed player B. C. Wright (US) and W. V. Eaves (Australia) 6–3 3–6 1–6 6–1 6–3.*

above *Miss M. Coles at Wimbledon in 1910. She is getting well forward to the ball, but with her straw hat her overhead can hardly have been effective. The pony-roller can be seen on the right of the picture.*

others to the game they made so famous.

At Wimbledon in 1895, the year that a loss of thirty-three pounds was suffered and the nadir of its fortunes, all three were competitors. This was the year when Dr W. V. Eaves, the apostle of international play, missed getting his name on the roll of Wimbledon champions by a single stroke. Since Pim was not defending, the title was at stake in the all-comers' final between Eaves and Wilfrid Baddeley. Eaves won the first two sets 6–4 6–2 and led 6–5 40–30 in the third. He put a lob over the baseline, and Baddeley, quietly confident against a tired opponent, won the last three sets 8–6 6–2 6–3. This was the second occasion the Wimbledon singles was won from match point down; the first man to do so had been W. Renshaw in 1889.

The first notable Doherty success was in 1897 when Reggie won the Wimbledon singles and, with Laurie, the doubles. Reggie did not lose a set in singles. In the semi-final Wilfrid Baddeley, thrice a title holder, was knocked out with only six games to his credit; Eaves, in the all-comers' final, retired exhausted after winning eight games; in the challenge round Mahony won only eleven games.

Reggie, in 1898, resisted the challenge of brother Laurie, who just survived when Mahony led 5–4 in the fifth set and had three match points before Doherty coolness prevailed at 14–12. Reggie won 6–1 in the fifth set against his brother after a contest that, according to contemporaries, was good but unexciting. In 1899 Reggie lost the first two sets in the challenge round against A. W. Gore, although he went on to win. He had been involved in a road mishap not long before while Laurie, even more unfit, did not that year enter for the singles. The next year Gore defeated Laurie but he in turn lost to S. H. Smith, the forehand terror merchant from Stroud; however, Reggie withstood him in the challenge round.

Reggie finally stood down in 1901. With declining health he lost in four sets to Gore who, in an earlier round against G. W. Hillyard, had been match point down and was saved with a net cord shot. Hillyard had eliminated Laurie and it looked like the eclipse of the Dohertys.

But Laurie came into his own in 1902 during the semi-final. Mahony, fighting with all the fervour of an Irishman against the English, volleyed like a demon to lead 6–4 6–4 and only a hair's breadth advantage with his passing shots pulled Laurie through the third set 8–6. By then Mahony had burnt himself out and after two games in the fourth set he retired exhausted. Having grasped back the title Laurie Doherty did not let go. Frank Riseley challenged in 1903 and in 1904 but he could not win a set. Nor could either Norman Brookes in 1905 or Riseley in 1906 take more than one set.

Doherty supremacy in doubles was marred only in 1902, when Laurie, with relatively weak support from his brother, could not hold the dashing sorties, based on the 'one up, one back' combination of Smith and Riseley; there were sixty-three needle games before the fifth set was decided after the twentieth game. With Reggie back in form, the Doherty ascendancy was resumed the following year, and continued until 1906 when Smith and Riseley won again at last. Reggie's indifferent health was again the weak link – he died four years later – and it was the last Wimbledon championship at which either brother was a serious competitor.

The Wimbledon stage, though capacious, was not large enough to contain the Doherty talents. Laurie Doherty was the first overseas competitor to win the official American singles title. His unique performance of 1903 was not equalled until René Lacoste in 1926, and was repeated only once again by Lacoste and later by Henri Cochet, Fred Perry and Frank Sedgman.

Laurie won the British covered court singles title for six years running, the doubles no less than nine times with Hillyard as a partner and with his brother fourteen other times. He won the Monte Carlo singles four times and Reggie six. The American doubles went to them twice. One cannot delve into the tennis record of the turn of the century without being struck by the overwhelming supremacy of the Dohertys.

Success should not be measured on financial grounds alone, but it is significant that a Wimbledon loss in 1895, their first year there, was turned to a profit of £1,300 in 1904. The Renshaws turned lawn tennis from a pastime into a sport, the Dohertys transformed it into a spectator's sport.

In ten years they were beaten as a pair only four times. Smith and Riseley were thrice winners, twice at Wimbledon and once, in 1903, at Monte Carlo. They lost to G. C. Ball-Greene and Hillyard in 1897 at Bad Homburg. There can be no other pair with such consistency of skill for so long a spell.

Between the departure of the Dohertys and the first world war the leading role in the lawn tennis drama was shared not by brothers but by two who might well have been. They were

Mlle Broquedis of France, Olympic Gold Medallist of 1912. She dominated the women's singles in the outdoor Olympic champion-ships in Stockholm by beating the Norwegian Molla Bjurstedt who, in turn, became champion of the United States several times. Mlle Broquedis was champion of France in 1913 and 1914.

above *Dorothea Lambert Chambers winning her seventh Wimbledon singles title in the challenge round against Edith Larcombe in 1914.*

left *J. C. Parke, a top tennis player who was also an Irish rugby international.*

Norman Brookes and Anthony Wilding, whose exploits brought the fame to Australia that it has strived successfully to perpetuate throughout the years. Brookes and Wilding in fact represented Australasia since Wilding was a New Zealander, but not until 1923 did the countries split forces in the Davis Cup. Brookes was an Australian though he learnt his first important lessons at the feet of Dr W. V. Eaves. His first tournament was in Melbourne in 1891 when he was fourteen and his first major success in 1902 when he was singles champion of Victoria.

Wilding, like many other fine players, was a Cambridge man. He was six years younger than Brookes and of the eight Wimbledon championships between 1907 and 1914, Wilding won the singles four times and Brookes twice.

In the doubles Brookes and Wilding played twice at Wimbledon in 1907 and 1914 and won on both occasions. As a Davis Cup team they played together for five years and on the last four occasions 1907, 1908, 1909 and 1914, they won the cup for Australasia winning both singles and doubles between them. Their joint Davis Cup record was forty-eight matches played, thirty-five matches won with Brookes winning two more singles than Wilding.

Brookes, a left-hander and the first overseas challenger to win the men's singles at Wimbledon, first played there in 1905. His daring volleying caused havoc in all rounds except the last. Gore, a fine baseliner, fell to the Australian's break service and sharply angled volleys in three sets. The redoubtable forehand of S. H. Smith was turned aside by a fifth set margin of 7–5 in the all comers' final. In the challenge round Laurie Doherty turned back the invasion by lobbing. Good as Brookes was, and he became even better with more penetration and pace of shot, he was not quite up to the Doherty standard. But, then, who was?

He returned to win in 1907. Doherty had retired and so had both Smith and Riseley, but to compensate for this weakening of home defences there was other overseas strength in the field. It was toughest for Brookes in the early rounds. Wilding held him for five sets and so did the American, Karl Behr, a famous volleyer, but the later rounds were far easier.

For thirty years, from 1877 to 1906, the singles at Wimbledon had been won by Englishmen or Irishmen. Brookes broke the spell and only two Englishmen have won since, Gore and Fred Perry. The ubiquitous Dr Eaves started rather more than he could have guessed when, in the

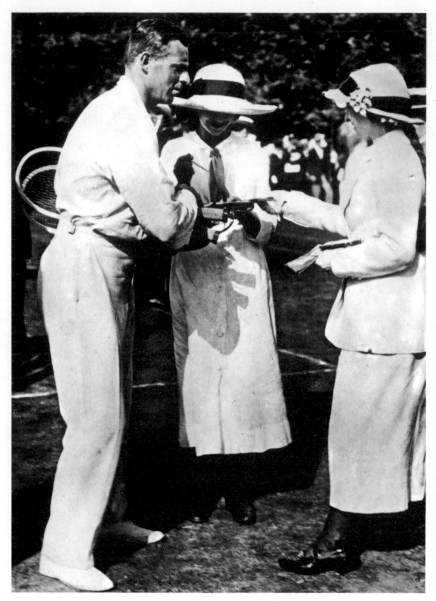

1890's he helpfully coached young Brookes in the subtleties of English lawn tennis.

Brookes was the dashing volleyer, darting, daring and a man of inspiration; Wilding was never a natural player but taught himself to be a great one by hard work and rigorous discipline. He made almost a fetish of physical fitness. Yet, despite his fitness, he could not endure great heat and his second Wimbledon victory in 1911 owed something to luck. Roper Barrett came to the challenge round after a terrific five set all-comers' final against C. P. Dixon in which he suffered slight sunstroke. It was equally hot when he played Wilding, and the wily Roper Barrett held an indifferent Wilding to two sets all before retiring. Wilding was just on the point of announcing his own withdrawal when Barrett resigned.

Wilding played his two finest matches at Wimbledon against Americans. In 1910 he met Beals C. Wright in the all-comers' final and won 4–6 4–6 6–3 6–2 6–3. In 1913 Maurice McLoughlin, born in Carson City, came with his California learnt game to cause havoc with his tremendous service, the most deadly shot of its kind to that date. As soon as McLoughlin had set foot on the boat for England, Americans gleefully declared the Wimbledon trophy was as good as halfway back across the Atlantic. The 'Californian Comet' did all his supporters declared he would until he met Wilding in the challenge round. The New Zealander won in three very tough sets. Wilding's last match was against McLoughlin in the Davis Cup challenge round in 1914, just after the start of the war in which Wilding was killed.

As has been said, Brookes and Wilding held the stage in place of the Dohertys but, while they did so, lawn tennis continued to expand. The Davis Cup proved a great stimulus and the game became international. Belgium and France joined America and Britain in 1904, Australasia and Austria in 1905. In 1913 Germany, Canada and South Africa were also challengers.

In the United States the dominant figure was W. A. Larned, until McLoughlin blazed through everything just before the war. Larned climbed a laborious ladder to fame and had played a great deal before he became American champion in 1901. He won again in 1902, bowed to the skill of Laurie Doherty and did not win again until 1907 when he held his position for five years. As seven-fold champion Larned equalled the record of R. D. Sears, though the latter did it in unbroken sequence. In 1912 the challenge round, instituted in 1884, was abolished.

Beals Wright, U.S. champion in 1905, was the American most feared abroad. It is worthy of record that W. J. Clothier, winner in 1906, made one of the most remarkable recoveries on record. In the quarter final against F. B. Alexander he trailed 2–5, was 0–40 down in the fifth set and yet went on to win.

Larned's swan song came in 1911 when, having beaten McLoughlin in the challenge round, he did not choose to enter the knock-out tournaments of later years. Some fourteen or so years earlier M. D. Whitman and Holcombe Ward had invented and had terrorised the game with the deadly spinning service. McLoughlin created the cannonball delivery and arrived on the East Coast from California with the effect of a cyclone. McLoughlin won in 1912 and in 1913, but in 1914 he lost in the final to R. N. Williams whom he had beaten in the same match the year before.

Williams was a great half-volleyer. Generally speaking half-volleyers have few imitators, but Williams played much lawn tennis in Europe. A little fellow from Lyons used to watch him, vowing that this was the way he would play. The little fellow was Henri Cochet and in due course, when Cochet was performing his legendary exploits, an·impudent youngster, with his nose stuck over the canvas at the back of the court, declared that there was the master he would follow. Perry was the youngster's name and with him the school of daring genius appears to have ended.

One of the first lawn tennis courts to be built in France was put down for the benefit of the Renshaws at Beau Site, Cannes. The Dohertys were equally fond of the riviera, and the season there, though tending to fluctuate according to the prosperity of the world at large, has been important ever since.

The first championship of France was played in 1891 and was won by a man called Briggs, whose first name or initial is unknown to the French authorities. He was, presumably, a Frenchman for, until 1925, the French championship was closed to foreigners.

The two great French players of the pre-1914 era were M. Decugis and A. H. Gobert. Decugis has a unique record in championship play. Between 1902 and 1920 Decugis won the French singles eight times, the doubles fourteen times in a row and the mixed doubles seven times. Add to this five world hard-court championship titles, one Olympic title, the Wimbledon doubles

left *Tony Wilding was the teenagers' idol at Wimbledon in 1914, the year he lost to Norman Brookes. Wilding was killed by shellfire at Neuve Chapelle on 9 May 1915, aged thirty-one.*

right *Edith Larcombe, a great woman player during the early years of the century. She won the Wimbledon singles in 1912. She had been a finalist in 1903 and she was again finalist in 1914. She was still a keen Wimbledon competitor in 1919 when she was forty years old.*

title, and there is a total of thirty-six major championships, a unique achievement among men, and among women surpassed only by Mlle Suzanne Lenglen.

Decugis was primarily a hard court player but he also played well on wood and won seventeen titles on covered courts in England and France. He learned much of his lawn tennis in England at the Connaught Club. His first success was in handicap doubles in 1897 at Brighton where he played with Mahony and he was boy champion at Queen's Club the same year. As for Gobert, eight years younger than Decugis, he was one of the world's best performers on wood. Seven British titles and seventeen French national titles came his way before and after the first world war.

Decugis and Gobert showed their doubles skill to the world by winning Wimbledon in 1911, the first French success there. They were both daring volleyers standing almost over the net, and they were not troubled until the semi-final where they survived the loss of the first two sets against E. O. Pockley and S. N. Doust. After losing only five games in the all-comers' final, the Frenchmen won the challenge round in the fifth set from Wilding and M. J. G. Ritchie.

The German championships, prior to 1914, were a popular event and the tournament at Bad Homburg had a riviera air. The first German championship was in 1893. The English champions there were Hillyard in 1897 and 1900, and M. J. G. Ritchie in 1903 through 1906 and 1908, an American, C. Hobart, won in 1899 and a Frenchman, Decugis, in 1901 and 1902.

The first great German player was Otto Foitzheim, champion in 1907, in 1909 through to 1911, in 1921 and in 1925 eighteen years after his first victory. Froitzheim played at Wimbledon in 1914 when he reached the all-comers' final and put Brookes in trouble. The Australian, despite a lead of 2–0 and being 5–4 ahead in the third set, was forced to a fifth set of 8–6. The year before, the German doubles team F. W. Rahe and H. Kleinschroth, had all but taken the doubles, losing finally to Roper Barrett and Dixon.

There were some doughty women before the first war. The incredible Miss Lottie Dod won her last Wimbledon championship in 1893. Her successor was Mrs Blanche Hillyard, the former Miss Bingley, who had previously won in 1886 and 1889, but she had lost consistently to Miss

Dod in the challenge round every time that prodigious athlete competed. Mrs Hillyard won the singles six times. Mrs Charlotte Sterry, the former Miss Cooper, won five times, first in 1895. Mrs Dorothea Lambert Chambers, the former Miss Douglass, won seven times, first in 1903 and for the last time in 1914. A reasonable order of priority would be Mrs Lambert Chambers, Miss Dod, Mrs Hillyard and Mrs Sterry. The very top place of a pre-1914 ranking list, however, can be claimed by a cheery little Californian, Miss May Sutton.

Miss Sutton, one of many sisters all of whom delighted in their expertise on the court, takes pride of place not only as the first American but the first overseas player to win a championship at Wimbledon. At her first attempt, at the age of eighteen in 1905, her top spin forehand toppled all defences and she did not lose a set.

The challenge round was perhaps not a fair test of the relative merits of Miss Sutton and Mrs Lambert Chambers since the latter had a sprained wrist; Mrs Lambert Chambers had her revenge the next year. Even so, the American was again invincible in 1907, the year all three Wimbledon titles went overseas, and Miss Sutton had already won the American singles in 1904 when she was only sixteen.

Miss Lambert Chambers made thirteen attempts to win the Wimbledon singles between 1902 and 1920 and she was beaten only six times. As late as 1925 she reached the semi-final of two doubles events at Wimbledon. The same year she went to America with the Wightman Cup team, won her cup singles, and afterwards reached the quarter-finals of the American national singles.

Mrs Sterry won her first singles at Wimbledon in 1895. In 1912, eighteen meetings later, she reached the all-comers' final and lost to the champion, Mrs Larcombe.

Mrs Hillyard was even more remarkable. She played at the first Wimbledon open to women in 1884 and lost to the first champion Mrs Maud Watson. During the next eighteen years Mrs Hillyard either won the singles or went down before the champion. But in 1912, no less than twenty-nine Wimbledons after her first challenge, she reached the singles semi-final where she went down, albeit rather easily, to the eventual champion.

In America the national women's singles was more widely shared than its sister event in Britain. There were fourteen different champions between 1887 and 1908 and only Mrs E. H. Moore won more than three times, the first in 1896, the fourth in 1905. Perhaps the best of five set matches were less conducive to a long life. Mrs Maud Barger Wallach, winner in 1908, was then thirty-eight years old. She had not taken up the game until she was thirty.

Subsequently American women began to emulate the consistency of the British. During the twenty meetings between 1909 and 1929 there were only four champions, Mrs Hazel Wightman who won four times, Mrs Mary Browne three times, Mrs Molla Mallory seven times and Miss Helen Wills six times. Mrs Mallory was forty when she won for the seventh time in 1926.

On 24 May 1899, at Compiegne in France, a baby girl was born to M. and Mme Lenglen and christened Suzanne. She showed a rare talent for lawn tennis and her father coached her assiduously. In 1913 she won the championship of Picardy and the singles at Lille. The following year she did brilliantly and was talked about as a prodigy. She won the Beau Site tournament at Cannes and also the two Carlton tournaments there. In Paris she won both the singles and doubles with the American Miss Elizabeth Ryan, and was runner-up of the mixed doubles in the world's championship on hard courts. All this at the age of fifteen. Here, assuredly, was Miss Lottie Dod all over again. In fact it was not, it was something greater. But with the first war, international lawn tennis came to an end and it was not until five years later that lawn tennis began to appreciate that a prima donna had come onto its stage.

Lawn tennis reached full international status on 20 October 1912 when the International Lawn Tennis Federation was founded in Paris. Prior to that the British Lawn Tennis Association had effectively been the world governing body, and the first I.L.T.F. president was Mr R. J. McNair, chairman of the British L.T.A. The founder members attending the first annual general meeting in March 1913, were Australasia, Austria, Belgium, Denmark, France, Germany, Great Britain, Netherlands, Russia, South Africa, Spain, Sweden and Switzerland.

Though the international federation was first mooted in 1911 by an American, Douane Williams, the United States did not at first join. It did not do so until after the first world war, when the federation ceased to designate such events as Wimbledon as 'World Championships'. The Davis Cup, first played between the United States and the British Isles in 1900, had

grown by 1914. Belgium and France took up the challenge in 1904, while Australasia and Austria came in the following year. Germany, Canada and South Africa had followed in 1913.

The first Olympic Games in Athens in 1896 featured lawn tennis. The gold medalist, J. P. Boland, appears to have had no other claim to sporting fame. But the Olympics added nothing to lawn tennis and lawn tennis little to the Olympics. When Wimbledon was the setting for the 1908 Olympic tournament the women's singles produced eight walk-overs and five matches. After World War I lawn tennis was played in Antwerp in 1920 and in Paris in 1924, but subsequent differences over the definition of amateurism brought an end to lawn tennis as an Olympic event.

The Golden Years—

On the lawn tennis court two qualities make for greatness, playing skill and personality. If lawn tennis is considered an art, then Suzanne Lenglen stands as its supreme exponent.

She was described as an extrovert who thrived on public adulation, a poser perhaps, but this was inherent in her. She demanded complete attention from everyone and always received it. She was dramatic in all she did and had to take the centre of the stage, even in so simple a thing as entering a room. She was never still, even whilst talking but was always on her toes, bubbling with energy. She could talk about anything for she was highly intelligent though not cultured.

Suzanne Lenglen was a lawn tennis perfectionist. She was fit, supple and strong. Her footwork, her most striking asset, was that of a ballet dancer for, if need be, she could get across the court in wide light leaps. Wonderful timing enabled her to get virile pace into her drives. Her ball control was supreme and her father, who trained her, used to put a handkerchief on the court and reward her in centimes when she found the target, and penalise her when she failed.

It is said she never served a double fault for five years. Her favourite tactics were the exploitation of the basic weakness on the backhand of practically every player. Down her own forehand line she would play the ball, first very short, then deeper, and finally very deep. She was a most able volleyer when she wished, with a round arm action, not the stab or chop.

All her wonderful technical skill would have been of slight importance had it not been for her facility of concentration, a vital factor. She concentrated from point to point and this was undoubtedly the reason for her remarkable freedom from error and long series of overwhelming victories. Her 1921 match against Molla Mallory apart, Suzanne Lenglen was not beaten in singles throughout the whole of her career from 1919. Her supremacy was exemplified by her record in 1925 in sixteen tournaments. She played in seven singles matches and in only two matches did she lose more than two games. In the final of the French Championships Kitty Godfree held her to 6–1 6–2.

In winning the French women's singles championship Suzanne Lenglen, in five matches, lost a total of only seven games. At Wimbledon a month later she won with the loss of only five games in five matches, with Miss Ryan she won the women's doubles for the loss of sixteen games in six matches, and with Jean Borotra she won the

mixed, losing one set in the semi-final against Randolph Lycett and Mrs Lycett. She also won two doubles events in the French championships, conceding only one set in the women's doubles whilst partnering Mlle Didi Vlasto.

In the early days of her career Suzanne Lenglen nearly always played her important matches with Papa and Mama glued to the side of the court. Mama sat there saying nothing. Papa growled advice, watching intently and he would toss cognac soaked sugar at his daughter before she played a vital point.

In France she became a national heroine. An avenue in Nice, where she lived, was named after her. Her house was subsidised by the municipality. High society flung open its doors and she could tour Europe like a great Princess, passing from château to château, from schloss to schloss, living a life, when she wanted to, of champagne and diamonds. Papa was always in the background and when tournament secretaries wanted his daughter to play it was he they approached.

If lawn tennis is now a great public spectacle it is largely because of Suzanne Lenglen. Even before the war there was pressure at the Worple Road ground of the All England Club for better accommodation. This pressure would doubtless have increased without the advent of Suzanne Lenglen, but this great player and fantastic personality from France made the spectators' accommodation hopelessly inadequate. Everything about her was sensational. Skirts were getting shorter, but those of Suzanne were shorter than any others, and moreover she wore less underneath than was the custom at the time.

Before 1914 nobody among the general public bothered much about women's lawn tennis. Whilst Suzanne Lenglen was at Wimbledon there was a tendency not to bother about anything else. The All England Club moved to bigger spheres, to the triangle of ground between Church Road and Somerset Road in 1922. It was at one of the early meetings there that the referee, pursuing a policy of strict fairness and impartiality, scheduled a match of hers on No. 4 court rather than one of the show courts. The result was a near riot and pandemonium. Hedges were trampled down, canvas torn away and the experiment was never repeated.

When Suzanne Lenglen came to her first Wimbledon in 1919 she was not unknown, for she had the five-year-old fame of having been the world hard court champion in 1914 at the age of fifteen. Good, yes, but surely hardly so good as Mrs Lambert Chambers, seven times holder of

The incomparable Suzanne Lenglen two months before her fifteenth birthday in 1914. She had already won the hard court championship of the world.

above right *Suzanne during a mixed doubles with Gerald Patterson in 1920. Only she could have played a backhand volley flying through the air.*

below right *Suzanne playing with René Lacoste in 1925.*

"Pour le Sport"

the championship? Such was British opinion.

Leaping about the court Suzanne Lenglen lost only six games in four matches. Then Elizabeth Ryan, herself a great player, forced her to two close sets. (The American had beaten her before the war. Their post-war singles meetings totalled, it is reputed, thirty-nine, and Miss Ryan never won). That brought Suzanne Lenglen to the all-comers' final where the renowned power of consistent return of Mrs Phyllis Satterthwaite was of no avail against her skill.

The challenge round against Mrs Lambert Chambers was perhaps the greatest women's match of all time. The Frenchwoman's career, one can see now, hinged on its outcome. She won, after two match points against her, 10–8 4–6 9–7. Had she not won it she would perhaps not have been as great as she was. That extra spark of confidence, the essential quality of all champions, would have been missing. Invincibility

A famous match between Henri Cochet and 'Big' Bill Tilden in the Wimbledon semi-final of 1929 when Cochet won 2–6 4–6 7–5 6–4 6–3 after Tilden had led 5–1 in the third set. They are seen **above** *spinning their rackets for ends, on the* **left** *Tilden in play, and finally* **below** *Tilden congratulating Cochet.*

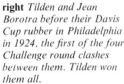

right *Tilden and Jean Borotra before their Davis Cup rubber in Philadelphia in 1924, the first of the four Challenge round clashes between them. Tilden won them all.*

below *Tilden had ambitions as a playwright and actor. He had little success. Here he is playing a part in a film called* Highbinders.

would have belonged to Mrs Lambert Chambers, not to her.

But win she did, and she settled to her unique career. When, in 1920, she defended the Wimbledon singles it was again against Mrs Lambert Chambers. It cannot be said that Mrs Lambert Chambers was less good than she had been, at least not to any degree, for she beat both Mrs Mallory and Miss Ryan easily in earlier rounds. In the final Suzanne Lenglen allowed her to win just three games, and for the next half decade it was rare for anyone to do more.

Suzanne Lenglen, who had won two Wimbledon titles in 1919, won all three in 1920 and did not drop a set throughout. She took two events in 1921, three again in 1922 without the loss of a set, though the challenge round in the women's singles was then abolished and she had to play through. In 1923 she lost only in the mixed doubles. In 1924; having reached the semi-final of the singles, jaundice made her withdraw. Her come-back in 1925 won her three titles again and her singles win was the most devastating in the annals of the game.

So much for her record on grass. Up to 1923 the major event on hard courts was the world championships held at Paris in 1912, 1913, 1914, 1920, 1921 and 1923, and at Brussels in 1922. Suzanne followed her twofold success of 1914 by winning three events in 1921, again in 1922, and two events in 1923. In her native French championships she, who had won the mixed doubles in 1914, was unbeaten in three events in 1920, 1921, 1922, 1923, 1925 and 1926. With the two Olympic titles won in 1920 there is a grand total of forty-six major titles won by the most talented lawn tennis player the world has known.

Her only failure, if it can be called that, was in 1921 when she was persuaded to pay her only visit to America. Sick from her journey she was hurried onto court for her first match against, of all opponents, Molla Mallory, the US Champion. She retired after losing the first set 6–2, leaving the Americans to regard her as a 'quitter'. When she met Mrs Mallory at Wimbledon the following year in the final she took her revenge 6–2 6–0.

Her other famous clash against an American was with Helen Wills at Cannes in 1926. It was a match that held the interest of the world and Suzanne was a convincing winner 6–3 8–6.

Being wise after the event it is now easy to see that sooner or later the prima donna temperament of Suzanne would clash with the strong personality of the late F. R. Burrow, the most

above *The Australians Gerald Patterson and James Anderson. Patterson was the Wimbledon singles champion in 1919 and in 1922; he was also Australian champion in 1927.*

left *The pigtailed Helen Wills was US junior champion in 1921 and 1922;* below, *at the age of eighteen, she is looking characteristically poker-faced.*

Helen Wills, later Helen Wills Moody and then Helen Wills Roarke, the American invincible. She set a record by winning the Wimbledon singles eight times, and the US singles seven times.

below Helen (left) with another outstanding US champion, Molla Mallory, also seven times singles winner.

famous, the most efficient and the most dictatorial referee Wimbledon ever had. The irresistible force met the immovable body in 1926.

Mr Burrow was an efficient referee because he commanded tournaments as a captain does his ship. He was fair, firm and exacted complete obedience. He was also man of the world enough to know when to yield to greatness, and because of her unique standing in the game Mlle Langlen was never treated like other competitors. As a matter of special courtesy she used to be escorted to the referee's office to be told at what time she was wanted the following day. Even though the matter was put so politely, referee Burrow expected to receive assent to his ruling with similar courtesy.

The evening before the day in question no-one, through some mischance, came to escort Mlle Lenglen for the little ceremony. Mlle Lenglen was piqued at this oversight, for it put her in the same position as any other competitor, bound by a reasonable but rigid rule to find out for herself or himself what time she or he is required on court.

Similarly Mr Burrow, busy with the multifold cares of Wimbledon, knew full well that Mlle Lenglen had not been informed in the usual way. He saw no reason to leave the bridge to go chasing after her and, being told that Queen Mary was coming down to see Mlle Lenglen in action, he drew up his schedule for the Frenchwoman to play in a singles match on the Centre Court as well as in a doubles at 4.30 p.m., a match that had been planned long before.

Queen Mary arrived but not Mlle Lenglen. When the Frenchwoman did turn up it was three-thirty and she in a state of Gallic frenzy and near hysteria. Though declaring she would on no account play her singles before her doubles, it was obvious she was in no condition to play at all that day. In fact she did not. That was the first Wednesday.

On the Thursday, she and her doubles partner, Mlle Vlasto lost to the Americans Miss Ryan and Miss M. K. Browne, after twice being within a point of winning it. Because of the rain the fateful singles did not take place until Friday, when Mlle Lenglen, though complaining of illness, beat Mrs Evelyn Dewhurst easily.

On Saturday came the end of Mlle Lenglen's unrivalled achievements at Wimbledon. Jean Borotra and she came onto the Centre Court for a mixed doubles and the crowd, still smarting under the discourtesy they felt she had shown to Queen Mary, came near to booing a former idol.

Elizabeth Ryan and Randolph Lycett. Miss Ryan won nineteen doubles titles, a unique record.

above *Miss Ryan with Dorothea Lambert Chambers at Wimbledon in 1919. Both were beaten by Suzanne Lenglen – Miss Ryan in the semi-final and Miss Lambert Chambers in the challenge round. The tournament scene in the 1920s and early 1930s would not have been the same without the ubiquitous 'Bunny' Ryan. She is seen* **above right** *with her dog and* **right** *as an eager spectator in 1925.*

Borotra worked to try and save the situation, doing everything but stand on his head to restore good humour. He succeeded, but that was the last time Mlle Lenglen appeared as a competitor at Wimbledon. A spell had broken. She turned professional and toured America with Mary Browne in a series of matches in which, as always, she was never beaten.

It seems she did not greatly enjoy exhibition play. Later she founded a lawn tennis school in Paris, and died of jaundice in 1938.

Commanding presence though she had, Suzanne Lenglen did not have the centre of the lawn tennis stage to herself. Throughout all Suzanne's histrionic performances was the burly figure of William Tatem Tilden. Tilden shares with Mlle Lenglen the distinction of possibly being the greatest player of all time. Before the footlights he stands out as a wonderful player, with every stroke and shot at his command, the most versatile of all great players. His private life, alas, was marred by tragedy that prevented his living normally and which, when he was beyond middle age, caused him twice to be sent to prison. For Tilden, like Oscar Wilde, was homosexual and the fact was brought into the light of world publicity largely through his own fault. In his egotism there were facets of Tilden's character no-one could admire. In all else he was honest, forthright and most worthy, loyal to the point of being quixotic. He is surely the only professional who, out of his own earnings, would refund money to the local promoters of his exhibition matches when public support did not come up to expectation.

He is the only leading actor on the lawn tennis stage who was an actor on the genuine stage as well. Though not a great success he was not entirely a failure. He dabbled in novel writing too, again without great success or failure. He wrote much on lawn tennis and wrote well. If the name of 'classic' can ever be given to an instructional book then Tilden's *The Art of Lawn Tennis,* alongside René Lacoste's *Lacoste on Tennis,* must be awarded that distinction. Tilden devoted his life to lawn tennis, but he was no muscle-bound dunderhead, rather a man of culture and of intellect.

The first great year for Tilden was 1920 when he was twenty-seven years old. It was the American trip to Europe in quest of the Davis Cup that touched off the spark which made him for the next decade a universal genius of the game. He was accompanied by Bill Johnston, and he

and Tilden – a burly, shambling figure in a long, woolly sweater beloved by the cartoonists of the day – became at once 'Big Bill' and 'Little Bill', as great and as famous a partnership as the Renshaws, the Dohertys or Brookes and Wilding.

Tilden won the Wimbledon singles, the first American man to do so. He beat J. C. Parke, who had put out Johnston in the previous round, then Colonel A. R. F. Kingscote, who represented the home resistance, and in the all-comers' final, the Japanese Z. Shimizu. The last was an odd encounter, for Tilden, winning 6–4 6–4 13–11, trailed 1–4 in the first set, 2–4 in the second, and 2–5 in the third. In the challenge round he quelled the Australian, Gerald Patterson, an opponent he was to face many times in subsequent years in important matches.

Tilden went on to win all his Davis Cup matches in Europe, and he returned to America to win the national singles, beating Norman Brookes in the final. For the first time since Laurie Doherty in 1903, the Wimbledon and American singles were held by the same man. Tilden, still accompanied by Johnston, went to New Zealand at the end of the year for the Davis Cup challenge round against Australasia. Brookes and Patterson were no match for the two 'Bills' and America won back the trophy she had held only once since 1903.

Tilden was unbeaten in any vital singles match in 1920. Nor was he beaten, in fact, until six years later when René Lacoste at last checked an invincibility almost as great as that of Suzanne Lenglen. Tilden returned to Europe in 1921. In Paris the world hard court title fell to him. His Wimbledon title was retained, though only by a hair's breadth. He kept his American title and won both his Davis Cup singles in the challenge round. Tilden did not come back to Europe until 1927, but in 1922, 1923, 1924 and 1925 he did not taste defeat in either the Davis Cup challenge round nor the American national singles.

Lacoste's challenge was at last successful in 1926 and in 1927, France, at long last, won the Davis Cup from the United States, though before that Tilden had been beaten by Lacoste in the French championships and by Henri Cochet at Wimbledon.

So by 1927, it can be said that Tilden's glorious reign had come to an end, but since he was then thirty-four it was not surprising. But in 1928 the wheel turned full circle for Tilden won against Lacoste in the challenge round at Wimbledon; it was the Frenchman's last year in the game.

It is said the 'old 'uns' never come back. Tilden

did. He regained the American singles, for the seventh time in 1929 and, in 1930, came back again to Wimbledon, after three failures, to win at the age of thirty-seven. An incredible performance, even though there was a measure of luck when Wilmer Allison, unseeded, put Cochet out of the way and reached the final. Tilden later played his last challenge round in the Davis Cup, his eleventh in succession and two more than anyone else has ever done; a record unlikely to be equalled or surpassed.

Australia, since the time of Norman Brookes, has never wanted for great players. At Wimbledon's revival after the first world war Brookes was ready to lay aside his mantle of world supremacy, he did so to a young compatriot Gerald Patterson, whose big serving and super-speed carried him through the all-comers' singles with the loss of only one set, and through the challenge round against Brookes with ease. Patterson had the pace of Maurice McLoughlin but not the guile of Tilden, who settled the question of American superiority the following year. With Tilden absent in 1922, he won again. His first Australian singles title was won as late as 1927.

Randolph Lycett, who played the first singles final at the new Wimbledon against Patterson in 1922, was an Australian who adopted British allegiance. One of his distinctions was to win the mixed doubles at Wimbledon three times with Miss Elizabeth Ryan, and he also took the men's doubles three years running, from 1921 to 1923, with three different partners, Max Woosnam, John Anderson and Leslie Godfree. He was defeated by the Japanese, Z. Shimizu, in the Wimbledon quarter-final in 1921 on a broiling day. Shimizu won 6–3 9–11 3–6 6–2 10–8, emotionless, cool and sober. Not so Lycett, who fortified himself with gin and then champagne to provide a lively knockabout spectacle. The wonder was that he finished the match.

That last championship at Worple Road was a hectic affair. Shimizu used all guile against Lycett, but he failed narrowly to reach the all-comers' final. Manuel Alonso, a fine free moving player and perhaps one of Spain's greatest players, beat him 3–6 7–5 3–6 6–4 8–6. In the other semi-final Brian Norton, a South African, beat the American F. T. Hunter in five sets, and won against Alonso in the final 5–7 4–6 7–5 6–3 6–3 after Alonso had led 5–2 in the third set. Norton then reached match point against Tilden in the challenge round, but he finally lost and it almost seemed as though he did

not want to win.

In the United States at this time the Americans swore that the greatest woman player was Molla Mallory, the best of a triumvirate which included Hazel Wightman and Mary K. Browne. In fact she reigned supreme, and there was some excuse when her uncompleted match against Suzanne Lenglen in 1921 was hailed by Americans as a victory on her merits. It is an odd fact that Mrs Mallory who learned the game in Norway – the first three of her seven American singles titles were won as Miss Bjurstedt – was never at her best in Europe.

The expansion of lawn tennis administration reflected the growth of the game. In 1922 the All England Club moved from Worple Road to its new venue a mile or so away in Church Road. The new site took two years to prepare at a cost of little under £140,000 and the venture was not without its detractors. But its success, in every aspect, financial and otherwise, was immediate, despite dreadful weather that caused the first meeting to overrun its schedule by three days. The money was raised by means of debenture shares, the dividends being not in cash but in centre court seats. The original shareholders never had cause to regret their investment.

In the United States the new stadium at Forest Hills, New York, was finished in 1923, the opening event was the first Wightman Cup contest between English and American women. The national American championships, singles and mixed doubles, had moved to Forest Hills in 1921, the men's singles coming from Newport, the women's from Philadelphia. The men's and women's doubles went to Boston.

The French national championships alternated at first between the Racing Club, in the Bois de Boulogne, and St Cloud. France's Davis Cup victory in 1927 gave the incentive and financial impetus to build the Stade Roland Garros at Auteuil, where the trees, that overhang the outside courts and the harsh concrete surrounding the main arena, give an atmosphere as notable as that of Wimbledon.

The Australian championships have so far missed the opportunity to create a unique setting. They have always been held in peripatetic fashion between Sydney, Melbourne, Adelaide and Brisbane. State rivalry – and it needs to be remembered that the state championships are older

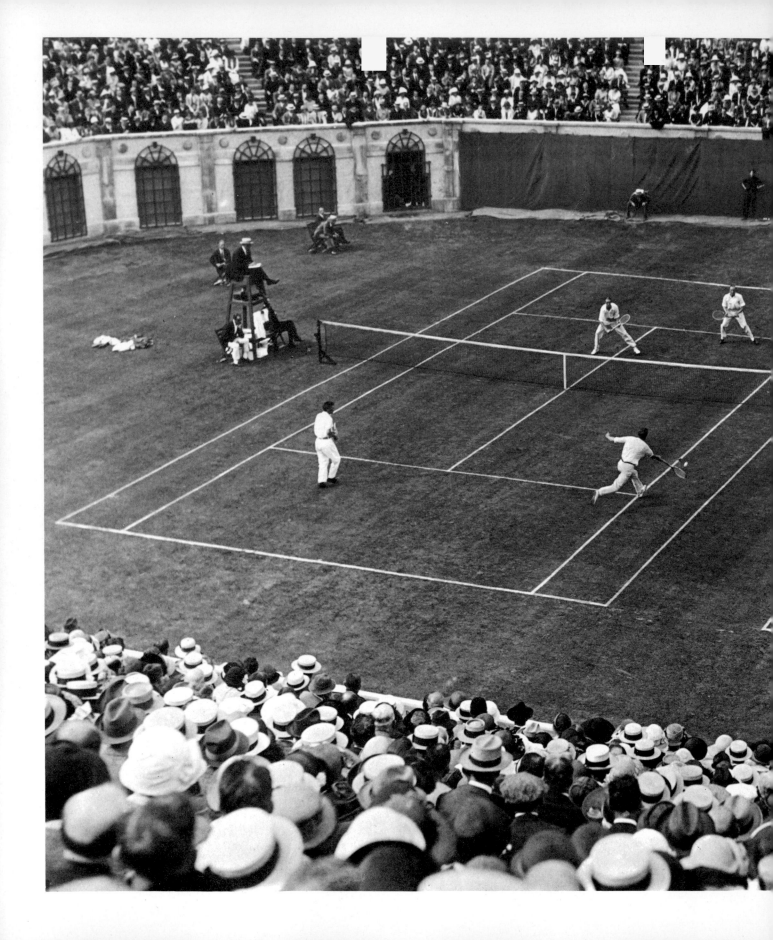

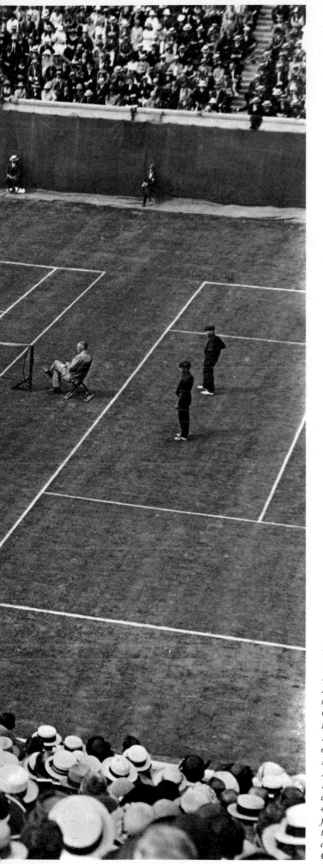

The Stadium Court at the West Side Club, Forest Hills, New York. It is 2 September 1923, the middle day of the Davis Cup Challenge Round between the United States and Australia, and the score is one all. 'Big' Bill Tilden and Norris Williams beat James Anderson and John Hawkes 17–15 11–13 3–6 6–3 6–2 and America won the tie 4–1 to keep the Davis Cup for the fourth successive time. It was the longest doubles played in the Challenge Round until 1958.

than the national meeting – has held back the creation of a permanent venue.

The period between the wars was a golden age, great in playing skill, rich in personality. Just when it reached its peak is a matter of opinion. Perhaps 1927 was the most remarkable year in the history of the game. Though from a British viewpoint, the mid-thirties, when Fred Perry was Wimbledon champion, when Dorothy Round was also champion there, when Peggy Scriven was champion of France and when Britain held the Davis Cup, was a time of glory and unique achievement. Certainly by 1939 the golden age was passing and when, after the war, the game went from success to success it was the triumph of specialists rather than personalities.

For two decades the courts were crowded with striking characters: Elizabeth Ryan, who rarely failed to appear, Betty Nuthall the infant wonder, Jack Crawford, the gentle Australian Ellsworth Vines, Donald Budge who combined the power of a bulldozer with hair spring delicacy, Willmer Allison, John Van Ryn, George Lott, Baron von Cramm Germany's elegant master, Señorita de Alvarez, Cilli Aussem, the long-legged Hilda Krahwinkel, the dour Simone Mathieu, the impish Anita Lizana from Chile, Bunny Austin, the incomparable Frenchmen Jacques Brugnon, René Lacoste, Jean Borotra and Henri Cochet, the sad Helen Jacobs, the beautiful Bobby Heine and hosts of others. And of course, Helen Wills.

Her career began in 1922 at seventeen when she reached the final of the American championship. She was beaten 6–3 6–1 by Molla Mallory, who thus acquired the rare distinction of defeating both Suzanne Lenglen and Helen Wills, wins that were both avenged. This was the only defeat sustained in singles by Helen Wills in the American nationals until she retired to Mrs Helen Jacobs in the final of 1933. She won seven times in 1923, 1924, and 1925, then in 1927, 1928 and 1929, and again in 1931.

She first played at Wimbledon in 1924, reached the final and lost 4–6 6–4 6–4 to Kitty Godfree, an occasion memorable in retrospect as the only time Miss Wills lost a Wimbledon singles. She came back in 1927 and won, the first of her unique series of victories in 1928, 1929, 1930, 1932, 1933, 1935 and 1938 – eight times in all. She took the French championships in 1928, 1929, 1930 and 1932. She was, in 1927, the first woman to win both Wimbledon and Forest Hills and, in 1928, the first to win those two and

above *Señorita de Alvarez with Suzanne Lenglen (left) at Wimbledon in 1926. Soon after this Suzanne turned professional.*

left *The captivating Lili de Alvarez of Spain, genius of the half-volley. She was three times a finalist at Wimbledon – in 1926, 1927 and 1928 – but never the champion. She took an earlier ball than any other woman player.*

above right *The great runner-up, Helen Jacobs. Six times a finalist at Wimbledon and only once a winner, twice a French finalist and never a winner. She did better in her own championships at Forest Hills where she won four out of her eight finals.*

centre right *Two notable British doubles pairs of 1928: Ermyntrude Harvey and Eileen Bennett, Peggy Saunders and Phoebe Watson.*

below right *From the time of the Dohertys, Wimbledon was never short of spectators and in 1927 they witnessed Henri Cochet's memorable cliff-hanging triumph.*

at Paris besides, a performance she repeated the following year.

From 1922 to 1938 is a long career. Mrs Mallory beat her in 1922 and Mrs Godfree in 1924, both in the Wimbledon championships, and Mrs B. C. Covell defeated her in the Wightman Cup. Suzanne Lenglen had her victory in 1926 at Cannes. In 1933 Miss Jacobs won. Kay Stammers had a victory at Beckenham in 1935. Mary Hardwick at Weybridge and Mrs Sperling at Queen's Club in 1938. These alone mar a famous record.

Unlike Suzanne Lenglen, who was as light as a gazelle, Helen Wills was heavy-footed. She was graceful so long as she did not have to run. Her service was nothing remarkable and could not compare, for instance, with the stinging deliveries of Alice Marble or Louise Brough. Her volleying was no more than adequate, her smashing never sure and she rarely made a shot on the half volley. For these reasons her doubles and singles skills were poles apart.

Between June 1927, when at Wimbledon in the first round, Gwen Sterry held her to 6–3 3–6 6–3, and July 1933, when Miss Round won the second set 8–6 in the Wimbledon final, Helen Wills did not lose a set. Such was the assertive power of her trenchant drives on either wing, such was her freedom from error and such was her cold, unswerving determination that she crushed opposition like a machine.

She was known as 'Poker Face' and was most aptly called. Helen Wills was magnificent in her beauty but it was of an icy kind. Neither on nor off the court did she show emotion in public except, most rarely, a fleeting Mona Lisa smile. She appeared a robot designed relentlessly to pound the ball for ever. One could never imagine that the possibility of defeat existed in her mind, but what thoughts and emotions lay within the chill splendour of her outward form were never revealed.

Elizabeth Ryan lost a Wimbledon final to both Suzanne Lenglen and Helen Wills. There was no world class player in twenty years against whom 'Bunny' Ryan did not play. The story of this Californian is the story of over two decades of lawn tennis, the story of the greatest woman doubles player of all time who, though never a singles champion, won more Wimbledon titles than any player, before or since.

Miss Ryan, the supreme exponent of the forehand chop, a great volleyer and a master doubles tactician, gained her first Wimbledon title, the doubles with Miss A. M. Morton, in 1914. Her

above *Lacoste playing in the right-hand court with Borotra.*

left *The 'Four Musketeers' who took France to the top of the tennis world. From left to right: René Lacoste. Henri Cochet, (the non-playing captain Pierre Gillou), Jacques Brugnon and Jean Borotra with the Davis Cup they won for the first time.*

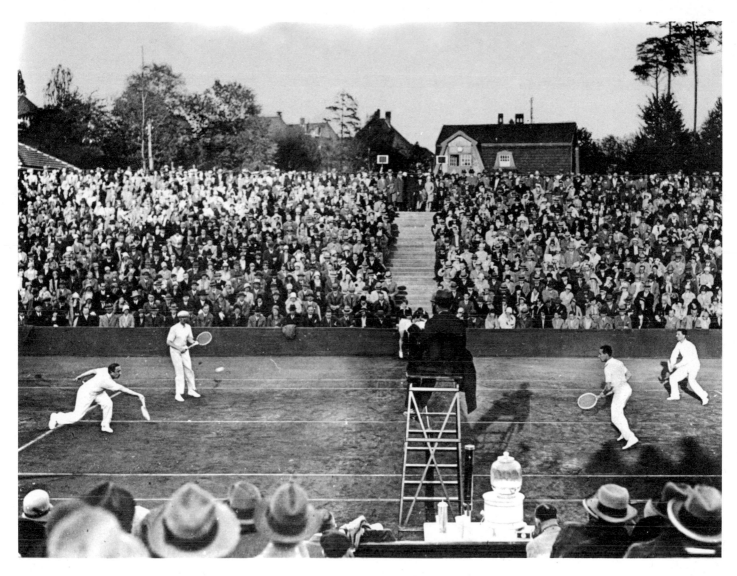

Berlin, 1929. The men's doubles final at the Rot-Weiss Club, when Henri Cochet and Jacques Brugnon (right) beat D. Prenn and H. Moldenhauer (left) 4–6 6–2 6–3 10–8

last was in 1934 in the same event with Mme Mathieu. Her first major success was in 1913 when she won the mixed in the world hard court championship at Paris. She then partnered Max Decugis. At that time another Californian, Ellsworth Vines, was not one year old. In 1933 Vines and Miss Ryan won the mixed doubles at Forest Hills.

Between 1914 and 1934 there were only two years when Miss Ryan did not win a doubles championship at Wimbledon. Twelve times she won the women's doubles and seven times the mixed. Miss Morton, her partner in 1914, had played at Wimbledon in 1901. She partnered Jean Borotra who played at Wimbledon in 1927.

Miss Ryan took nineteen titles at Wimbledon. How many other tournaments she won is almost beyond calculation, for she was perhaps the most fervent player the world has known. The doubles game was her forte yet, in sixteen playing years between 1913 and 1932, she won at least 130 singles cups. Most of them were in England or Europe, for though American she played but rarely in the United States and was domiciled in London.

The most sensational drama in lawn tennis took place in 1927, when every championship was a vintage match, when every final was a memorable one, when France won the Davis Cup and when Helen Wills plucked the two laurels of Wimbledon and Forest Hills. Excitement hardly ceased throughout the twelve months.

Beginning with the Australian Champion-

left *Strawberries and cream at Wimbledon in 1931.*

below left *Leslie and Kitty Godfree, the only married couple to win the mixed doubles. Wimbledon 1926.*

below *George VI, then Duke of York, was a competitor at Wimbledon in 1926. He and Wing Commander Louis Greig were beaten in the first round of the doubles.*

above The great runner, Hilda Krahwinkel of Germany, whose stamina made her champion of France in 1935, 1936 and 1937.

below *Sir Herbert Wilber-force, Wimbledon doubles finalist in 1888, guided the destinies of Wimbledon as All England Club chairman between the wars – seen here in 1932 with Sir Maurice Jenks, Lord Mayor of London.*

ships held in Melbourne, Gerald Patterson, who despite two Wimbledon titles had never won his native championship, finally did so by beating the holder, John B. Hawkes, in the longest final ever played. Patterson won 3–6 6–4 3–6 18–16 6–3, after Hawkes, at 13–12 and 16–15, had thrice been within a stroke of victory.

In the French championships at St Cloud the women's singles was memorable for a classic quarter-final between the South African Miss Bobbie Heine, and the Spaniard Señorita de Alvarez. A beautiful match between two beautiful players was won by Bobbie Heine, then seventeen, 3–6 7–5 7–5 after de Alvarez had twice been at match point at 5–4 in the second set and had cast away her chances with a double fault. This graceful drama was but an aperitif for the thunderous men's final in which Lacoste beat Tilden, 6–4 4–6 5–7 6–3 11–9, after match point against him.

At Wimbledon, Cochet, incredibly, impudently and incomprehensibly, won after losing the first two sets to F. T. Hunter, the American, in the quarter-final, he then lost the first two sets and trailed 1–5 in the third against Tilden in the semi-final, and finally after again losing the first two sets and surviving six match points beat Borotra in the final. That was not all at Wimbledon that astonishing year. In the doubles final both Tilden and Hunter had their revenge. They beat Brugnon and Cochet 1–6 4–6 8–6 6–3 6–4, after Cochet had led 5–4 and had two match points on his own service in the third set.

Across the Atlantic, Messieurs Lacoste, Cochet, Brugnon and Borotra, after trailing 1–2, won the Davis Cup for France. In the American Championships, Lacoste beat Tilden in the singles final winning 11–9 6–3 11–9, after Tilden had led 7–6 and 40-love on his own service in the first set and was also 5–2 with two set points in the third set.

Between 1924 and 1929 no-one but a Frenchman won the Wimbledon singles. No foreigner took the French title from 1925, when it first became an open meeting, until 1933. For three years running, 1926 to 1928, the American singles was won by a Frenchman; in 1928 Cochet won in France and America, Lacoste won at Wimbledon, and Borotra in Australia. For five out of nine years the Wimbledon doubles went to France. Lacoste won once with Borotra, Brugnon twice with Cochet and twice with Borotra.

These Frenchmen, firmly united by patriotism, had little in common but the ability to play doubles with Brugnon. He was the perfect partner, a consummate tactician and the master of a shot that, like Miss Ryan's chop, is almost a lost art. That was the low, attacking lob. One might have thought that he and Miss Ryan would have teamed to make a wonderful mixed pair, but Brugnon's only real success in that event was with Suzanne Lenglen, that dominant personality. Of his three male partners he was least successful with Lacoste with whom he did not play in a major event after 25 May 1926 when, in the Davis Cup at Prague, they beat J. Kozeluh and M. Zemla 6–2 3–6 6–8 6–2 7–5.

The trio, Cochet, Borotra and Lacoste, were as different from each other as they were from every other player. Lacoste was the theorist who saw every rally as a problem in geometry which he preferred to work out at the back of the court, and he saw every opponent as a mixture of strength and weakness that could be systematized in his notebook beforehand. Painstaking and studious he liked to blueprint every match before he played it.

Borotra too was a planner, but whereas Lacoste had a different plan for every opponent this prodigious athlete from the land of the Basques had a master plan for all. It was based on the assumption that it is possible, for some of the time, to out-volley the opposition with a sufficient output of energy from the forecourt. Since Borotra, in his early days, hardly had a ground stroke worthy of the name, his wins or defeats depended largely on how well he apportioned his energies, whether he retained sufficient ammunition for critical sets and for the vital games of those sets.

As for Cochet, it is difficult to imagine he planned a match strategically, tactically or in any other way. He had the touch of an angel and a genius for easy stroking of the ball as though he were nonchantly flicking a badminton shuttle. His facility for the half-volley was uncanny and most of the time he used that shot for choice; it meant he could dispose himself in no-man's land, tactically the worst but geometrically the best position on the court, and deal with what came with the minimum of effort.

The best known British player in the late nineteen-twenties should have been Kitty Godfree who won the Wimbledon singles in 1924 and 1926, beaten only by Suzanne Lenglen and, later, by Helen Wills. But to the man in the street lawn tennis meant Betty Nuthall, she was a fabulous junior who, as a senior, was partnered by the beautiful and graceful Eileen Bennett.

Betty Nuthall, publicised to an unprecedented degree, never quite fulfilled her original promise. While she served underhand she rated as an infant prodigy, but she struggled to learn an overhead delivery and was never the same afterwards. Both she and Miss Bennett stood on the verge of greatness for years but never managed to take the final step. Perhaps it does Miss Nuthall an injustice, for she did have one very fine achievement in winning the American singles title in 1930, the first British woman ever to do so and the first overseas winner apart from Molla Bjurstedt, whom Americans understandably claim as their own.

A grand little player came from Germany, Cilli Aussem, who won her native championship first in 1927 and again in 1930 and 1931. Since Miss Wills did not come to Europe in 1931 there were titles to win and Fräulein Aussem won them both. At the Stade Roland Garros she beat Miss Nuthall in the final to hoist the German flag abroad. It flew high at Wimbledon when there was an all German women's singles final and Fräulein Aussem, neat and deft, beat Fräulein Krahwinkel for the major crown. Then, in the hour of her triumph, she was stricken with appendicitis and the lawn tennis courts hardly saw her again.

The all-German match was the only singles final seen at Wimbledon in 1931. The men's title was won by young Sidney Wood, who at nineteen was given a walk-over from his fellow American, Frank Xavier Shields, who wished to nurse an injury and save himself for the Davis Cup in Paris. Wood, who had been a junior prodigy, never afterwards got further than the last eight at Wimbledon, and though he reached the final at Forest Hills in 1935 he won only seven games from Wilmer Allison.

The American who looked as though he might be as great a king as Tilden was Ellsworth Vines. In 1932 the talent of this tall Californian, aged twenty-one, shone brilliantly but it did not last. He won at both Wimbledon and Forest Hills with shots of lightning speed, having won in America the previous year as well. Then came the Australian, Jack Crawford, to prove the limitations of power-play. He beat Vines in the final at Wimbledon in 1933 in a classic match, one of the longest played at that stage. His win, 4–6 11–9 6–2 2–6 6–4, exemplified the resilience and eventual superiority of ground

above *Two favourites of the early 1930s: Betty Nuthall (left) and Cilli Aussem.*

left *The Australian Jack Crawford (left) and the American Ellsworth Vines in 1932.*

below *Outside Wimbledon in 1933.*

above *Ellsworth Vines in 1933. By then his tremendous pace and accuracy of the previous year had begun to diminish.*

right *Don Budge (left) and Gottfried von Cramm in 1937. Budge won both the Wimbledon and US finals against von Cramm.*

stroke purity against sheer speed.

Crawford, in turn, had to fight hard against Perry. With his flapping shirt sleeve and flat topped racquet he brought the atmosphere of the Dohertys back to the game. In 1933 he won the singles both in France and at Wimbledon. At Forest Hills he lost in the final to Perry. In 1934 he came within one point of winning the French title for the second time. The German, Baron Gottfried von Cramm, beat him 6–4 7–9 3–6 7–5 6–3 with strokes as classic in style but with more bite than his own. At Wimbledon Crawford lost the final to Perry. Had Crawford won the American final in 1933 he would have been the first man to hold the four major championships at the same time. His sequence ran thus: Australian champion, French champion and Wimbledon champion, U.S. finalist, Australian finalist, French finalist and Wimble-

don finalist.

America had its great doubles players in the golden nineteen-thirties, successors to pairs like Tilden and Hunter, Richards and Williams. Allison and Van Ryn did noble duty, as did Lott and Stoefen and Lott and Van Ryn. George Lott must rank among the great doubles men of all time, alongside Brugnon, Quist, Bromwich and Sedgman, though he did not achieve so much.

Gottfried von Cramm, immaculate in style, impeccable in court manners, will always rate among the aristocrats of lawn tennis. He twice won the French championships in 1934 and 1936, but large scale victory eluded him, he was five

times beaten in a major singles final, three times by Perry and twice by Budge. For three years running, 1935 to 1937, he lost the final at Wimbledon.

Germany had no better ambassador but the Nazis used him ill. He was sent to prison by the Gestapo in 1938. He rates as one of the sublime failures but survived to show classic worth to the post-war world.

Talent was well dispersed. Japan had a fine player in Jiro Satoh, successor to Shimizu of the nineteen-twenties. He was thrice a quarter-finalist at Wimbledon, twice a semi-finalist, the last in 1933, when he beat Bunny Austin. In

1934 he committed suicide by jumping overboard when travelling with his Davis Cup team to Europe; in Japanese eyes, of course, it was an honourable end.

Italy had G. de Stefani, a skilful ambidextrous player, and H. L. Morpurgo. Czechoslovakia produced Roderick Menzel, one of the few men Perry disliked playing against; he brought down many good men without gaining a major title. Menzel was as hot tempered as von Cramm was calm. In 1935 he flung down his racquet and stalked off the court in a semi-final at Rome when he was leading two sets to one and 4–2 in the fourth set against the Italian, G. Palmieri,

because the audience was barracking. Menzel assumed German allegiance in 1938.

When Arthur Wentworth Gore died in 1928 it seemed as though the last link with English success in major championship singles of the twentieth century had passed away. He, who won Wimbledon in 1909, cannot have known that the doings of an obstreperous youngster at the Herga Club, Harrow, presaged the renaissance of English lawn tennis. The lad in question, Frederick John Perry, was six weeks old when Gore last won at Wimbledon.

The social historian may find significance in

far left *The last of the British all-time greats: Fred Perry, son of a Labour M.P., who helped kill the image of lawn tennis as the prerogative of the upper classes.*

left *The Davis Cup Challenge Round at Forest Hills, 13 August 1914. The opening singles – Tony Wilding for Australasia versus Norris Williams for the United States. Wilding won 7–5 6–2 6–3. Wilding is on the left.*

that the supreme honour in lawn tennis, a game confined mainly to the middle and upper classes before the first war, was won after a British lapse of twenty-five years by the son of a Labour member of parliament. Perry was educated at Ealing County School and his home background was one of zealous service to the trade union and co-operative movement in the tradition of Kier Hardie and John Burns.

Perry did for British lawn tennis what Nelson did for the British navy. He created a tradition that has become a legend. One does not need to be British to hail him as one of the great players of all time; the facts speak for themselves. As a youngster he did a foolish thing. He emulated Henri Cochet, an inimitable individualist. Perry himself happened to be a genius so he got away with it. The dangers inherent in hitting a rising ball, in adopting the 'continental' grip, unchanged between forehand and backhand, which spell doom to the normal aspirant, were overcome with a wrist more strong, an eye more acute and a body more lithe than the ordinary first class athlete. It is significant that at table tennis, a game demanding quick reactions, Perry was world champion in 1929.

The vital part of Perry's career was from 1930 through to 1936 during which he won the Wimbledon singles three times, the American singles three times as well as the French and Australian titles. He was, incidentally, the first man to gain all four major championships, though, unlike his successor Donald Budge, he never held them at the same time. Since his entire game was based on a tiny margin of error he was, like Cochet, never immune from defeat. Both Laurie Doherty and Budge, as well as Tilden, had a more consistent succession of victories, though Perry's record is outstanding.

Yet Perry held supremacy at a time when, more than Doherty, Budge, or even Tilden, there were never so many quality rivals to contend against. In his time major championships were won by Sidney Wood, Cochet, Ellsworth Vines, Jack Crawford, Gottfried von Cramm, Willmer Allison and Adrian Quist. In vital encounters Perry beat Wood three times out of five, Cochet one out of two, Vines one out of two, Crawford seven times out of nine, von Cramm three times out of five, Allison three times out of four, Quist four times out of four, and Budge three times out of five. All these men were giants.

In seven years Perry played ninety-one important matches. He lost twenty-three but only

above 'Noblesse oblige'. Baron Gottfried von Cramm, probably the best German player of all time and notable for his impeccable sportsmanship.

left von Cramm with Count and Countess Reventlow (Barbara Hutton), later to become his wife.

below In 1933 Fred Perry, Bunny Austin, Pat Hughes, Harry Lee and H. Roper Barrett display the Davis Cup after the first British win for 21 years.

right *Lawn tennis crowds behave well – most of the time. Not here – Wimbledon, 1938, where rain stopped play in the Inter-Zone final of the Davis Cup.*

below *Nor at Forest Hills in 1941, when Frank Kovacs won his semi-final against Don McNeill.*

six between 1934 and 1936 when he was at his peak. He was beaten by Stefani, Crawford, Allison, von Cramm and twice by Budge. He was injured when he lost to Allison in the semi-final of the American championship in 1935.

Perry became a professional at the end of 1936 having contributed more to the prosperity of the British game than anyone. His last big match was the final of the American championship at Forest Hills when he beat Budge 2–6 6–2 8–6 1–6 10–8. The mighty Budge was close on Perry's heels and, in the last singles Perry played as an amateur, the final of the Pacific South West championship at Los Angeles, Budge won 6–2 4–6 6–2 6–3.

H. W. Austin, whose name will always be coupled with Perry's in relation to the British glories of the nineteen-thirties, had a foot in the world game before Perry forced his way in, and he was on the scene three years after Perry left it. He won his first open singles and got his Cambridge blue while Perry, three years his junior, was writing lines at school. Perry blustered a noisy way to the top. Austin, helped by willing hands, reached the last rung of the ladder but one, but he never stood on the highest platform of the game.

Austin was a beautiful player, a gentle artist with the grace and style of his Cambridge predecessor Laurie Doherty. He was immaculate on the drive, both left and right, and equally immaculate on the volley. But, judged by the same standards, his service and smashes were poor. He lacked the devil of a champion, the bite of a world beater. Perry was as strong as a horse and as fit as a Derby winner. Austin was slight and not robust, his stamina always suspect. Perry was the successor to Cochet, Austin to René Lacoste.

The highlights of Austin's career were widely spaced. His first Wimbledon final was 1932, his second in 1938 and in both years his victor was at the peak of shattering form. Those who saw Ellsworth Vines in 1932 are unlikely to forget the speed and power of the tall Californian, who flayed the ball with devastating zest not shown before and not revealed again, even by Vines himself. It is doubtful if the Dohertys or Brookes, or Wilding, or Tilden, or even Cochet in his most supreme moments, could have held the game Vines played that year.

In the final he beat Austin 6–4 6–2 6–0. The last point was the supreme cannon ball delivery. Vines tossed the ball up and swung his racquet. The ball disappeared. There was the

above *Bunny Austin (right) was thoroughly thrashed by Ellsworth Vines in the Wimbledon final of 1932. When Vines served his last ace, it was so fast that Austin never knew which side of him it passed.*

left *Even an English summer is sometimes hot: Wimbledon first aid in action, 1937.*

The general standard of British women's lawn tennis was probably at its peak in the 1930s. Dorothy Round was the Wimbledon singles champion in 1934 and 1937, but she was never better than semi-finalist at Forest Hills.

'pling' as it met the gut. There was a thump and a sudden eddy of net and canvas at the Royal Box end of the centre court. Austin did not even swing his racquet, for he had no idea whether the ball was going to left or right. All that was seen, for which the service linesman must have been profoundly thankful, was a burst of chalk rising from the service line, the only clue to the passage of what must have been the fastest ball ever struck.

Six years later Austin met with a like fate from Donald Budge, who beat him 6–1 6–0 6–3.

Budge lost only forty-eight games in seven matches and did not drop a set, a feat which had not been achieved since Reggie Doherty in 1897.

Austin, though never senior wrangler of the game, was consistent. For nine years running, from 1931 to 1939, he reached the last eight at Wimbledon and he was there ten times in all, a record unequalled since the first war. In twelve years from 1928 he never failed to rank among the ten best in the world.

The apogee of British lawn tennis was 1934,

left *The Californian Alice Marble with her aggressive play added a new dimension to the women's game. Four times US champion, she won all three events at Wimbledon in 1939 and in the singles final overwhelmed the British Kay Stammers (right) 6–2 6–0.*

below left *Uniformed messenger boys paid to queue for tickets in 1937 – and the Wimbledon pony-roller, minus pony, in use in 1938.*

right *In the Wimbledon final of 1938 Don Budge (seen in action far right) crushed Britain's Bunny Austin 6–1 6–0 6–3. Later* **(below right),** *Budge went into the laundry business with Sidney Wood.*

the most triumphant year in a quarter of a century. For the first time since 1913, the challenge round of the Davis Cup was held at Wimbledon and Britain kept the trophy. Peggy Scriven became French champion for the second time. Perry won Wimbledon, the American title for the second time and that of Australia besides. Dorothy Round became Wimbledon women's singles champion, a successor to Mrs Godfree who had won in 1926.

Like Mrs Godfree, who won in 1924 when Suzanne Lenglen was not playing and again two years later when the French queen abdicated, Miss Round reigned in the absence of the mon-

arch, for Miss Wills was not defending.

Dorothy Round gained the universal soubriquet, 'the Sunday school mistress', for she refused to play in the French championships on a Sunday. Catholic France took the incident more calmly than non-conformist England.

Miss Wills resumed suzerainty a year later. Miss Round might have met her in the semi-final but she was beaten in the quarter-final by the Australian, Joan Hartigan. In 1936 Miss Round failed again, once more in the quarter-final, losing to her old rival Fräulein Krahwinkel, now Mrs Sperling and the wife of a Dane. The winner's popularity was not enhanced

when, during the match, Miss Round asked permission to leave the court to fix a broken shoulder strap and received an abrupt refusal.

The revival of Miss Round's glory in 1937 was the greater since Perry had turned professional. Miss Jacobs in the quarter-final, then Mme Mathieu and, finally, Miss Jadwiga Jedrzejowska were beaten and Miss Round became champion again.

The nineteen-thirties were grand days for British women. Miss Round was the best stylist, strong and fluent. There was also Peggy Scriven, determined but with no style at all. Was there ever such a gawky ill-equipped champion? A left-hander, she had an appalling service, a monstrously defensive backhand and her only winning shot, and that cumbersomely styled, was on the forehand. Yet she had the quality of Lottie Dod, of Mrs Lambert Chambers, of

Suzanne Lenglen, of Helen Wills with her dour determination not to lose. She and Miss Round had a memorable clash in the British hard court final of 1934. Six times Miss Scriven came within a point of winning but Miss Round won 6–2 2–6 8–6.

Miss Scriven never won at Bournemouth. The arid centre court at Auteuil was the scene of her two greatest triumphs in 1933 and in 1934 when she won the French title. The irony of her first win, when she beat Mme Mathieu in the final 6–2 4–6 6–4, was that she had no official status. The English team had not included her and she paid her own expenses. The next year she played a dour match against Helen Jacobs, and won 7–5 4–6 6–1 in the longest women's final up to that time. It ended in the dark.

Kathleen Stammers would have topped any British popularity poll from about 1934 on. She

No less than four Wimbledon and two US finals were played out between Helen Jacobs and Helen Wills Moody. Miss Jacobs won only once – at Forest Hills in 1933. Their last big clash was the Wimbledon final of 1938 when Miss Jacobs was beaten 6–4 6–0.

above *An aerial view of the All England Club in 1935.*

right *Under Mussolini, Italian tennis players had little choice but to pay their respects to the regime. This photograph was taken in 1929.*

had a sparkling personality and a sparkling, if imperfect, game. Like Miss Scriven she was left handed, but as graceful and mobile as Miss Scriven was awkward. She hit piercing winners on the forehand but it took her years to achieve a safe defensive backhand. She had her famous win over Helen Wills at Beckenham in 1935, but players like Mrs Sperling and Miss Jedrzejowska tended to have her measure. But she had the edge most of the time on Miss Scriven and Señorita Lizana, who were her final opponents in three hard court championship victories, the first in 1935, the last in 1939.

The apex of Miss Stammers' achievement was 1939. She reached the semi-final of the Wightman Cup, beating Miss Jacobs on the way. There arduously, she beat Sarah Palfrey and got to the final. British hopes did not live long. Alice Marble, her third American opponent in a row, devastated her 6–2 6–0, and Miss Stammers, though twice a Wimbledon champion at doubles with Miss James, never won a major singles.

Donald Budge, born in California in 1917, succeeded Perry and Tilden as the great mogul of the game. Perhaps he was the best of all time. That is a matter of opinion. He dwarfed his rivals and, if his reign were shorter than Perry's and much briefer than Tilden's, his two years' invincibility, continuously put to the test in the four quarters of the globe, was entire. He was the first man to hold the four big championships, Australia, France, Wimbledon and America, at the same time. He was the first man, in comparable conditions, to win the Wimbledon singles without losing a set, the first to win all three events, the only one to do so two years running, and he was unique in winning all three for the total loss of only one set. He was the first man to be a triple winner both at Wimbledon and in America.

Budge beat Perry at Los Angeles in the autumn of 1936, the last amateur singles Perry played. Since Perry had beaten him in the semi-final at Wimbledon and in the final at Forest Hills too much should not be made of that. Yet for the next twenty-four months no-one won against Budge in an important singles. He had thirty-four testing matches against strong players and won the lot. Only twelve players lasted more than three sets, only three the full distance.

Budge, a master player, was more dominant at his peak than any other player. He rolled out his power shots with ruthless effect. His backhand, timed as no backhand was ever timed before, had all his weight behind it and it was a killing stroke. It was said he had a forehand weakness, but opponents sought in vain to exploit it, just as they strived to use the more obvious backhand vulnerability of Perry. Facing the power game of Budge was like trying to stop a tank with a machine gun.

It is not without interest to note the two opponents who extended Budge to five sets: von Cramm who managed it twice and a rising youngster, Jaroslav Drobny.

Alice Marble, born in California in 1914, succeeded Suzanne Lenglen and Helen Wills as empress of the game. Some hold her to be greater than both, but it is a matter of opinion. That she could have beaten both is fairly certain but whether she could consistently have done so is another matter. Her overhead work, service, smash and volley, had the lithe, unchecked action from muscles developed young in pitching a baseball. Imagine a clean limbed young lad playing good, aggressive lawn tennis and there you have Alice Marble, a tomboy as a little girl and still the tomboy at Forest Hills and Wimbledon. Once she had a champion's status and the confidence that springs therefrom, she was murderous and few survived long against her.

No player becomes a champion without travail and disappointment. Her first major success, the American singles in 1936, came at the age of twenty-three. Ill health dogged Miss Marble all along. On her first visit to Europe in 1933 she collapsed while playing in the French championships. She had anaemia, was threatened with T.B. and hospitalised for two years. No athletic career could have seemed more completely at an end. That so virile a game was produced from so frail a physique is one of the wonders of sport.

She came to Wimbledon, as American champion, for the first time in 1937. She won the mixed doubles with Budge but the real prize eluded her. Miss Jedrzejowska beat her in the semi-final and she failed at Forest Hills as well. At Wimbledon in 1938 she won both doubles, the women's with Miss Sarah Palfrey and the mixed again with Budge, but Miss Jacobs brought her down in singles, again at the semi-final stage. Judged then as a candidate for all time greatness one would have said Miss Marble was a failure, just as one would have said of Perry in 1933. When the margin of error permitted is so small, the balance between defeat and victory is precarious.

Perhaps the turning point that transformed Miss Marble from a gallant failure into an established success was a remarkable semi-final match she played against Miss Palfrey in the American championship in 1938. She led 5–1 in the first set but lost it 5–7. She trailed 2–5 in the second set, had two match points against her, but won it 7–5. She lagged 1–3 in the final set, eventually gained at 7–5. It was not stoutness in defence that saved Miss Marble. It was persistent aggression, heroic faith in her natural volleying game that achieved such a close triumph. In the final against the Australian, Miss Nancye Wynne, majestic in style and power but frail in consistency, Miss Marble lost only three games. Miss Marble was American champion for the next two years.

Her Wimbledon triumph was in 1939. She won all three events and in singles had the most overwhelming victory since Miss Wills in 1932.

The year Miss Marble was triple champion at Wimbledon in 1939, was the year Robert Lorimer Riggs, then twenty-one, also won three events. This was a remarkable performance since he had never played there before and even more remarkable in that Riggs, by his own telling, went to a bookmaker beforehand and backed himself to do so. But then Riggs was a remarkable player, a mischievous genius.

Looking back on lawn tennis between the two wars the dominance of the United States is undeniable, whatever yardstick be adopted. The Wimbledon championship makes the most convenient frame of reference since it never failed to have a representative international entry. Measuring by singles titles one sees:

Men		*Women*	
U.S.	9	U.S.	10
France	9	France	6
G.B.	3	G.B.	4
Germany	3	Germany	1

More representative of national strength, perhaps, is to compare the last eight of the singles at Wimbledon. This is most conveniently done from 1922, when the challenge round was abolished. The figures that matter are:

Men		*Women*	
U.S.	42	G.B.	51
G.B.	32	U.S.	38
France	24	France	16
Australia	13	Germany	13

By 1939 the tournament system in the major championships had become more or less standardised. In the United States the challenge round was abolished in 1912 and the holder required to play through; an innovation altogether more fair. At Wimbledon the old system lingered on until the change of venue to Church Road where, with the new ground, conservative opposition faded.

The system of 'seeding' the draw originated in the United States. Britain ventured such modernity in 1924 when overseas competitors were precluded from meeting each other in the early rounds. Full seeding in order of merit was not introduced at the Wimbledon championship until 1927.

The Growth of Professionalism –

In the world as a whole lawn tennis, which had been put in cold storage in 1939, resumed in 1946. In the United States it had never ceased, and the major championships there had continued without a break. Inevitably some nations were slower than others in regaining the international scene. The fervour of post-war patriotism was reflected in the expulsion both from the Davis Cup and from the International Federation of Germany and Japan. But by 1951 they were back in the comity of lawn tennis nations.

The standard of play was set by Australians and Americans. Indeed the dominance of the men of these nations made the Davis Cup a closed competition as far as the rest of the world was concerned. Every Challenge Round between 1946 and 1959 was played between them. Even so, the event continued to attract a growing entry. By 1939, forty-one nations were competing, by 1967 the number was sixty-two and the arrangement of the competition became increasingly complex. The international calendar became fuller in every respect.

As for the standard of play, American expertise among the women was a revelation. The first international event to be staged was the Wightman Cup at Wimbledon in June 1946, and the British assumed that their representatives were world class. The Americans, Pauline Betz, Margaret Osborne, Louise Brough and Doris Hart, scored a devastating victory, winning by 7-nil and never losing a set in the process, a display of shattering superiority.

The virile game of Alice Marble was the basis for this widespread American skill. As it happened Miss Betz, the best of the original quartet that astonished the world, did not play in the leading events after 1946, for the U.S.L.T.A. declared her a professional on the grounds that she had discussed the terms of a professional contract. Miss Betz won both Wimbledon and Forest Hills in 1946 and one suspects she would have been invincible for many years had she continued.

Few players other than Americans won many important events after 1946. At Wimbledon there was only one non-American in the last four of the women's singles during the whole of the next decade, and in the US championships there were only three. Even in the French championships, whose slow courts least favour the serve and volley technique so ably exploited by the Americans, had only two non-American winners in the same period.

1946–1967

above *Jack Kramer won the men's singles at Wimbledon in 1947 having lost the previous year because of a blistered hand. He is receiving the trophy from George VI; also in the royal box are Princess Margaret and Queen Elizabeth, the Queen Mother.*

left *Yvon Petra of France (left) surprised the world by winning Wimbledon in 1946.*

right *Petra's serves actually smashed straight through the poor quality post-war net at Wimbledon.*

left *Bob Falkenburg was reckoned a 'freak' Wimbledon champion in 1948. But he was a bold player and in the final he beat John Bromwich 7–5 0–6 6–2 3–6 7–5 after surviving three match points in the fifth set.*

below *Naval ratings from Chatham acting as stewards during the torrential rain of the 1947 Wimbledon.*

above *An American who became a virtual European Budge Patty. His great year was 1951, when he became champion of both France and Wimbledon. He played little in the United States and had relatively small success there.*

right *Ted Schroeder (right) won the US singles in 1942 and, seven years later, won Wimbledon at his first and only attempt. In the quarter-final he was match point down to Frank Sedgman, who is congratulating him here at the end of the match. Sedgman's first big success was two years later when he won the US title.*

The Wimbledon championships of 1946 were a little surprised by their own success. Parts of the stands round the centre court were cordoned off where a time-bomb had left a gaping hole. Equally surprising the men's singles winner, Yvon Petra of France. The American Jack Kramer was the overwhelming favourite, but a badly blistered hand brought about his defeat in his match against the Czech Jaroslav Drobny. The Australian Geoff Brown played in the final against Petra. Brown, of medium height and slight in build, had one of the most devastatingly fast services of all time which projected the ball like an uncoiling spring. Petra hardly seemed of the same class, but in the final Brown made the odd tactical error of slow balling which was for him an alien game. He was two sets down before he saw his error and eventually he lost in the fifth set.

Kramer, who won the US title later in 1946 and also Wimbledon and the US title in 1947, had an all-round strength, few weaknesses, a capacity of tremendous concentration. His excursions into the amateur game were but the means to an end, the stepping stone to the rich prizes of a professional career. At Wimbledon in 1947 he did not equal the 1938 record of Donald Budge who did not drop a set, but, through yielding one set to the Australian Dinny Pails in the semi-finals, he gave away fewer games than any champion – Donald Budge excepting – before or since. Only thirty-seven games were taken against him. With his compatriot, the tall Bob Falkenburg, he won the doubles without losing a set, a unique record.

Kramer's successors at Wimbledon were Falkenburg, Ted Schroeder, Budge Patty and Dick Savitt, all Americans. Falkenburg in 1948 had the luck of a poker player, he drew a joker on the last card when he survived three match points in his final against the gentle Australian John Bromwich. He was 2–5, 15–40 down in the fifth set, and he salvaged all the vital points with fast and daring cross court passing shots that were hit or miss gambles from the moment he struck the ball. For spectators, Bromwich's defeat was an almost tearful occasion for he was a favourite with the crowd, and they disliked Falkenburg's habit of deliberately losing sets to conserve his energy.

Schroeder was another gambler. This pipe smoking Californian could have walked straight out of a western. He was a supreme individualist and his first and only Wimbledon challenge in 1949 was hectic. In his quarter-final against the

above *The rugged Vic Seixas had his greatest successes in 1953 as champion of Wimbledon and of the United States in 1954.*

below *Gardner Mulloy (left) and Budge Patty won the Wimbledon men's doubles in 1957 as an unseeded pair. Mulloy was forty-three years old.*

above *Seixas never missed a chance to go up to the net – on this occasion he went right into it.*

above *Jaroslav Drobny was the greatest 'outsider' ever to win the Wimbledon singles. After two defeats in the final, three losses in the semi-final, he finally acquired the title in 1954 as the no. 11 seed. He was thirty-two years old.*

right *Drobny at the end of the most memorable match of 1953, when he beat Budge Patty 8–6 16–18 3–6 8–6 12–10 after four hours and fifteen minutes. The All England Club presented both players with a gold cigarette case in recognition of their battle.*

left and right *The Austrian Freddie Huber astonished the world in the mid-1950s by his extraordinary acrobatic exploits in mid-court. He was a superb touch artist but his extravagant temperament prevented him from reaching the top.*

below *One of the many great Californians: Louise Brough, an outstanding volleyer, she was US champion in 1947 and won Wimbledon four times.*

below *Doris Hart, the US champion in 1954 and 1955, Wimbledon winner in 1951 and a player of rare grace.*

left *Maureen Connolly, one of the all time 'greats', dominated the women's game from 1951 to 1954 and she was the first woman to win the 'Grand Slam', in 1953. She had won the Wimbledon singles three times when a broken leg caused her to retire in 1954; she was not then twenty years old.*

left *The American Gussie Moran pioneered a revolution in fashion on the court. Her display of lace panties in 1949 marked the start of a new era.*

below *One of Wimbledon's more exotic fashions.*

above *Lew Hoad failed to win only one of the major championships, that of the United States, while Ken Rosewall* **(above right),** *seen in a characteristic pose, won all the major championships except Wimbledon. They are seen playing in a doubles* **(right).**

far right *Rod Laver in 1962, the year when he won the championships of Australia, Italy, France, Wimbledon, Germany and the United States.*

Australian Frank Sedgman he survived a match ball against him at 5–4 and again at 6–5 in the final set. On the first occasion, Schroeder, footfaulted on his first delivery, scraped a winning volley off the wood. On the second, he risked all with a fast backhand down the line.

For all his erratic brilliance, Schroeder won the American singles only once at a war-time meeting in 1942. He maddened his super-specialist colleagues by not bothering to play at Forest Hills, preferring to sell refrigerators in California. Following his rollicking Wimbledon success he did appear at Forest Hills in 1949 and, though he did not win, he became involved in the longest final to date, and was finally beaten by Ricardo Gonzales 16–18 2–6 6–1 6–2 6–4. Yet Schroeder was the chief architect of American Davis Cup victories from 1946–1949.

Patty's real triumph was less in winning Wimbledon than in becoming French champion a few weeks before. Lithe and debonair, he was a Californian who had taken French nationality and the French looked upon him as one of their own. No player had a sounder forehand.

After Patty came Savitt, another man like Schroeder, to take the Wimbledon crown at his first assault. He had met the full force of partisanship in Australia as a visiting American, and at Wimbledon he seemed ready to assume that English crowds would be as avid to see him lose. So somewhat truculently he rolled out the penetrating strength of perhaps the best backhand since that of Budge, and emerged as champion.

In 1948 and 1949 the US champion was the swarthy Gonzales, a big man with a big game. Yet for all his weight of shot he had delicacy of touch as well. Perhaps the greatest indictment of the division of the game into its two classes, professional and amateur, was the effect it had on his career. He became a professional in 1949 and it barred him from the best setting of the game. Even so, Gonzales showed in a more restricted field a stature which elsewhere would probably have earned him the classification as the greatest player of all time. He had a memorable encounter against Sedgman at Wembley in 1956, winning by 4–6 11–9 11–9 9–7 after a masterpiece of a match.

Sedgman, the singles champion of Australia in 1949 and 1950 was a super-specialist and the product of Australian zest for sport. In 1951 Forest Hills was won by an overseas player, the first since Fred Perry in 1936, when Sedgman,

potentially the best player in the world for two years, burst through to classic success. His last three rounds were meteoric. Tony Trabert won seven games in the quarter-final, Art Larsen, a genius of a touch player who had won the year before, took four games in the semi-final. In the last match Vic Seixas only wrested six games and the most one-sided US final would have been unique had not Sedgman repeated it against Gardner Mulloy twelve months later. Mobility was Sedgman's greatest talent, as well as a fore-hand of rare quality, and his splendid footwork enabled him to make every shot seem easy. In 1952 in France, Drobny beat Sedgman, but at Wimbledon Sedgman's talents were at their sharpest on the lightning turf, and there he was as much the master of Drobny as Drobny had been him at Auteuil in France. Sedgman was triple champion in 1952, the first since Riggs in 1939.

In 1953 Ken Rosewall, with his classic back-hand and service gentle enough to defy all the tenets of the service-volley theories, won the Australian and French titles; but the Wimbledon winner was the resolute Vic Seixas who had been in the US final but who had been beaten by his fellow-American Tony Trabert. The match of the year was played at Wimbledon and the joint heroes were Patty and Drobny. They met in the third round and such a conflict had never been seen at the All England Club before. They began at five o'clock and finished at twilight, Drobny winning 8–6 16–18 3–6 8–6 12–10, a total of ninety-three games lasting four hours fifteen minutes. Patty had three match balls in the fourth set and three more in the fifth, and the standard of play never fell below the highest. Drobny staggered through two more rounds to the semi-final where he lost to the Dane, Kurt Nielsen, but his chances of the title had been killed by the physical demands of that earlier encounter.

Two years later at Lyons in France, Drobny and Patty, who were often touring companions, had another outstanding cut and thrust. There, on a fast wood court, they split the final after four hours thirty-five minutes with the score, in terms of Drobny, 21–19 8–10 21–21. That was a total of 100 games and, in the best of a five-set match, they might have gone on far longer.

Drobny, a left-hander who first appeared at Wimbledon as a stripling before the war, took some time to reach the top rung of the ladder. A quarter-finalist at Wimbledon in 1946, a finalist against Schroeder in 1949, quarter-finalist again in 1950, finalist against Sedgman in 1952, semi-finalist in 1953, he could not crack the best lawn tennis nuts. His fine skill on hard courts made him French champion in 1951 and 1952.

Finally Drobny beat Lew Hoad, Patty and Rosewall to become Wimbledon champion in 1954. He had been a refugee from Czechoslovakia for three years, although he was in the bizarre situation of holding an Egyptian nationality at Wimbledon that year, and later he became a British citizen. He was the most popular winner for years, and won after a splendid final against Rosewall 13–11 4–6 6–2 9–7, which was one of the longest ever played.

In 1951 Forest Hills threw up a remarkable winner in the women's singles. This was Maureen Connolly, aged only sixteen. She was no volleyer, her serve was nothing out of the way, but her driving was superb, especially on the backhand. She came from San Diego, California, and was a natural left-hander who had adapted herself to the other wing.

When she came onto the scene Miss Osborne (later Mrs du Pont), Louise Brough and Doris Hart had dominated all important play. Miss Connolly forced them into second place. In the years 1952, 1953 and 1954 she assumed the mantle of greatness that had belonged to Suzanne Lenglen and to Helen Wills Moody. In that time she lost on four occasions, to Miss Hart at South Orange, New Jersey, in 1952, to Miss Hart again in the final of the Italian championships in 1953, to Shirley Fry in Los Angeles five months later and to Beverly Fleits in La Jolla, California, early in 1954.

Otherwise she was invincible. She won Wimbledon in 1952, 1953 and 1954, Forest Hills again in 1952 and 1953, France in 1953 and 1954. She also won the Australian singles in 1953, and so in that year became the first woman to win the 'Grand Slam' of the four traditional major championships. After winning the US clay court championship in 1954 she broke her leg in a riding accident and never played competitive tennis again. She became a coaching professional. She was not twenty years old when her accident put her from the game. Tragically, for she was a charming and lovable person, she died in 1969 at the age of thirty-four.

At Wimbledon in both 1953 and 1954 Miss Connolly lost no sets and conceded only nineteen games. This complete superiority was accomplished with relatively limited technical skills, and only in the latter years could it be said that her overhead was becoming really competent. Had her career continued she would probably have risen to heights unequalled since Suzanne Lenglen. As a doubles player she was far short of her singles skill, and indeed, this otherwise tremendous performer, when she played in the Wimbledon women's doubles final with Julie Sampson in 1953 against Shirley Fry and Doris Hart, had the intimidating experience of losing 6–0 6–0.

Miss Connolly's backhand drive was assuredly the fastest and most accurate shot of its kind ever played by a woman. What position she should occupy among the all-time greats is necessarily a matter of opinion, but that Miss Connolly ranks among them is certain.

So perhaps do two of her contemporaries among the men, Rosewall and Hoad. As two Australian seventeen-year-old novices, they first appeared on the international scene in 1952 when their apprentice skill was sufficiently mature to make them doubles semi-finalists in the championships of France, Wimbledon and America.

In his career as an amateur Rosewall won the Australian singles in 1953 and 1955, the French singles in 1953, the American singles in 1956. Hoad won the Australian singles in 1955, the French title in 1956, and Wimbledon in 1956 and 1957. Rosewall never won at Wimbledon and Hoad never won the American title, and it was Rosewall's victory over Hoad in the US final of 1956 that prevented Hoad from achieving the 'Grand Slam'.

Rosewall was the quiet perfectionist and the more consistent of the two, Hoad was perhaps the most dynamic shot-maker that ever was. Rosewall epitomised the classic lawn tennis game, but no-one could presume to imitate Hoad unless they were possessed of a wrist of steel. He was a law unto himself.

In the opinion of those who saw it, the Wimbledon final of 1957, in which Hoad beat his compatriot Ashley Cooper, was perhaps the greatest example of killing lawn tennis ever played. Hoad won 6–2 6–1 6–2, and Cooper, who was to be champion the next year, was made to look little more than a beginner. By that time Rosewall had turned professional, and Hoad did so immediately Wimbledon finished.

It would have been appropriate if Hoad and Rosewall had won the 'Grand Slam' as a doubles pair, a feat performed only by Sedgman

top left *Althea Gibson, the first black player to get to the top. She was invincible at Wimbledon and Forest Hills in 1957 and 1958 before turning professional.*

below left *The rivalry between Maria Bueno and Margaret Smith (later Mrs Court) was the major motif of the 1960s.*

left *Maria Bueno, the fiery and graceful champion from Brazil.*

above and right *Margaret Smith won the second of her two successive finals against Maria Bueno at Wimbledon in 1965.*

above *The evergreen Ken Rosewall – here the first open champion of France in 1968 – fifteen years after his original success.*

left *The super athlete and perpetual runner-up, Roy Emerson. He won at last in 1964 at Wimbledon when he beat Fred Stolle 6–4 12–10 4–6 6–3. He won again a year later, while Stolle lost three consecutive finals.*

below *Emerson with his Wimbledon trophy. He also took the US title in 1964.*

The Spaniard Manuel Santana used the top spin drive from both wings to add a new dimension to the game with shots that had seemed impossible. Surprisingly he did as well on grass as on hard courts and, having been French champion in 1961 and 1964, was champion of the United States in 1965 and of Wimbledon in 1966. He provided the inspiration for another touch genius: the Rumanian Ilie Nastase.

and Ken McGregor in 1951. They could well have done so in 1953 when, having taken the Australian, French and Wimbledon titles, they did not compete for the American title. Similarly in 1956, when they won in Australia, Wimbledon and the US, they did not play together in the French match.

The supply of outstanding Australian men players did not cease when Hoad and Rosewall turned professional. In 1958 Harry Hopman, the outstanding guide and mentor of young Australians, had under his wing a red-headed Queenslander, Rod Laver. He was left-handed and not physically very impressive. If anything, his companion Bob Mark, who was much burlier, appeared to have more potential. But in 1959 Laver's lawn tennis began to make its mark. At Wimbledon, though unseeded, he reached the final where he lost to the Peruvian, Alex Olmedo. At Forest Hills he was a quarter-finalist, losing to Ron Holmberg.

In 1960 Laver came again, this time as champion of Australia. Again he reached the Wimbledon final, losing to his fellow left-hander Neale Fraser, whom he had beaten to take his own national title. Laver also reached the US final, and there too he lost to Fraser.

In 1961 Laver lost the Australian final to Roy Emerson's athletic energies, and in France he reached the semi-final before yielding to the artistic craft of the Spaniard Manuel Santana, whose first major success was gained at this championship. But at Wimbledon, Laver, playing in the final for the third year running, won the title for the first time. However, a few weeks later, he was defeated by Emerson in his second American final.

In 1962 Laver achieved a good deal more. He became champion extraordinary. He beat Emerson to win the Australian title at the beginning of the season, he went to Rome for the Italian meeting and beat Emerson in another final. In France in his quarter-final, he was match point down against Martin Mulligan, an Australian expatriate living in Italy, but survived and went on to reach the final. There he again beat Emerson. At Wimbledon Laver met the unseeded Mulligan in the final and won easily. At Hamburg he took the German championship in his stride, winning against Santana in the final match. That left one big event, the American championships at Forest Hills, and Laver won the final there yet once more against Emerson.

Don Budge in 1938 had won the 'Grand Slam'.

This was more than that, it was the six major championships: Australia, Italy, France, Wimbledon, Germany and America. To complete Laver's awesome record for that year it should be added that he won all his rubbers in the Challenge Round of the Davis Cup. Indeed Australia was always a victor in the Davis Cup with Laver in the side.

Laver spent the next five years as a professional player, and his status and standards remained undiminished. He was to rise to great heights when the game became open in 1968, but 1962 was a year when Laver's achievements, both quantitatively and qualitatively, assured him a unique niche in the history of the game.

In 1958 an eighteen-year-old Brazilian, Maria Esther Bueno, came to Europe for the first time. She competed in the Italian championships in Rome and, after surviving match points in an early round against the British holder Shirley Bloomer, she won the title. The grace of her game was exceptional, with no apparent effort she generated hot pace on every stroke, service, drive and volley. She evinced the same contempt for the ball as Gonzales, and her personality was imperious allowing herself little margin of error. She was an artist striving for perfection every time she hit the ball. This was both her strength and weakness, for if her timing were awry there was no safety margin.

In 1961 eighteen-year-old Australian, Margaret Smith, also ventured to Europe for the first time, winning the Monte Carlo tournament. She was strong, muscular and super-fit, an athlete in every inch. The rivalry between the super-artist Miss Bueno and the super-athlete Miss Smith provided a major *motif* in the game for seven years.

Neither had the virtual invincibility of Suzanne Lenglen, Helen Wills Moody or Maureen Connolly. Miss Bueno had no second line game on which to fall back if she were playing badly. Miss Smith for long suffered from inhibiting tension on the big occasion.

Miss Bueno established herself among lawn tennis aristocrats by winning Wimbledon at her second attempt in 1959. It made her a national heroine of Brazil. A statue was erected to her and her portrait appeared on a postage stamp.

Miss Smith won the US title in 1962, and Wimbledon at her third attempt in 1963. The Australian Lawn Tennis Association hardly gave her the honour which was her due. Clinging to an outmoded concept of amateurism,

left *Pietrangeli, like many leading tennis players, takes an active interest in encouraging youngsters.*

below *Pietrangeli is seen shaking hands with one of his many admirers, Pope Paul VI.*

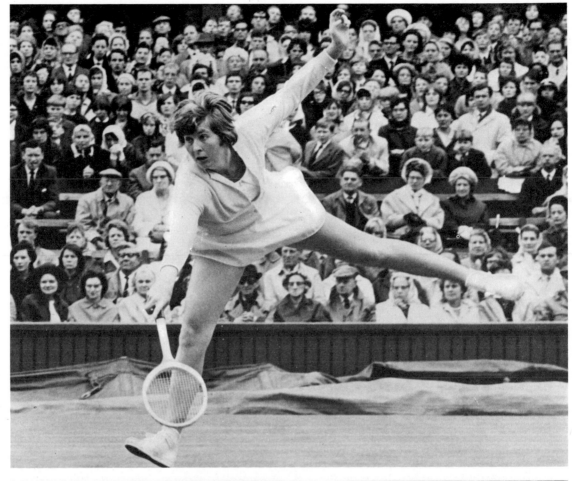

right *Christine Truman's courageous spirit and sportsmanship went straight to the hearts of the British public. Great was their disappointment when she just failed to win the Wimbledon women's singles in 1961.*

below *The enterprising journalist who snapped this picture of sleeping lineswoman Dorothy Cavis-Brown made front page news during the 1964 Wimbledon Championships; the officials were considerably embarrassed.*

they even wrote around to the tournaments organisations declaring that she must not be given private hospitality. Yet in due course the outstanding success of Miss Smith brought a new concept of women's lawn tennis to Australia, raising it from the second-class status it had always had to parity with the men.

So far as their rivalry was concerned, the athlete was more successful than the artist. In the course of their careers Miss Bueno and Miss Smith met twenty-one times, and the Australian was the victor on seventeen occasions.

Nine of their matches were major contests in the final of important championships. The first was the Italian championships of 1962, which Miss Smith won, the last in 1968, was the US National Amateur Championship in Boston, also won by Miss Smith, by then Mrs Barry Court. In between, they played for the Australian title once, the French title once, the Wimbledon title twice, the German title twice and the US title when it was at Forest Hills.

Miss Bueno won twice. She beat Miss Smith 7–5 6–4 for the American title in 1963 and she won 6–4 7–9 6–3 to win Wimbledon in 1964. Had it not been for the Australian's gymnastic-like exploits at the net, Miss Bueno would certainly have won more than she did. As it was Miss Bueno won twenty-four major titles, in the course of a career which in its latter years was plagued by sickness and injury.

Between 1960, when she first won the Australian title, and 1972, when she won the US mixed doubles open championship five months after giving birth to a son, Mrs Court collected more championships than anyone, man or woman, in the history of lawn tennis.

If one recognises the major events as the championships of Australia, South Africa, Italy, France, Wimbledon, Germany and America, Mrs Court acquired no less than eighty-three titles. At one time or another she was triple champion at every one of these meetings save only Wimbledon. In 1970 she emulated Miss Connolly by taking the 'Grand Slam', which she had already acquired in mixed doubles with the Australian, Ken Fletcher, in 1963.

If the measure of greatness were purely statistical, then Mrs Court would rank as the finest woman player of all time. She, more than anyone, epitomised professionalism in the game, even if her status until 1968 was technically that of an amateur. She actually played no more tournaments than an enthusiast like Bunny Ryan between the wars, but her matches were organised on a vastly more intensive level as she flew from one country to another, and the average standard of opposition was a good deal higher. In twelve years, from 1961 to 1972, it was only in 1967 that she did not travel the world.

The dedicated professionalism of Mrs Court echoed the outlook of most of the leading men players. A typical example was the Australian Roy Emerson, a fleet-footed athlete who from the age of seventeen onwards took to travelling around the world from one tournament to another as a way of life. He made himself the number one player in the world in 1964 and 1965, winning the Wimbledon singles, but he had served a long apprenticeship. He totalled thirty-five major titles, notably taking his native title six times out of the seven between 1961 and 1967. In France he set the remarkable record of taking the men's doubles every year from 1960 to 1965, twice with Neale Fraser and once with Rod Laver, as well as with Manuel Santana, Ken Fletcher and Fred Stolle.

A contrast to Emerson was the Spaniard Santana, a young artist the very reverse of rugged athleticism. His happy personality made him a tremendously popular Wimbledon champion in 1966, following his success as French champion in 1961 and 1964, and as American champion in 1965. Santana's exquisite gift of controlling the ball on the racquet strings made him a master of cross court shots from either wing which seemed quite impossible to perpetrate. He had a knack of finding inspiration only after losing the first two sets, as he did when he took his first French title against another fine touch artist, the Italian Nicola Pietrangeli, who was determined to win for the third year running. Santana was so exhausted physically and mentally at the end of the match, that he could not jump the net as victor, and had to crawl beneath it. He then burst into tears on his opponent's shoulder.

It was mainly because of Pietrangeli that the Australian–American pattern of the Davis Cup was broken. That was in 1960 when Italy beat the United States in the Inter-zone final. But Italy put up a poor showing in the Challenge Round, and did even less well the next year. It marked a decline of the Challenge Round in Australia as a major sporting occasion.

In 1963 the International Federation celebrated its jubilee. Curiously it still did not exert

A controversial champion: the Californian Karen Susman, an aggressive all-court player, was criticized for her 'stalling' tactics, her careful conservation of energy between the rallies. She never won the US title but triumphed at Wimbledon in 1962 when she beat the Czech Vera Sukova in the final 6–4 6–4.

Françoise Durr, ungainly in style, put French women's tennis back on the map after a long spell. She won her own championship at the Stade Roland Garros in 1967 and was German champion that same year.

above *Until they split up in 1971, Billie Jean King (left) and Rosemary Casals were the world's outstanding women's doubles pair.*

right *The spectators on the roof had a free view. They are watching the Czech Jan Kodes in the French Championships at the Stade Roland Garros, Paris, in 1972.*

direct control over the major international event, the Davis Cup, administered by its own annual meeting of participating nations. The personnel of the two international bodies were much the same; the difference came in the system of voting. Whereas the Davis Cup nations operated by one nation, one vote, the I.L.T.F. had varied voting strength, ranging from the twelve possessed by Great Britain, the United States, France and Australia, to the one possessed by some countries and to the associate members who have no vote at all.

To mark its fifty years of sometimes uneasy control of the world game, the I.L.T.F. inaugurated in 1963 the Federation Cup. This for women was the equivalent of the Davis Cup, a world team championship. Its playing format was different, for the event was to be staged within a week at one venue, instead of having the ties spread throughout the whole season. The first Federation Cup was staged by Great Britain at Queen's Club, just before the Wimbledon championships, and it was not particularly successful. But at other centres it thrived. Between 1963 and 1971 the United States and Australia shared the honours, and it was not until 1972 that South Africa, on its own courts in Johannesburg, broke their dominance.

The British game in the twenty-two years

from 1946 to 1967 occupied a respectable second place with the women more successful in the international field than the men. Tony Mottram, a Midlander, came back from wartime service in the R.A.F. to pick up what had looked like a promising career. For a decade he gave a useful best, and perhaps his finest achievement was in becoming a quarter-finalist at Wimbledon in 1948. For years this stood out as a lonely achievement, for no British rival did as well in any of the three major tournaments until 1958, when Bobby Wilson got equally far at Wimbledon.

Wilson, who had good touch and talent, played better at Wimbledon than anywhere, for he never became a rugged competitor and some of his Davis Cup efforts abroad were lamentable. He was also a quarter-finalist at Wimbledon in 1959, 1961 and 1963. Greater international success was achieved by Mike Sangster, a big server from Torquay, who made himself a semi-finalist at Wimbledon and Forest Hills in 1961 and a semi-finalist also in Paris in 1963. Curiously, Sangster had less success when he began to rely less on his booming service because his ground strokes had become more secure.

Roger Taylor, a left-hander from Yorkshire, raised the British standard when he became one of the last four at Wimbledon in 1967. In November 1966 Taylor had been engaged in a remarkable match in the King's Cup, the international team championship on indoor courts which Britain had won from 1964 to 1967, during the tie between Britain and Poland. At Warsaw the court was very fast wood and the lighting poor. Under these conditions serving strength predominated to an absurd degree, and Taylor's winning score against Wieslaw Gasiorek was 27–29 31–29 6–4. Though only a best of three sets, their 126 games created a record as the longest singles ever played.

British women had to concede to the superiority of the Americans. Susan Partridge was champion of Italy in 1952, Joy Mottram champion of Germany in 1954. In 1955 Angela Mortimer from Torquay, which has produced a number of British players, made herself champion of France, and in the same year Pat Ward was champion of Italy and finalist at Forest Hills. Shirley Bloomer won both the Italian and French titles in 1957, and Christine Truman did the same in 1959.

No player before or since has been taken to the hearts of the British public as was Christine Truman. Her game consisted of a courageous spirit and a natural forehand. Her court manners were perfect, her disposition lovable. She was the heroine of the Wightman Cup match of 1958 when, at Wimbledon, Great Britain won that elusive trophy for the first time since 1930. The key rubber was taken when Miss Truman beat Althea Gibson after losing the first set. Miss Gibson, a coloured player, tall and strong, was currently the number one player of the world, and the odds against the seventeen-year-old girl from Woodford Green enormous. Nevertheless Miss Truman played a 'blinder' she won and became a national heroine overnight.

That year, 1958, Miss Mortimer reached the Wimbledon final and was beaten by Miss Gibson. In 1961 Miss Mortimer reached the final again, but so did Miss Truman: the first all-British Wimbledon final since 1914. Miss Mortimer, a persevering baseliner, was well enough liked, but 14,000 spectators yearned for a Miss Truman victory for they felt that it was that charming girl next door who was on court. Alas for their hopes, Miss Truman slipped over when in the lead in the final set and was not afterwards in the match.

When Britain gained the Wightman Cup victory in 1958, the victory was not finalised until Ann Haydon had beaten Mimi Arnold. Miss Haydon hardly got the credit she deserved for this, since her success was taken for granted. Miss Haydon, a left-hander from Birmingham, was a table tennis player of the highest rank until she turned to the outdoor game. She won the French Championship in 1961 and repeated the performance five years later, taking the Italian title as well. That year the British Wightman Cup side, victorious for the second time at Wimbledon in 1960, went to defend the trophy in Chicago. There had never been better prospects of British success on American soil. But the British team, numbering the champion of France, the champion and runner-up at Wimbledon, failed to contain an American side that consisted entirely of junior or young players. One of the American players was Billie Jean Moffitt.

1967 was the end of an epoch in lawn tennis. In that year Francoise Durr, despite an extraordinarily gawky style, enough to give any coach a nightmare, won the French championship, the first Frenchwoman to do so since Nellie Landry in 1948 – if one excluded Mme Landry since she was Belgian born – and Simone Mathieu in 1939. Billie Jean King, as

Miss Moffitt had now become, won Wimbledon for the second successive year, beating Ann Jones, the former Miss Haydon, in the final. Mrs King also won Forest Hills against the same opponent.

Emerson, pursuing his tireless athleticism, took the titles of Australia and France, and John Newcombe those of Wimbledon and America. In the professional ranks Gonzales, Laver, Hoad and Rosewall were the men of might.

In August 1968, the All England Club broke a long tradition and for the first time in its history professionals played on the Centre Court. The tournament was a resounding success. Hoad beat Gonzales in the first round, subsequently losing to Rosewall who went down in the final to Laver. It seemed that a precedent had been set for a major professional tournament every year. As events worked out the face of lawn tennis changed before twelve months had passed.

Tennis as Big Business—

As early as the first Wimbledon Championship in 1877 lawn tennis had been a spectator sport, but it was essentially a middle-class game and there was no such thing as an amateur problem prior to 1914. Indeed, so rigidly was a strict amateur code taken for granted, that in 1910 the British Lawn Tennis Association solemnly sat in judgement on the case of an indigent player who exchanged a prize voucher for food instead of some trinket.

After 1919 the former clear cut social distinctions began to break down. Both Suzanne Lenglen and 'Big Bill' Tilden benefited discreetly from their status as crowd drawing personalities. One reason why lawn tennis ceased to be part of the Olympic Games after 1924 was a differing view about the concept of amateurism. But, by and large, adherence to an amateur status was real between the two world wars, save only for a few leading players famous enough to merit undercover payments necessary to support them. Certainly the nominal distinction between amateurs and professionals was rigid.

Both Mlle Lenglen and Tilden became professionals in due course and stepped outside the traditional game. Henri Cochet also left the amateur ranks, though he was subsequently reinstated. Ellsworth Vines became professional as did Fred Perry and Donald Budge. They became touring professionals, playing mainly at exhibition matches, though professional tournaments at Madison Square Garden in New York and at the Empire Pool and Sports Arena at Wembley, London became important events in themselves.

The effort to maintain amateurism in any real sense after 1946 became increasingly impossible. The payment of expenses of varying amounts, often quite large, became an essential prerequisite for staging any worthwhile tournament. Even so, the attraction of a guaranteed income given by a promoter could outweigh the uncertainties of life as a free-lance amateur living on expenses. The winning of Wimbledon or Forest Hills became a preliminary to the bigger money of the touring circus and the list of amateur champions changing status lengthened.

Of the fifteen men who ranked as world number one between 1946 and 1967 only five kept their amateur status. Among those who became professional were Jack Kramer, Ricardo Gonzales, Frank Sedgman, Tony Trabert, Rex Hartwig, Ken Rosewall, Lew Hoad, Ashley

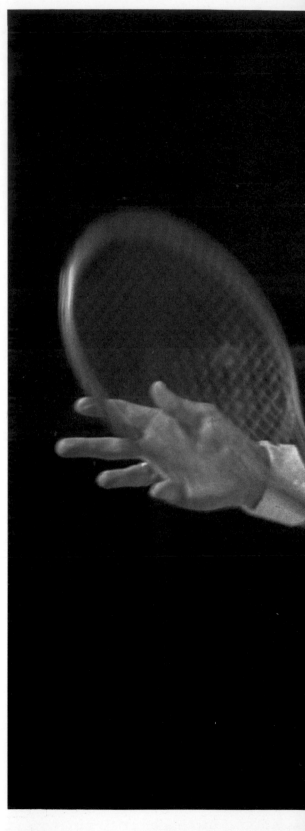

Rod Laver, small and unassuming, is considered one of the greatest players of all time. Already a 'Grand Slam' winner in 1962, he repeated his achievement in 1969, when he won all four open championships of Australia, France, Wimbledon and the United States. His prize money in 1970 amounted to more than $200,000. The next year he became the first professional to earn more than one million dollars.

above *What many black Americans have done on the sports track and in the games field, Arthur Ashe, son of a policeman, did on the tennis court. He was the first Negro in the American Davis Cup team and won the first US Open Championship in 1968. In 1975 he won at Wimbledon, beating Jimmy Connors in straight sets in a surprise victory.*

left *Ricardo Gonzales (right) had a great triumph in 1969 at the age of forty-one when, at Wimbledon, he beat his fellow American Charles Pasarell 22–24 1–6 16–14 6–3 11–9 after five hours twelve minutes.*

The imperious Lew Hoad, Australia's most dynamic player, forthright in manner and in stroke, here points an accusing finger at the net judge.

The finest German player since Gottfried von Cramm, Wilhelm Bungert. He played brilliantly to reach the Wimbledon final in 1967.

*Virginia Wade has brought
an imperious boldness to the
court, rare in a British
player. No one could have
been more English than the
daughter of an archdeacon
and a graduate in
mathematics, but her game
has the aggressive qualities
of an American's.*

Ann Jones brought more shrewdness to the court than Virginia Wade and made herself Britain's most successful post-war player. Italian champion in 1966, French champion in 1961, 1966, and Wimbledon champion in 1969.

Cooper, Mal Anderson, Mervyn Rose, Alex Olmedo, Barry MacKay, Earl Buchholz, Louis Ayala, Fred Stolle, Dennis Ralstan and Rod Laver.

The absurdity of a so-called amateur game merely fed the professional ranks and there was no common ground for either class to meet the other. The situation provoked the desire for reform long before it was carried out. The first realistic attempt to open tournaments like Wimbledon and Forest Hills to both categories was made by Great Britain, France, Australia and the United States at the meeting of the International Federation in Paris in 1960. It failed by a mere five votes to get the necessary two-thirds majority; the subsequent history of

the game's administration might have been different had it gone through.

It was felt by many, however, that the open tournament was not in itself enough. What was disturbing was the degeneration of the amateur status to a technicality, implying nothing more than adherence to the discipline of the amateur ruling bodies. The desire to abolish hypocrisy was stronger in Great Britain than elsewhere, and nowhere more so than in the traditional heart of conservative thinking: the All England Club.

The catalyst which provoked a British revolution and subsequent reform came about in the late summer of 1967. The Austrian L.T.A. complained to Britain about Roger Taylor. It

If looks could kill, Billie
Jean King would not have
needed three sets to beat
Ann Jones. In 1972 she
became champion of France,
Wimbledon and the United
States and dropped only one
set. By 1975 Mrs King had
equalled Elizabeth Ryan's
41-year-old Wimbledon
record of 19 titles.

left Billie Jean King being
welcomed at Brighton by the
Whitehawk School Band.

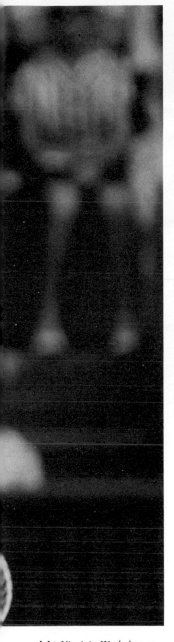

right *Virginia Wade lost to the unseeded Australian Judy Dalton at Wimbledon in 1971, though she won the Australian title that year. She has never seemed to play her best before her home crowd.*

was alleged he had agreed to play there but had chosen instead to take up a better financial offer from Canada. The details of what Taylor had or had not done are irrelevant, but what stuck in the gullet of the British was that they were being asked to suspend Taylor, an amateur, for not carrying out what was in effect a professional contract. Taylor was doing no more than every other amateur of his standing took as a natural way of life.

The L.T.A. had, since 1960, pressed the I.L.T.F. without success to abolish the outmoded amateur-professional distinction. Following the upset over Taylor, a triumvirate of Derek Penman then chairman of the L.T.A. Rules Committee, Derek Hardwick L.T.A. vice-chairman, and Eric Attewell L.T.A. chairman, moved that Britain should act alone. Herman David and Ted Avory of the All England Club had long advocated such a course. The L.T.A. President, Judge Carl Aarvold, gave the rebels his support. The L.T.A. secretary Basil Reay opposed the motion.

In December 1967, at the annual meeting of the L.T.A., the motion abolishing the amateur-

professional distinction as from the first day of the next British Hard Court Championships, at Bournemouth on 22 April 1968, was approved. This was in defiance of the Federation rules and an overt act of rebellion against the world's governing body. But dissent at the L.T.A. meeting was only about the tactical detail of the revolution, not its principle.

For the International Federation there were only two courses, either to expel Great Britain or to acquiesce. At a special meeting in Paris in March 1968 it acquiesced, each nation was to make its own rules about amateurism, save only for the restriction of prize money to players over eighteen years old.

Accordingly, from 22 April 1968 lawn tennis became entirely open. The game, freed from its hypocrisy and supported by increasing commercial sponsorship, should have lived happily ever after. It did not.

In Dallas, Texas, Mr Lamar Hunt, son of one of the richest oil millionaires in the world, took control of the purely commercial World Championship Tennis Incorporated. It had a jet age concept of what lawn tennis should be, far removed from the traditional form of the game.

Many, if not most, of the world's leading men players signed generous contracts with W.C.T. Their legal commitments removed them from the control of the International Federation and as such they were barred from playing in the Davis Cup. The liberality of W.C.T. contracts proved a bugbear. All prize money won by the contracted men was retained by them. Unless additional fees were paid there was nothing for W.C.T. when its players took part in tournaments. A dispute about fees and the degree to which the W.C.T. should take part in the running of tournaments led to a Federation ban on W.C.T. men as from 1 January 1972. This was back to square one.

A compromise was reached in time for W.C.T. contract men to play in the U.S. Open Championships in September 1972. The W.C.T. was given a special position in the game since they were allowed to stage fully sanctioned tournaments between January and May each year, and in return they agreed to cease placing players under contract in the hope and expectation that in due course the writ of Federation discipline would apply to all.

In the early 1900's Laurie and Reggie Doherty exploited their skill to the extent of being given tea in a special V.I.P. tent. In 1972 the Rumanian

Rosemary Casals being warned off the court by referee Mike Gibson for wearing a tennis dress with a Virginia Slims cigarette design.

above *The supreme woman athlete: the Australian Margaret Court. In an awesome record of achievement, Mrs Court has won every title, singles, doubles and mixed of every major championship. Her tally of major singles titles amounts to 35, and of titles in general to 92.*

right *Evonne Goolagong and Margaret Court with Billie Jean King and Rosemary Casals before their Wimbledon final in 1971. Billie Jean King and Rosemary Casals won 6–3 6–2.*

overleaf *Evonne Goolagong played in the United States for the first time in 1972. Her happy temperament brought her less success in a rugged competitive climate than in Europe the previous year.*

Ilie Nastase, as a freelance player, made something like £90,000. Amateurism began to die when Suzanne Lenglen's papa bet with tournament secretaries that his daughter would not play.

The game's first open tournament was the British Hard Court Championships at the West Hants Club, Bournemouth and its novel status gave it an important international aura it had never possessed before. The total prize money was £5,440 with £1,000 to the men's singles winner, £300 to the women's. During the course of the meeting the British left-hander Mark Cox achieved fame by beating two of the most notable professionals: Gonzales and Emerson. The gap between the old amateur and

Billie Jean King had her first major overseas success at Wimbledon in 1962 when she beat the number 1 seed Margaret Smith (Mrs Court). Through the years Mrs King beat Mrs Court 13 times and lost 21 times.

Chris Evert, from Fort Lauderdale, Florida, made a spectacular entry to the international game in 1971, at the age of 16, when her precocious skill was the main reason for America's Wightman Cup success. By 1975 her skills had made her the top women's earner – grossing $412,977 for the year.

professional standards was less than many had supposed. None the less the final was between two professionals of long standing, Rosewall and Laver, with Rosewall the winner.

The exploits of Rosewall combined with those of Laver to make the dominant pattern of early years of the open. That Laver should bring back to the historic venues an even fuller measure of his rich skill was not surprising for there was only a five-year gap and he was twenty-nine years old in 1968. But Rosewall was thirty-four that year, and had played against none but his professional colleagues since 1956.

The first major open tournament was the French Championships in Paris in 1968. Rosewall won it after a splendid final against Laver. It

was fifteen years since he had been champion of France in 1953, a proven master on the demanding rubble surface. The following year, 1969, he was in the final again, but on this occasion Laver was too good. It seemed then that the evergreen Rosewall was on the decline at last. But Rosewall's majestic artistry took him to the final of Wimbledon in 1970. The crowd yearned for him to win for, like Gonzales, if ever a great player deserved the accolade of a Wimbledon singles title it was he. Newcombe, the last of the amateur champions at Wimbledon in 1967, was too good. It was Rosewall's third appearance in the Wimbledon men's singles final. The first occasion had been in 1954, sixteen years before.

Six weeks or so later Rosewall avenged his

One of the best matches played anywhere in 1971 was between the Australian Ken Rosewall and the Texan Cliff Richey in the 1971 Wimbledon quarter final. The thirty-six-year-old Rosewall (left) won after four hours – 6–8 5–7 6–4 9–7 7–5. In 1974, Rosewall was a finalist at Forest Hills and at Wimbledon – and was defeated both times by Jimmy Connors.

*The Australian John
Newcombe's fine rugged
game came into its own in
1967 when he won both the
US and Wimbledon titles.
He won Wimbledon again in
1970 and 1971.*

left *By 1971 Roy Emerson, aged 34, had lost some of his edge. But he was still pressing forward, and in winning the doubles with Rod Laver he took his fifth Wimbledon title.*

right *Ilie Nastase of Rumania, the most colourful, the most artistic and the most controversial of modern players. Not as consistent as some of his contemporaries, at his best he is untouchable. His sometimes excessive clowning and his displays of temperament have not always endeared him to other players or to the crowds; yet even after one of these lapses this most exciting of players can quickly change the onlookers' mood into ecstatic appreciation.*

Stan Smith leaping the net after his close Wimbledon final victory over Ilie Nastase in 1972. Nastase appears deeply dejected and whilst Stan Smith does his best to console him there is evident joy in his victory as he kisses the trophy, a compensation for his failure the previous year against John Newcombe.

Wimbledon defeat against Newcombe in the semi-final of the US Open at Forest Hills, and he went on to win the final against another Australian, the left-hander Tony Roche. It was his second tenure as American Champion. The last had been fourteen years before in 1956, when he had thwarted Hoad's bid for the 'Grand Slam'. Early in 1972 Rosewall brought off the most remarkable example of his ability to span the years. He won the Australian title for the fourth time; the first occasion had been in 1953.

Laver was the first open champion of Wimbledon in 1968 which meant that, allowing for the five years from 1963 to 1967 when he was barred entry as a professional, he was unbeaten there since 1960. But Forest Hills in 1968 was dominated by the former amateurs. Arthur Ashe, mercurially brilliant, beat the Dutchman Tom Okker in the last match.

1969 was the first full year of open lawn tennis. Laver reached a peak of excellence and achievement and for the second time in his career won the 'Grand Slam'. As in 1962 he won all the major singles events for which he entered, and he added to these the championships of Italy and Germany. In 1969 he also won the championship of South Africa. This awesome record established the red-headed Queenslander as probably the most outstanding player of all time.

It also helped to establish him as the wealthiest player of all time, for the rewards of the game grew more and more. In 1970 Laver won no major title, for the spark of his genius had begun to dim, but none the less he earned more than 200,000 US dollars in prize money alone. Even so he remained a modest man.

In the 1969 Wimbledon there was a first round match between forty-one-year-old Gonzales and Charles Pasarell. The latter, from Puerto Rico, had beaten Santana in the opening round in 1967 when the Spaniard lost his title defence on the first day. Gonzales, aggrieved because the referee was reluctant to stop play in the fading light, lost the first two sets 22–24 1–6. When it resumed the next afternoon Gonzales won 16–14 6–3 11–9, surviving seven match points in all, including two games when he was love–40. This was a total of 112 games played over five hours and twelve minutes.

Another inordinately long match took place in the same year at the Edgbaston-Priory Club in Birmingham during the Davis Cup tie between Britain and Germany. In the doubles, Wilhelm Bungert and Christian Kuhnke beat Mark Cox and Peter Curtis 10–8 17–19 13–11 3–6 6–2 to make the longest rubber in the history of the competition. For Great Britain it was a notable Davis Cup year. Mainly because of Cox and Graham Stillwell there was greater success than in any post-war year, and Britain reached the inter-zone final against Rumania at Wimbledon, where only the genius of Ilie Nastase, then being shown for the first time, prevented British participation in the Challenge Round.

The match of 112 games at Wimbledon and the 95 games of the Davis Cup in Birmingham undoubtedly gave a spur to those advocating a reform in lawn tennis scoring. The impetus came mainly from the United States, and in 1970 the American Open meeting used a tie break scoring system. At six games all, sets were decided on the basis of the best of the next nine points. The method was controversial. It meant that if the tie break went to four points the next rally was a decisive issue for both sides; small satisfaction to the loser if it were determined by such freak of luck as a net cord.

Wimbledon in 1971 adopted a more conservative system. Here the tie break came into operation at eight games all and never in a final set. Furthermore the tie break was the best of twelve points, the deuce principle of the game retained by the winner having to be at least two points in front.

Administratively the onset of open lawn tennis proved uneasy, not to say chaotic. The conflict of interest between the amateur controlled International Federation and the commercially inspired World Championship Tennis, inspired the I.L.T.F. to promote the Grand Prix in 1970. This was a series of point-linked tournaments carrying large bonus prizes, and its object was to discourage players from joining with W.C.T. by giving an additional incentive to remain under the discipline of their national associations. It was financed by commercial sponsorship and each participating tournament allocated ten per cent of its prize money to the general fund. A Masters' tournament at the end of the year pitted the leaders against each other.

The Texan Cliff Richey was the first Grand Prix victor, and the American Stan Smith the winner of the Masters' event which was staged in Tokyo. In 1971 Smith won the Grand Prix and Nastase the Masters', this time held in Paris. Smith, a cool and able match player, six feet four inches tall, and Nastase, volatile in tempera-

left By 1973, Jan Kodes, from Czechoslovakia, had become one of the best known of the Eastern European players. He had been a semi-finalist in the Men's Singles at Wimbledon in 1972 (defeated by that year's champion, Stan Smith), and he had been a finalist in 1971 U.S. Open Championships (also beaten by Stan Smith). He had won the French Championship twice and had been runner-up for three years in succession in the Italian Championships.

ment but a brilliant touch player with incredible shots he learned from Santana, loomed as giants of the game. Smith was a runner-up at Wimbledon to Newcombe in 1971, but he won the American title a little later. In 1972 he won Wimbledon, beating Nastase in the best final for many years, but Nastase won over Ashe at Forest Hills.

Smith and Nastase were also the leading rivals in the Final Round of the Davis Cup in Bucharest in 1972. The last Challenge Round was played in 1971 after which, with some nostalgic regret, the challenge round system with the holder standing out was abolished. Nevertheless the United States played through the competition to win once again against Rumania whom they had beaten in the Challenge Rounds of 1969 and 1971. The Final Round in Rumania was the first time the destiny of the Davis Cup was decided in Europe since the US beat Great Britain in 1937.

Players under contract to W.C.T. were not eligible for the Davis Cup. Because of this the status of that long standing competition somewhat declined. For the first seven months of 1972, W.C.T. contract men were barred from all but their own events, so it meant that both the French and Wimbledon championships that year functioned as though the clock had been put back to 1967.

Open lawn tennis made little difference at first to the women, save only that money-making became legal and the amounts greater. The Texan Nancy Richey was the first open champion of France in 1968 and Mrs King won the Wimbledon singles for the third year running. British prestige was enhanced when, in America, Virginia Wade took the first open title at Forest Hills by beating Mrs King in the final.

The Americans rather muddled their introduction of the open game for they hankered to retain an amateur status. While Forest Hills was made an open tournament, the old US National Championship, started in 1881, was carried on at the Longwood Cricket Club at Chestnut Hill, near Boston. Accordingly for two years from 1968 to 1969 there were two American championships, the old National meeting and the new Open event.

Margaret Court dominated events of 1969 with the exception of Wimbledon. There Ann Jones, the former Miss Haydon, had her ultimate triumph and a reward for a long effort. After

above *Rosemary Casals, playing with Billie Jean King, formed a doubles partnership unrivalled at Wimbledon since World War II, except perhaps by that of Louise Brough and Mrs du Pont.*

being an unsuccessful finalist in 1967, an unsuccessful semi-finalist in 1958, 1960, 1962, 1963, 1966 and 1968 and an unsuccessful quarter-finalist in 1959 and 1964, she beat both Mrs Court and Mrs King to take the crown; the first British winner since Miss Mortimer in 1961.

In 1970 Mrs Court equalled the record of Maureen Connolly and won the 'Grand Slam'. It was her ninth time as Australian champion, her fourth as French, her third as Wimbledon and her sixth, if the overlapping meetings be counted, as American. She also took the South African title. There was nothing really left for this all-conquering Australian to do, save only to become 'Grand Slam' winner in women's doubles and to be triple champion at Wimbledon. In 1971 she was, for the third time, in all three finals at Wimbledon. She won none.

Her conqueror at Wimbledon in the singles was an entrancing new personality in the game: Evonne Goolagong. She was Australian and, unique among players, partly aboriginal. She brimmed with natural talent. Her weakness was to enjoy the game and not mind too much whether she won or lost. Nevertheless in her second year on the international circuit she won the French championship at her first attempt, and Wimbledon as well. She was probably one of the most popular winners there, at nineteen years old.

A year later Miss Goolagong found the ultimate opposition a little sterner. In both Paris and at Wimbledon she took her title defence as far as the final and submitted to the all-round expertise and rigorous professionalism of Mrs King. The latter ended 1972 as champion of France, Wimbledon and America and no doubt would have taken the Australian title in addition had she cared to enter. A Grand Prix, but no comparable Masters' event, was started for women in 1971, and Mrs King became the winner. The rewards for women, though less than those of the men, were considerable. Mrs King earned more than 100,000 US dollars in prize money in 1971.

While earnings continued to rise among both men and women, 1973 proved traumatic for administrators. This was the year of the Wimbledon boycott.

In September 1972 the leading men players of the world organized themselves into the Association of Tennis Professionals. Its first president was the South African Cliff Drysdale, and Jack Kramer, the former Wimbledon champion, was appointed its executive director. From the first it sought to achieve for players a share in the administration and discipline of the professional game. Early in the season the Yugoslav Nikki Pilic ran foul of his own Yugoslav L.T.A. when he failed to turn out for a Davis Cup tie. His national association suspended him. In due course the International Lawn Tennis Federation was asked to endorse the suspension and Pilic continued to play in the French Championships while his 'sentence', as it were, was under review.

A little embarrassingly Pilic prospered in the French meeting and reached the final, where he was beaten by Ilie Nastase. His suspension was then regarded as beginning from the end of the meeting. Despite this Pilic went straight from Paris to Rome to compete in the Italian Championships and the Italians allowed him to play. By this time A.T.P. had made it clear that they regarded this suspension of one of their players as invalid.

The Wimbledon meeting became the trial of strength. The Wimbledon authorities made it clear that they would not fly in the face of the ruling of the I.L.T.F. In turn Pilic appealed to the British High Court for his entry to be accepted. A judge in chambers ruled that Wimbledon's action was perfectly legal. A.T.P. then called upon its members to withdraw from the Championships. With three exceptions they did so. The men's events at Wimbledon saw the scratching of 79 players. The Rumanian Ilie Nastase, the British Roger Taylor and the Australian Ray Keldie were the only A.T.P. members who did not follow their association's boycott. All were subsequently fined by A.T.P. for the breach of discipline. Wimbledon had been emasculated. It all happened at the last moment and the draw had to be postponed and the seeding re-done. The meeting should have been in ruins. Yet it went ahead quite smoothly and the chairman of the Championships, Herman David, went out of his way to say at the belated draw, 'There will be no recriminations.' There was no difficulty in making up the numbers from among the players who had been placed in the qualifying rounds.

The reaction of the British public was on the side of Wimbledon and against the players. The most surprising aspect of the affair was the huge support for the 1973 meeting. The total attendance was 300,172, the second highest figure to date. The main 'blackleg' players, Nastase and Taylor, were greeted as heroes. Along with the Czech Jan Kodes, who was not an A.T.P. member, they were the only members of the original seeding list of 16 to survive into the new and abbreviated roll of eight which had to be prepared.

Despite its diminished quality the men's singles proved an entrancing event. Teenage spectators came in vast numbers. One of their cult figures was Nastase. Another was the barely seventeen-year-old Swede Bjorn Borg, and both Borg and Nastase had to have a police escort wherever they went. Patriotic hopes demanded that Taylor do well and he by no means did badly, getting to the semi-final where he lost narrowly to Kodes. Nastase, who on form should have taken the event in his stride, failed in the fourth round. Kodes made himself Wimbledon champion when he beat the Soviet Alex Metreveli in the final. The general feeling was that though the field as a whole was hardly worthy of Wimbledon standards the calibre of the champion was.

The Wimbledon dispute was basically a struggle for power, with Wimbledon an innocent victim of events. In due course A.T.P. did achieve its share of administrative power as part of the Men's Professional Council. If there were any bitterness it was not much and left no trace. That Wimbledon could be so successful in so diminished a field stressed the value of the event as a whole compared with the value of individual players.

Another significant aspect of 1973 was in the women's game. Mrs Court, though unsuccessful at Wimbledon, won the singles titles in Australia, France and Forest Hills, three magnificent jewels bedecking a crown more heavily encrusted than that of any other player, man or woman. She won the French title by beating Chris Evert in one of the best women's finals seen for many a year, taking it 6–7 7–6 6–4, having missed a lead of 4–1 in the first set for which she had two set points and recovering from 3–5 in the second set.

A year later Miss Evert started winning great championships. The astonishing career of Mrs Court was nearly, though not entirely, at an end. In the U.S. meeting in 1973 Mrs Court again met Miss Evert, this time in the semi-final, and she

Françoise Durr, always so much a part of the Wimbledon doubles scene, crowned her career in 1976 when, partnered by the Australian Tony Roche, she took the mixed doubles victory.

Margaret Court, at Wimbledon in 1975, demonstrating the power which carried this magnificent player through sixteen years of top class tennis.

above *The young American, Vitas Gerulaitis, surprised Wimbledon in 1975 when, unseeded and partnered by Sandy Mayer, he won the men's doubles. The following year he reached the quarter-finals in the singles.*

right *Jimmy Connors, the top money earner of 1975 ($600,273) was favourite to win the Wimbledon championship of 1976; but, as victory had eluded him in the previous year's final, even a place in the finals of 1976 escaped his grasp.*

won 7–5 2–6 6–2. She went on to win the final from Miss Goolagong by 7–6 5–7 6–2. That was her last major singles title. In 1975 Mrs Court won the women's doubles at Forest Hills with Virginia Wade. She was 33 years old.

The career of Mrs Court between 1960, when she won the Australian singles for the first time, and 1975, is unparalleled, her record of championships unsurpassed. The major titles of the world may be taken as those of Australia, South Africa, Italy, France, Wimbledon, Germany and the United States, with those of the last country being duplicated with both 'National' and 'Open' meetings in 1968 and 1969. At one time or another the incredible Mrs Court won every event, singles, women's doubles and mixed doubles, at all these meetings. Her tally of singles titles amounts to 35 and of titles in general to 92.

The notable contemporary rivals of Mrs Court were Maria Bueno, Billie Jean King and Ann Jones. Against Miss Bueno, the more majestic player, Mrs Court won 16 times, lost 6. Against Mrs King, probably the more complete player technically, she won 21 times, lost 13. Against Mrs Jones her wins were 9, her losses 3.

Mrs King won the Wimbledon singles in 1973, the U.S. singles in 1974 and the Wimbledon singles again in 1975. The last was a particularly memorable achievement. As Miss Moffitt this Californian had taken her first Wimbledon title, the women's doubles with Karen Hantze, in 1961. When she won the singles in 1975 it gave her that event for the sixth time, this in itself being a unique post-war achievement. More than that, however, it gave her a Wimbledon title for the nineteenth time, her tally amounting to six singles, nine women's doubles and four mixed doubles.

Thus after a lapse of forty-one years the record of another Californian, Elizabeth Ryan, was equalled. In 1934 Miss Ryan, an indefatigable competitor, won the women's doubles with the French Simone Matthieu, this being her 12th triumph in that event which, added to seven mixed doubles championships, gave her 19 Wimbledon titles in all.

From the start in 1975 Mrs King avowed it was her last effort in the singles. In 1976 she gave herself two chances to break the record, competing in the mixed with Sandy Mayer and in the women's doubles with a familiar partner, the Dutch Betty Stove, with whom she had won in 1972. Her challenge in the mixed lasted no longer than the second round. Record hopes in the other doubles lasted right up to the final.

There Mrs King and Miss Stove were beaten, 7–5 in the third set, by Miss Evert and Martina Navratilova. Youth was triumphant here and the shared record of 19 Wimbledon titles remained as it was.

By 1973 the Virginia Slims circuit of tournaments in the United States had become a very lucrative and major part of the women's game. More than anywhere Miss Evert built up her reputation as a great player in the classic mould, with impeccable driving, accuracy and control. Her unorthodoxy was with her double-fisted backhand. In 1974 she took one of the major traditional titles for the first time.

This was the Italian title. She also won the French. Then she took the Wimbledon singles as well, to leave no doubt about her supremacy. But her own national title at Forest Hills eluded her. She had to wait until 1975 before she pulled that one off, by which time she had had to give best to Mrs King at Wimbledon. Miss Evert revived her Wimbledon fortunes in 1976, despite signs earlier that year that Mrs Roger Cawley, as Evonne Goolagong had become, was fulfilling her undeniable talents at her expense.

Miss Evert, who became twenty-one years old in December 1975, earned prize money that year that would have been unbelievable a few years earlier. Six players gained more than $100,000. They were:

Chris Evert	$412,977
Martina Navratilova	185,518
Virginia Wade	153,576
Evonne Cawley	145,254
Billie Jean King	124,900
Margaret Court	105,646

There was a marked change of fortune in the Wightman Cup contest between the women of America and Great Britain. With some misgivings there was a change in the British venue in 1974 because calendar changes made it impracticable to maintain the event at Wimbledon. It was staged indoors at the Deeside Leisure Centre in North Wales. Admirably led by Virginia Wade the British were far too strong for the visitors. More surprisingly the British, again with Miss Wade at the head, kept the trophy a year later, winning for the first time in America – at an indoor arena in Cleveland, Ohio – since 1925.

A minor hurricane blew in the men's game in 1974 in the person of the twenty-year-old Jimmy Connors, a brave, rather brash and undeniably effective American. He won the Australian title.

Bjorn Borg, despite continual treatment for a torn stomach muscle, delighted his fans at Wimbledon in 1976 by his dismissal of an unusually listless Ilie Nastase in the final of the championship.

above *Not what it seems. A smiling Ilie Nastase, defeated in the 1976 Wimbledon final, puts a comforting arm round his conqueror, Bjorn Borg, overcome with emotion.*

left *One of the world's top earning players, Arthur Ashe was a popular winner at Wimbledon in 1975. The scoreboard shows only too clearly the margin of his victory over Jimmy Connors.*

That was more or less by the way. He came to Wimbledon and hit with uninhibited skill to become the champion. He went to Forest Hills and did the same. The astonishing thing was that in both cases the finalist against him was the Australian Ken Rosewall, thirty-nine years old. Rosewall was twenty years removed from his first Wimbledon singles final. At both Wimbledon and Forest Hills Rosewall had the misfortune to be entirely routed in the last match. Indeed he won only two games in the U.S. match, making it the briefest of its kind of all time. But until the last matches he was superb. How did he remain so evergreen?

Connors was a young winner. The champion of Italy and France in 1974 was vastly younger. The Swede Bjorn Borg, not the prettiest of players stylistically, won the Italian title when he was seventeen, the French title when he was only just turned eighteen.

Connors was double-fisted on the backhand. So was Borg. So was Chris Evert. The unorthodox had become the orthodox.

Connors did not sustain himself at Olympian heights. When he defended his Wimbledon title in 1975 he did so entirely from strength until the final match. There the negro Arthur Ashe, who had earlier won the W.C.T. championships in Dallas, craftily gave Connors the widely angled shots he disliked most, had a complete triumph. Nor could Connors keep his title at Forest Hills.

That was less surprising, for after 1974 a great change took place in the U.S. Open Championships at the West Side Club, Forest Hills, New York. For years there had been grumblings about the poor condition of the grass courts. The turf disappeared and was replaced by a hard court made of granite chippings. Forest Hills was now in line with Italy and the Stade Roland Garros, Paris, rather than Wimbledon and Australia. Inevitably the hard court tournament was won by a hard court expert. The Spanish left-hander, cheerful, skilled and sporting Manuel Orantes, became the champion of America, though not before being five times within a point of losing in the semi-final to the Argentinian Guillermo Vilas.

Both the Italian and French titles in 1976 were won by the Italian Adriano Panatta, a player of fluency and flair. What flair it proved to be! In the first round in Rome Panatta was eleven times within a point of losing to the Australian Kim Warwick. In the first round in Paris Panatta was within a point of losing to the Czech Pavel Hutka.

Wimbledon in 1976 went back to youth. Borg, playing magnificently and beating the other teenage idol Ilie Nastase in the final, won at the age of twenty years twenty-seven days. There were only two younger men's singles champions in the records, Wilfrid Baddeley, who was nineteen when he won in 1891, and the American Sidney Wood, who was also nineteen when he won on a walkover in 1931.

The Davis Cup, torn about by the refusal of some nations to compete against South Africa, reached a nadir of fortune in 1974 when India, getting to the final against the Union, was compelled by its government to concede a walkover. A year later Sweden triumphed in the final round against Czechoslovakia to provide the first winners from continental Europe since France in 1932.

While lawn tennis flourished as never before, the Davis Cup wrestled with its difficulties. There was even a brief spell in 1976 when the United States resigned from the competition because of objection to political interference and was with difficulty cajoled back into the fold.

In America too the onset of League Team Tennis in 1974, which put players under lucrative contracts, made it difficult for some traditional tournaments, especially those in Europe and particularly with women, to maintain their old standards of entry. Administratively the game became more and more complex.

If the earnings of some of the women players were big those of some of the men were bigger. The figures for 1975 were:

Jim Connors	$600,273
Arthur Ashe	338,337
Manuel Orantes	271,066
Guillermo Vilas	247,372
Bjorn Borg	229,875
Raul Ramirez	210,850
Ilie Nastase	210,793
Brain Gottfried	171,130
Rod Laver	165,321
John Alexander	158,650
Roscoe Tanner	145,659
Harold Solomon	140,200
Ken Rosewall	107,192
Adriano Panatta	105,963
Juan Gisbert	104,707

Lawn tennis had moved a long way since Wimbledon staged the first tournament in the world in 1877.

Wimbledon championships

MEN'S SINGLES

1877	s. finals	Spencer W. Gore d. C. G. Heathcote
		W. C. Marshall a bye
	final	SPENCER W. GORE d. W. C. Marshall 6–1 6–2 6–4
1878	s. finals	L. Erskine d. H. F. Lawford
		P. F. Hadow a bye
	final	Hadow d. Erskine
	challenge round	P. F. HADOW d. Spencer W. Gore 7–5 6–1 9–7
1879	s. finals	J. T. Hartley d. C. F. Parr
		V. St Leger Gould a bye
	final	J. T. HARTLEY d. V. St Leger Gould 6–2 6–4 6–2
	challenge round	w.o.
1880	s. finals	O. E. Woodhouse d. G. Montgomerie
		H. F. Lawford d. M. Butterworth
	final	Lawford d. Woodhouse
	challenge round	J. T. HARTLEY d. H. F. Lawford 6–0 6–2 2–6 6–3
1881	s. finals	W. Renshaw d. H. F. Lawford
		R. T. Richardson a bye
	final	Renshaw d. Richardson
	challenge round	W. RENSHAW d. J. T. Hartley 6–4 6–2 6–3
1882	s. finals	E. Renshaw d. H. F. Lawford
		R. T. Richardson d. F. Benson
	final	Renshaw d. Richardson
	challenge round	W. RENSHAW d. E. Renshaw 6–1 2–6 4–6 6–2 6–2
1883	s. finals	D. Stewart d. W. C. Taylor
		E. Renshaw a bye
	final	Renshaw d. Stewart
	challenge round	W. RENSHAW d. E. Renshaw 2–6 6–3 6–3 4–6 6–3
1884	s. finals	C. W. Grinstead d. E. Renshaw
		H. F. Lawford d. H. Chipp
	final	Lawford d. Grinstead
	challenge round	W. RENSHAW d. H. F. Lawford 6–0 6–4 9–7
1885	s. finals	E. Renshaw d. E. de S. H. Browne
		H. F. Lawford d. J. Dwight
	final	Lawford d. Renshaw
	challenge round	W. RENSHAW d. H. F. Lawford 7–5 6–2 4–6 7–5
1886	s. finals	H. F. Lawford d. T. R. Garvey
		E. W. Lewis d. H. W. W. Wilberforce
	final	Lawford d. Lewis
	challenge round	W. RENSHAW d. H. F. Lawford 6–0 5–7 6–3 6–4
1887	s. finals	H. F. Lawford d. H. Grove
		E. Renshaw w.o. C. Lacey Sweet
	final	H. F. LAWFORD d. E. Renshaw 1–6 6–3 3–6 6–4 6–4
	challenge round	w.o.
1888	s. finals	R. Renshaw d. W. J. Hamilton
		E. W. Lewis d. W. C. Taylor
	final	Renshaw d. Lewis
	challenge round	E. RENSHAW d. H. F. Lawford 6–3 7–5 6–0
1889	s. finals	H. S. Barlow d. W. J. Hamilton
		W. Renshaw d. H. F. Lawford
	final	Renshaw d. Barlow
	challenge round	W. RENSHAW d. E. Renshaw 6–4 6–1 3–6 6–0
1890	s. finals	W. J. Hamilton d. J. Pim
		H. S. Barlow d. E. W. Lewis
	final	Hamilton d. Barlow
	challenge round	W. J. HAMILTON d. W. Renshaw 6–8 6–2 3–6 6–1 6–1
1891	s. finals	W. Baddeley d. E. Renshaw
		J. Pim d. H. S. Mahony
	final	W. BADDELEY d. J. Pim 6–4 1–6 7–5 6–0
	challenge round	w.o.
1892	s. finals	E. W. Lewis d. H. A. B. Chapman
		J. Pim d. H. S. Mahony
	final	Pim d. Lewis
	challenge round	W. BADDELEY d. J. Pim 4–6 6–3 6–3 6–2
1893	s. finals	J. Pim d. H. S. Barlow
		H. S. Mahony d. A. Palmer
	final	Pim d. Mahony
	challenge round	J. PIM d. W. Baddeley 3–6 6–1 6–3 6–2
1894	s. finals	W. Baddeley w.o. T. Chaytor
		E. W. Lewis d. H. Baddeley
	final	W. Baddeley d. Lewis
	challenge round	J. PIM d. W. Baddeley 10–8 6–2 8–6
1895	s. finals	W. Baddeley w.o. H. Baddeley
		W. V. Eaves d. E. G. Meers
	final	W. BADDELEY d. W. V. Eaves 4–6 2–6 8–6 6–2 6–3
	challenge round	w.o.
1896	s. finals	H. S. Mahony d. H. A. Nisbet
		W. V. Eaves d. H. Baddeley
	final	Mahony d. Eaves
	challenge round	H. S. MAHONY d. W. Baddeley 6–2 6–8 5–7 8–6 6–3
1897	s. finals	W. V. Eaves d. S. H. Smith
		R. F. Doherty d. W. Baddeley
	final	Doherty d. Eaves
	challenge round	R. F. DOHERTY d. H. S. Mahony 6–4 6–4 6–3
1898	s. finals	H. L. Doherty d. C. Hobart
		H. S. Mahony d. A. W. Gore
	final	Doherty d. Mahony
	challenge round	R. F. DOHERTY d. H. L. Doherty 6–3 6–3 2–6 5–7 6–1
1899	s. finals	A. W. Gore d. H. S. Mahony
		S. H. Smith d. H. Roper Barrett
	final	Gore d. Smith
	challenge round	R. F. DOHERTY d. A. W. Gore 1–6 4–6 6–2 6–3 6–3
1900	s. finals	A. W. Gore d. H. L. Doherty
		S. H. Smith d. H. A. Nisbet
	final	Smith d. Gore
	challenge round	R. F. DOHERTY d. S. H. Smith 6–8 6–3 6–1 6–2
1901	s. finals	C. P. Dixon d. H. S. Mahony
		A. W. Gore d. H. Roper Barrett
	final	Gore d. Dixon
	challenge round	A. W. GORE d. R. F. Doherty 4–6 7–5 6–4 6–4
1902	s. finals	M. J. G. Ritchie d. S. H. Smith
		H. L. Doherty d. H. S. Mahony
	final	Doherty d. Ritchie
	challenge round	H. L. DOHERTY d. A. W. Gore 6–4 6–3 3–6 6–0
1903	s. finals	F. L. Riseley d. S. H. Smith
		M. J. G. Ritchie d. G. A. Caridia
	final	Riseley d. Ritchie
	challenge round	H. L. DOHERTY d. F. L. Riseley 7–5 6–3 6–0
1904	s. finals	F. L. Riseley d. S. H. Smith
		M. J. G. Ritchie d. P. de Borman
	final	Riseley d. Ritchie
	challenge round	H. L. DOHERTY d. F. L. Riseley 6–1 7–5 8–6
1905	s. finals	N. E. Brookes d. A. W. Gore
		H. S. Smith d. M. J. G. Ritchie
	final	Brookes d. Smith
	challenge round	H. L. DOHERTY d. N. E. Brookes 8–6 6–2 6–4
1906	s. finals	A. W. Gore d. A. F. Wilding
		F. L. Riseley d. S. H. Smith
	final	Riseley d. Gore
	challenge round	H. L. DOHERTY d. F. L. Riseley 6–4 4–6 6–2 6–3
1907	s. finals	A. W. Gore d. W. V. Eaves
		N. E. Brookes d. M. J. G. Ritchie
	final	N. E. BROOKES d. A. W. Gore 6–4 6–4 6–2
	challenge round	w.o.
1908	s. finals	A. W. Gore d. R. B. Powell
		H. Roper Barrett d. M. J. G. Ritchie
	final	A. W. GORE d. H. Roper Barrett 6–3 6–2 4–6 3–6 6–4
	challenge round	w.o.
1909	s. finals	M. J. G. Ritchie d. T. M. Mavrogordato
		H. Roper Barrett d. F. W. Rahe
	final	Ritchie d. Roper Barrett
	challenge round	A. W. GORE d. M. J. G. Ritchie 6–8 1–6 6–2 6–2 6–2
1910	s. finals	A. F. Wilding d. J. C. Parke
		Beals C. Wright d. A. H. Lowe
	final	Wilding d. Wright
	challenge round	A. F. WILDING d. A. W. Gore 6–4 7–5 4–6 6–2
1911	s. finals	C. P. Dixon d. M. Decugis
		H. Roper Barrett d. F. G. Lowe
	final	Roper Barrett d. Dixon
	challenge round	A. F. WILDING d. H. Roper Barrett 6–4 4–6 2–6 6–2 rt'd
1912	s. finals	A. H. Gobert d. M. Decugis
		A. W. Gore d. A. E. Beamish
	final	Gore d. Gobert
	challenge round	A. F. WILDING d. A. W. Gore 6–4 6–4 4–6 6–4
1913	s. finals	M. E. McLoughlin d. J. C. Parke
		S. N. Doust d. O. Kreuzer
	final	McLoughlin d. Doust
	challenge round	A. F. WILDING d. M. E. McLoughlin 8–6 6–3 10–8
1914	s. finals	O. Froitzheim d. T. M. Mavrogordato
		N. E. Brookes d. A. E. Beamish
	final	Brookes d. Froitzheim
	challenge round	N. E. BROOKES d. A. F. Wilding 6–4 6–4 7–5
1915–1918 not held		

1919	s. finals	G. L. Patterson d. M. J. G. Ritchie
		A. R. F. Kingscote d. C. S. Garland
	final	Patterson d. Kingscote
	challenge round	G. L. PATTERSON d. N. E. Brookes 6–3 7–5 6–2
1920	s. finals	Z. Shimizu d. T. M. Mavrogordato
		W. T. Tilden d. C. S. Garland
	final	Tilden d. Shimizu
	challenge round	W. T. TILDEN d. G. L. Patterson 2–6 6–3 6–2 6–4
1921	s. finals	M. Alonso d. Z. Shimizu
		B. I. C. Norton d. F. T. Hunter
	final	Norton d. Alonso
	challenge round	W. T. TILDEN d. B. I. C. Norton 4–6 2–6 6–1 6–0 7–5

(Challenge round abolished)

1922	s. finals	R. Lycett d. J. B. Gilbert
		G. L. Patterson d. J. O. Anderson
	final	G. L. PATTERSON d. R. Lycett 6–3 6–4 6–2
1923	s. finals	W. M. Johnston d. B. I. C. Norton
		F. T. Hunter d. F. G. Lowe
	final	W. M. JOHNSTON d. F. T. Hunter 6–0 6–3 6–1
1924	s. finals	R. Lacoste d. R. N. Williams
		J. Borotra d. L. Raymond
	final	J. BOROTRA d. R. Lacoste 6–1 3–6 6–1 3–6 6–4
1925	s. finals	J. Borotra d. H. Cochet
		R. Lacoste d. J. O. Anderson
	final	R. LACOSTE d. J. Borotra 6–3 6–3 4–6 8–6
1926	s. finals	J. Borotra d. H. Cochet
		H. Kinsey d. J. Brugnon
	final	J. BOROTRA d. H. Kinsey 8–6 6–1 6–3
1927	s. finals	H. Cochet d. W. T. Tilden
		J. Borotra d. R. Lacoste
	final	H. COCHET d. J. Borotra 4–6 4–6 6–3 6–4 7–5
1928	s. finals	R. Lacoste d. W. T. Tilden
		H. Cochet d. C. Boussus
	final	R. LACOSTE d. H. Cochet 6–1 4–6 6–4 6–2
1929	s. finals	H. Cochet d. W. T. Tilden
		J. Borotra d. H. W. Austin
	final	H. COCHET d. J. Borotra 6–4 6–3 6–4
1930	s. finals	W. T. Tilden d. J. Borotra
		W. L. Allison d. J. H. Doeg
	final	W. T. TILDEN d. W. L. Allison 6–3 9–7 6–4
1931	s. finals	S. B. Wood d. F. J. Perry
		F. X. Shields d. J. Borotra
	final	S. B. WOOD w.o. F. X. Shields scr.
1932	s. finals	H. E. Vines d. J. H. Crawford
		H. W. Austin d. J. Satoh
	final	H. E. VINES d. H. W. Austin 6–4 6–2 6–0
1933	s. finals	J. H. Crawford d. J. Satoh
		H. E. Vines d. H. Cochet
	final	J. H. CRAWFORD d. H. E. Vines 4–6 11–9 6–2 2–6 6–4
1934	s. finals	F. J. Perry d. S. B. Wood
		J. H. Crawford d. F. X. Shields
	final	F. J. PERRY d. J. H. Crawford 6–3 6–0 7–5
1935	s. finals	F. J. Perry d. J. H. Crawford
		G. von Cramm d. J. D. Budge
	final	F. J. PERRY d. G. von Cramm 6–2 6–4 6–4
1936	s. finals	F. J. Perry d. J. D. Budge
		G. von Cramm d. H. W. Austin
	final	F. J. PERRY d. G. von Cramm 6–1 6–1 6–0
1937	s. finals	J. D. Budge d. F. A. Parker
		G. von Cramm d. H. W. Austin
	final	J. D. BUDGE d. G. von Cramm 6–3 6–4 6–2
1938	s. finals	J. D. Budge d. F. Puncec
		H. W. Austin d. H. Henkel
	final	J. D. BUDGE d. H. W. Austin 6–1 6–0 6–3
1939	s. finals	R. L. Riggs d. F. Puncec
		E. T. Cooke d. H. Henkel
	final	R. L. RIGGS d. E. T. Cooke 2–6 8–6 3–6 6–3 6–2
1940–1945 not held		
1946	s. finals	Y. Petra d. T. Brown
		G. E. Brown d. J. Drobny
	final	Y. PETRA d. G. E. Brown 6–2 6–4 7–9 5–7 6–4
1947	s. finals	J. Kramer d. D. Pails
		T. Brown d. J. E. Patty
	final	J. KRAMER d. T. Brown 6–1 6–3 6–2

1948	s. finals	R. Falkenburg d. G. Mulloy
		J. E. Bromwich d. J. Asboth
	final	R. FALKENBURG d. J. E. Bromwich 7–5 0–6 6–2 3–6 7–5
1949	s. finals	F. R. Schroeder d. E. W. Sturgess
		J. Drobny d. J. E. Bromwich
	final	F. R. SCHROEDER d. J. Drobny 3–6 6–0 6–3 4–6 6–4
1950	s. finals	J. E. Patty d. E. V. Seixas
		F. A. Sedgman d. J. Drobny
	final	J. E. PATTY d. F. A. Sedgman 6–1 8–10 6–2 6–3
1951	s. finals	R. Savitt d. H. Flam
		K. McGregor d. E. W. Sturgess
	final	R. SAVITT d. K. McGregor 6–4 6–4 6–4
1952	s. finals	F. A. Sedgman d. M. G. Rose
		F. Drobny d. H. Flam
	final	F. A. SEDGMAN d. J. Drobny 4–6 6–2 6–3 6–2
1953	s. finals	E. V. Seixas d. M. G. Rose
		K. Nielsen d. J. Drobny
	final	E. V. SEIXAS d. K. Nielsen 9–7 6–3 6–4
1954	s. finals	J. Drobny d. J. E. Patty
		K. R. Rosewall d. M. A. Trabert
	final	J. DROBNY d. K. R. Rosewall 13–11 4–6 6–2 9–7
1955	s. finals	M. A. Trabert d. J. E. Patty
		K. Nielsen d. K. R. Rosewall
	final	M. A. TRABERT d. K. Nielsen 6–3 7–5 6–1
1956	s. finals	L. A. Hoad d. H. Richardson
		K. R. Rosewall d. E. V. Seixas
	final	L. A. HOAD d. K. R. Rosewall 6–2 4–6 7–5 6–4
1957	s. finals	L. A. Hoad d. S. Davidson
		A. J. Cooper d. N. A. Fraser
	final	L. A. HOAD d. A. J. Cooper 6–2 6–1 6–2
1958	s. finals	A. J. Cooper d. M. G. Rose
		N. A. Fraser d. K. Nielsen
	final	A. J. COOPER d. N. A. Fraser 3–6 6–3 6–4 13–11
1959	s. finals	A. Olmedo d. R. S. Emerson
		R. G. Laver d. B. Mackay
	final	A. OLMEDO d. R. G. Laver 6–4 6–3 6–4
1960	s. finals	N. A. Fraser d. R. Krishnan
		R. G. Laver d. N. Pietrangeli
	final	N. A. FRASER d. R. G. Laver 6–4 3–6 9–7 7–5
1961	s. finals	R. G. Laver d. R. Krishnan
		C. R. McKinley d. M. J. Sangster
	final	R. G. LAVER d. C. R. McKinley 6–3 6–1 6–4
1962	s. finals	R. G. Laver d. N. A. Fraser
		M. F. Mulligan d. J. G. Fraser
	final	R. G. LAVER d. M. F. Mulligan 6–2 6–2 6–1
1963	s. finals	C. R. McKinley d. W. Bungert
		F. S. Stolle d. M. Santana
	final	C. R. McKINLEY d. F. S. Stolle 9–7 6–1 6–4
1964	s. finals	R. S. Emerson d. W. Bungert
		F. S. Stolle d. C. R. McKinley
	final	R. S. EMERSON d. F. S. Stolle 6–4 12–10 4–6 6–3
1965	s. finals	R. S. Emerson d. R. D. Ralston
		F. S. Stolle d. E. C. Drysdale
	final	R. S. EMERSON d. F. S. Stolle 6–2 6–4 6–4
1966	s. finals	M. Santana d. O. K. Davidson
		R. D. Ralston d. E. C. Drysdale
	final	M. SANTANA d. R. D. Ralston 6–4 11–9 6–4
1967	s. finals	J. D. Newcombe d. N. Pilic
		W. Bungert d. R. Taylor
	final	J. D. NEWCOMBE d. W. Bungert 6–3 6–1 6–1
1968	s. finals	R. G. Laver d. A. R. Ashe
		A. D. Roche d. C. E. Graebner
	final	R. G. LAVER d. A. D. Roche 6–3 6–4 6–2
1969	s. finals	R. G. Laver d. A. R. Ashe
		J. D. Newcombe d. A. D. Roche
	final	R. G. LAVER d. J. D. Newcombe 6–4 5–7 6–4 6–4
1970	s. finals	J. D. Newcombe d. A. Gimeno
		K. R. Rosewall d. R. Taylor
	final	J. D. NEWCOMBE d. K. R. Rosewall 5–7 6–3 6–2 3–6 6–1
1971	s. finals	J. D. Newcombe d. K. R. Rosewall
		S. R. Smith d. T. W. Gorman
	final	J. D. NEWCOMBE d. S. R. Smith 6–3 5–7 2–6 6–4 6–4
1972	s. finals	S. R. Smith d. J. Kodes
		I. Nastase d. M. Orantes
	final	S. R. SMITH d. I. Nastase 4–6 6–3 6–3 4–6 7–5

1973	s. finals	J. Kodes d. A. Mayer
		A. Metreveli d. R. Taylor
	final	J. KODES d. A. Metreveli 6–1 9–8 6–3
1974	s. finals	J. S. Connors d. R. Stockton
		K. R. Rosewall d. S. R. Smith
	final	J. S. CONNORS d. K. R. Rosewall 6–1 6–1 6–4
1975	s. finals	A. R. Ashe d. A. D. Roche
		J. S. Connors d. R. Tanner
	final	A. R. ASHE d. J. S. Connors 6–1 6–1 5–7 6–4
1976	s. finals	I. Nastase d. R. Ramirez
		B. Borg d. R. Tanner
	final	B. BORG d. I. Nastase 6–4 6–2 9–7

WOMEN'S SINGLES

1884	s. finals	Miss M. Watson d. Miss B. Bingley
		Miss L. Watson d. Miss Leslie
	final	MISS M. WATSON d. Miss L. Watson 6–8 6–3 6–2
1885	s. finals	Miss B. Bingley d. Miss Guerney
		Miss M. Watson d. Miss E. F. Hudson
	final	MISS M. WATSON d. Miss B. Bingley 6–1 7–5
Challenge round introduced		
1886	s. finals	Miss A. Tabor d. Miss M. Shackle
		Miss B. Bingley d. Miss L. Watson
	final	Miss Bingley d. Miss Tabor
	challenge round	MISS B. BINGLEY d. Miss M. Watson 6–3 6–3
1887	s. finals	Miss L. Dod d. Miss B. James
		Mrs C. J. Cole d. Miss J. Shackle
	final	Miss Dod d. Mrs Cole
	challenge round	MISS L. DOD d. Miss B. Bingley 6–2 6–0
1888	s. finals	Miss Howes d. Miss Patterson
		Mrs G. W. Hillyard w.o. Miss Phillimore
	final	Mrs Hillyard d. Miss Howes
	challenge round	MISS L. DOD d. Mrs G. W. Hillyard 6–3 6–3
1889	s. finals	Miss L. Rice d. Miss Jacks
		Mrs G. W. Hillyard d. Miss B. Steedman
	final	MRS G. W. HILLYARD d. Miss L. Rice 4–6 8–6 6–4
	challenge round	w.o.
1890	s. finals	Miss Jacks d. Mrs C. J. Cole
		Miss L. Rice d. Miss M. Steedman
	final	MISS L. RICE d. Miss Jacks 6–4 6–1
	challenge round	w.o.
1891	s. finals	Miss L. Dod d. Miss B. Steedman
		Mrs G. W. Hillyard d. Miss M. Langrishe
	final	MISS L. DOD d. Mrs G. W. Hillyard 6–2 6–1
	challenge round	w.o.
1892	s. finals	Miss M. Shackle d. Miss B. Steedman
		Mrs G. W. Hillyard d. Miss Martin
	final	Mrs Hillyard d. Miss Shackle
	challenge round	MISS L. DOD d. Mrs G. W. Hillyard 6–1 6–1
1893	s. finals	Miss M. Shackle d. Miss L. Austin
		Mrs G. W. Hillyard d. Miss C. Cooper
	final	Mrs Hillyard d. Miss Shackle
	challenge round	MISS L. DOD d. Mrs G. W. Hillyard 6–8 6–1 6–4
1894	s. finals	Mrs G. W. Hillyard d. Miss Bryan
		Miss L. Austin d. Miss S. Robins
	final	MRS G. W. HILLYARD d. Miss L. Austin
	challenge round	w.o.
1895	s. finals	Miss Jackson d. Mrs Pickering
		Miss C. Cooper d. Mrs Draffen
	final	MISS C. COOPER d. Miss Jackson 7–5 8–6
	challenge round	w.o.
1896	s. finals	Miss L. Austin w.o. Mrs Horncastle
		Mrs Pickering d. Mrs Draffen
	final	Mrs Pickering d. Miss Austin
	challenge round	MISS C. COOPER d. Mrs Pickering 6–2 6–3
1897	s. finals	Mrs G. W. Hillyard w.o. Mrs Horncastle
		Mrs Pickering d. Miss R. Dyas
	final	Mrs Hillyard d. Mrs Pickering
	challenge round	MRS G. W. HILLYARD d. Miss C. Cooper 5–7 7–5 6–2
1898	s. finals	Miss Martin w.o. Miss Legh
		Miss C. Cooper d. Miss L. Austin
	final	MISS C. COOPER d. Miss Martin 6–4 6–4
	challenge round	w.o.

1899	s. finals	Mrs Durlacher d. Miss B. Steedman
		Mrs G. W. Hillyard d. Miss Tullock
	final	Mrs Hillyard d. Mrs Durlacher
	challenge round	MRS G. W. HILLYARD d. Miss C. Cooper 6–2 6–3
1900	s. finals	Miss C. Cooper d. Mrs G. Greville
		Miss Martin d. Mrs Evered
	final	Miss Cooper d. Miss Martin
	challenge round	MRS G. W. HILLYARD d. Miss Cooper 4–6 6–4 6–4
1901	s. finals	Miss Martin d. Miss A. M. Morton
		Mrs A. Sterry d. Miss Adams
	final	Mrs Sterry d. Miss Martin
	challenge round	MRS A. STERRY d. Mrs G. W. Hillyard 6–2 6–2
1902	s. finals	Miss M. E. Robb d. Miss D. K. Douglass
		Miss A. M. Morton d. Mrs G. Greville
	final	Miss Robb d. Miss Morton
	challenge round	MISS M. E. ROBB d. Mrs A. Sterry 7–5 6–1
		(replayed after overnight score 4–6 13–11)
1903	s. finals	Miss D. K. Douglass d. Miss T. Lowther
		Miss E. W. Thomson d. Miss A. N. G. Greene
	final	MISS D. K. DOUGLASS d. Miss E. W. Thomson
		4–6 6–4 6–2
	challenge round	w.o.
1904	s. finals	Mrs A. Sterry d. Miss A. N. G. Greene
		Miss A. M. Morton d. Miss C. M. Wilson
	final	Mrs Sterry d. Miss Morton
	challenge round	MISS D. K. DOUGLASS d. Mrs A. Sterry 6–0 6–3
1905	s. finals	Miss M. Sutton d. Miss A. M. Morton
		Miss C. M. Wilson d. Mrs G. W. Hillyard
	final	Miss Sutton d. Miss Wilson
	challenge round	MISS M. SUTTON d. Miss D. K. Douglass 6–3 6–4
1906	s. finals	Miss D. K. Douglass d. Miss B. Tulloch
		Mrs A. Sterry d. Miss T. Lowther
	final	Miss Douglass d. Mrs Sterry
	challenge round	MISS D. K. DOUGLASS d. Miss Sutton 7–3 9–7
1907	s. finals	Miss M. Sutton d. Miss L. Bosworth
		Miss C. M. Wilson d. Mrs G. W. Hillyard
	final	Miss Sutton d. Miss Wilson
	challenge round	MISS M. SUTTON d. Mrs Lambert Chambers 6–1 6–4
1908	s. finals	Mrs A. Sterry d. Miss D. Boothby
		Miss A. M. Morton d. Mrs Lamplough
	final	MRS A. STERRY d. Miss A. M. Morton 6–4 6–4
	challenge round	w.o.
1909	s. finals	Miss A. Morton d. Mrs H. Edgington
		Miss D. Boothby d. Miss M. Garfit
	final	MISS D. BOOTHBY d. Miss A. M. Morton 6–4 4–6 8–6
	challenge round	w.o.
1910	s. finals	Miss E. G. Johnson d. Mrs Lamplough
		Mrs Lambert Chambers d. Mrs R. J. McNair
	final	Mrs Lambert Chambers d. Miss Johnson
	challenge round	MRS LAMBERT CHAMBERS d. Miss D. Boothby
		6–2 6–2
1911	s. finals	Mrs Hannam d. Miss H. Aitchison
		Miss D. Boothby d. Mrs Parton
	final	Miss Boothby d. Mrs Hannam
	challenge round	MRS LAMBERT CHAMBERS d. Miss D. Boothby
		6–0 6–0
1912	s. finals	Mrs A. Sterry d. Miss E. D. Holman
		Mrs D. R. Larcombe d. Mrs G. W. Hillyard
	final	MRS D. R. LARCOMBE d. Mrs A. Sterry 6–3 6–1
	challenge round	w.o.
1913	s. finals	Mrs R. J. McNair d. Miss E. D. Holman
		Mrs Lambert Chambers d. Miss H. Aitchison
	final	MRS LAMBERT CHAMBERS d. Mrs R. J. McNair
		6–0 6–4
	challenge round	w.o.
1914	s. finals	Mrs D. R. Larcombe d. Mrs H. Edgington
		Miss E. Ryan d. Miss H. Aitchison
	final	Mrs Larcombe d. Miss Ryan
	challenge round	MRS LAMBERT CHAMBERS d. Mrs D. R. Larcombe
		7–5 6–4
1915–1918 not held		
1919	s. finals	Mrs P. Satterthwaite d. Mrs A. E. Beamish
		Mlle S. Lenglen d. Miss E. Ryan
	final	Mlle Lenglen d. Mrs Satterthwaite
	challenge round	MLLE S. LENGLEN d. Mrs Lambert Chambers
		10–8 4–6 9–7
1920	s. finals	Miss E. Ryan d. Mrs Parton
		Mrs Lambert Chambers d. Mrs F. Mallory
	final	Mrs Lambert Chambers d. Miss Ryan
	challenge round	MLLE S. LENGLEN d. Mrs Lambert Chambers 6–3 6–0

1921	s. finals	Mrs P. Satterthwaite d. Mrs Clayton
		Miss E. Ryan d. Mrs G. Peacock
	final	Miss Ryan d. Mrs Satterthwaite
	challenge round	MLLE S. LENGLEN d. Miss E. Ryan 6–2 6–0

(Challenge round abolished)

1922	s. finals	Mlle S. Lenglen d. Mrs G. Peacock
		Mrs F. Mallory d. Mrs A. E. Beamish
	final	MLLE S. LENGLEN d. Mrs F. Mallory 6–2 6–0
1923	s. finals	Mlle S. Lenglen d. Mrs A. E. Beamish
		Miss K. McKane d. Miss E. Ryan
	final	MLLE S. LENGLEN d. Miss K. McKane 6–2 6–2
1924	s. finals	Miss H. Wills d. Mrs P. Satterthwaite
		Miss K. McKane w.o. Mlle S. Lenglen
	final	MISS K. McKANE d. Miss H. Wills 4–6 6–4 6–4
1925	s. finals	Mlle S. Lenglen d. Miss K. McKane
		Miss J. Fry d. Mme Billout
	final	MLLE S. LENGLEN d. Miss J. Fry 6–2 6–0
1926	s. finals	Mrs L. A. Godfree d. Mlle D. Vlasto
		Sta E. de Alvarez d. Mrs F. Mallory
	final	MRS L. A. GODFREE d. Sta E. de Alvarez 6–2 4–6 6–3
1927	s. finals	Miss H. Wills d. Miss J. Fry
		Sta E. de Alvarez d. Miss E. Ryan
	final	MISS H. WILLS d. Sta E. de Alvarez 6–2 6–4
1928	s. finals	Miss H. Wills d. Miss E. Ryan
		Sta E. de Alvarez d. Miss D. Akhurst
	final	MISS H. WILLS d. Sta E. de Alvarez 6–2 6–3
1929	s. finals	Miss H. Wills d. Miss E. Goldsack
		Miss H. H. Jacobs d. Miss J. Ridley
	final	MISS H. WILLS d. Miss H. H. Jacobs 6–1 6–2
1930	s. finals	Mrs F. S. Moody d. Mme R. Mathieu
		Miss E. Ryan d. Frl C. Aussem
	final	MRS F. S. MOODY d. Miss E. Ryan 6–2 6–2
1931	s. finals	Frl C. Aussem d. Mme R. Mathieu
		Frl. H. Krahwinkel d. Miss H. H. Jacobs
	final	FRL C. AUSSEM d. Frl H. Krahwinkel 6–2 7–5
1932	s. finals	Mrs F. S. Moody d. Miss M. Heeley
		Miss H. H. Jacobs d. Mme R. Mathieu
	final	MRS F. S. MOODY d. Miss H. H. Jacobs 6–3 6–1
1933	s. finals	Mrs F. S. Moody d. Frl H. Krahwinkel
		Miss D. E. Round d. Miss H. H. Jacobs
	final	MRS F. S. MOODY d. Miss D. E. Round 6–4 6–8 6–3
1934	s. finals	Miss D. E. Round d. Mme R. Mathieu
		Miss H. H. Jacobs d. Miss J. Hartigan
	final	MISS D. E. ROUND d. Miss H. H. Jacobs 6–2 5–7 6–3
1935	s. finals	Mrs F. S. Moody d. Miss J. Hartigan
		Miss H. H. Jacobs d. Fru S. Sperling
	final	MRS F. S. MOODY d. Miss H. H. Jacobs 6–3 3–6 7–5
1936	s. finals	Miss H. H. Jacobs d. Panna J. Jedrzejowska
		Fru S. Sperling d. Mme R. Mathieu
	final	MISS H. H. JACOBS d. Fru S. Sperling 6–2 4–6 7–5
1937	s. finals	Miss D. E. Round d. Mme R. Mathieu
		Panna J. Jedrzejowska d. Miss A. Marble
	final	MISS D. E. ROUND d. P. J. Jedrzejowska 6–2 2–6 7–5
1938	s. finals	Mrs F. S. Moody d. Fru S. Sperling
		Miss H. H. Jacobs d. Miss A. Marble
	final	MRS F. S. MOODY d. Miss H. H. Jacobs 6–4 6–0
1939	s. finals	Miss A. Marble d. Fru S. Sperling
		Miss K. E. Stammers d. Mrs S. P. Fabyan
	final	MISS A. MARBLE d. Miss K. E. Stammers 6–2 6–0

1940–1945 not held

1946	s. finals	Miss P. Betz d. Miss D. Bundy
		Miss L. Brough d. Miss M. Osborne
	final	MISS P. BETZ d. Miss L. Brough 6–2 6–4
1947	s. finals	Miss M. Osborne d. Mrs S. P. Summers
		Miss D. Hart d. Miss L. Brough
	final	MISS M. OSBORNE d. Miss D. Hart 6–2 6–4
1948	s. finals	Miss L. Brough d. Mrs P. C. Todd
		Miss D. Hart d. Mrs W. du Pont
	final	MISS L. BROUGH d. Miss D. Hart 6–3 8–6
1949	s. finals	Miss L. Brough d. Mrs P. C. Todd
		Mrs W. du Pont d. Mrs H. P. Rihbany
	final	MISS L. BROUGH d. Mrs W. du Pont 10–8 1–6 10–8
1950	s. finals	Miss L. Brough d. Miss D. Hart
		Mrs W. du Pont d. Mrs P. C. Todd
	final	MISS L. BROUGH d. Mrs W. du Pont 6–1 3–6 6–1

1951	s. finals	Miss D. Hart d. Miss B. Baker
		Miss S. Fry d. Miss L. Brough
	final	MISS D. HART d. Miss S. Fry 6–1 6–0
1952	s. finals	Miss M. Connolly d. Miss S. Fry
		Miss L. Brough d. Mrs P. C. Todd
	final	MISS M. CONNOLLY d. Miss L. Brough 7–5 6–3
1953	s. finals	Miss M. Connolly d. Miss S. Fry
		Miss D. Hart d. Mrs D. Knode
	final	MISS M. CONNOLLY d. Miss D. Hart 8–6 7–5
1954	s. finals	Miss M. Connolly d. Mrs C. Pratt
		Miss L. Brough d. Miss D. Hart
	final	MISS M. CONNOLLY d. Miss L. Brough 6–2 7–5
1955	s. finals	Miss L. Brough d. Miss D. R. Hard
		Mrs J. G. Fleitz d. Miss D. Hart
	final	MISS L. BROUGH d. Mrs J. G. Fleitz 7–5 8–6
1956	s. finals	Miss S. Fry d. Miss L. Brough
		Miss A. Buxton d. Miss P. Ward
	final	MISS S. FRY d. Miss A. Buxton 6–3 6–1
1957	s. finals	Miss A. Gibson d. Miss C. C. Truman
		Miss D. R. Hard d. Mrs D. Knode
	final	MISS A. GIBSON d. Miss D. R. Hard 6–3 6–2
1958	s. finals	Miss A. Gibson d. Miss A. S. Haydon
		Miss A. Mortimer d. Mrs S. Kormoczy
	final	MISS A. GIBSON d. Miss A. Mortimer 8–6 6–2
1959	s. finals	Miss M. E. Bueno d. Miss S. Moore
		Miss D. R. Hard d. Miss S. Reynolds
	final	MISS M. E. BUENO d. Miss D. R. Hard 6–4 6–3
1960	s. finals	Miss M. E. Bueno d. Miss C. C. Truman
		Miss S. Reynolds d. Miss A. S. Haydon
	final	MISS M. E. BUENO d. Miss S. Reynolds 8–6 6–0
1961	s. finals	Miss A. Mortimer d. Miss S. Reynolds
		Miss C. C. Truman d. Miss R. Schuurman
	final	MISS A. MORTIMER d. Miss C. C. Truman 4–6 6–4 7–5
1962	s. finals	Mrs J. R. Susman d. Miss A. S. Haydon
		Mrs V. Sukova d. Miss M. E. Bueno
	final	MRS J. R. SUSMAN d. Mrs V. Sukova 6–4 6–4
1963	s. finals	Miss M. Smith d. Miss D. R. Hard
		Miss B. J. Moffitt d. Mrs P. F. Jones
	final	MISS M. SMITH d. Miss B. J. Moffitt 6–3 6–4
1964	s. finals	Miss M. E. Bueno d. Miss L. R. Turner
		Miss M. Smith d. Miss B. J. Moffitt
	final	MISS M. E. BUENO d. Miss M. Smith 6–4 7–9 6–3
1965	s. finals	Miss M. Smith d. Miss C. C. Truman
		Miss M. E. Bueno d. Miss B. J. Moffitt
	final	MISS M. SMITH d. Miss M. E. Bueno 6–4 7–5
1966	s. finals	Mrs L. W. King d. Miss M. Smith
		Miss M. E. Bueno d. Mrs P. F. Jones
	final	MRS L. W. KING d. Miss M. E. Bueno 6–3 3–6 6–1
1967	s. finals	Mrs L. W. King d. Miss K. M. Harter
		Mrs P. F. Jones d. Miss R. Casals
	final	MRS L. W. KING d. Mrs P. F. Jones 6–3 6–4
1968	s. finals	Mrs L. W. King d. Mrs P. F. Jones
		Miss J. A. M. Tegart d. Miss N. Richey
	final	MRS L. W. KING d. Miss J. A. M. Tegart 9–7 7–5
1969	s. finals	Mrs P. F. Jones d. Mrs B. M. Court
		Mrs L. W. King d. Miss R. Casals
	final	MRS P. F. JONES d. Mrs L. W. King 3–6 6–3 6–2
1970	s. finals	Mrs. B. M. Court d. Miss R. Casals
		Mrs L. W. King d. Mlle F. Durr
	final	MRS B. M. COURT d. Mrs L. W. King 14–12 11–9
1971	s. finals	Miss E. F. Goolagong d. Mrs L. W. King
		Mrs B. M. Court d. Mrs D. E. Dalton
	final	MISS E. F. GOOLAGONG d. Mrs B. M. Court 6–4 6–1
1972	s. finals	Mrs L. W. King d. Miss R. Casals
		Miss E. F. Goolagong d. Miss C. Evert
	final	MRS L. W. KING d. Miss E. F. Goolagong 6–3 6–3
1973	s. finals	Mrs L. W. King d. Miss E. F. Goolagong
		Miss C. Evert d. Mrs B. M. Court
	final	MRS L. W. KING d. Miss C. Evert 6–0 7–5
1974	s. finals	Miss C. Evert d. Miss K. Melville
		Mrs O. Morozova d. Miss S. V. Wade
	final	MISS C. EVERT d. Mrs O. Morozova 6–0 6–4
1975	s. finals	Mrs L. W. King d. Miss C. Evert
		Mrs R. Cawley d. Mrs B. M. Court
	final	MRS L. W. KING d. Mrs R. Cawley 6–0 6–1

1976 s. finals   Miss C. Evert d. Miss M. Navratilova
                        Mrs R. Cawley d. Miss S. V. Wade
      final   MISS C. EVERT d. Mrs R. Cawley   6–3 4–6 8–6

MEN'S DOUBLES

Played for the first five years at Oxford.
1879   L. R. Erskine & H. F. Lawford
1880   W. Renshaw & E. Renshaw
1881   W. Renshaw & E. Renshaw
1882   J. T. Hartley & R. T. Richardson
1883   C. W. Grinstead & C. E. Welldon

Played at Wimbledon
1884   W. RENSHAW & E. RENSHAW
                        d. E. W. Lewis & E. L. Williams   6–3 3–6 6–1 1–6 6–4
1885   W. RENSHAW & E. RENSHAW
                        d. C. E. Farrar & A. J. Stanley   6–3 6–3 10–8

Challenge round introduced
1886 final   C. E. Farrar & A. J. Stanley
                        d. H. W. W. Wilberforce & P. B. Lyon
     challenge round   W. RENSHAW & E. RENSHAW
                        d. C. E. Farrar & A. J. Stanley   6–3 6–3 4–6 7–5
1887 final   H. W. W. WILBERFORCE & P. B. LYON
                        d. J. H. Crispe & Barratt Smith   7–5 6–3 6–2
     challenge round   w.o.
1888 final   W. Renshaw & E. Renshaw
                        d. E. G. Meers & A. G. Ziffo
     challenge round   W. RENSHAW & E. RENSHAW
                        d. H. W. W. Wilberforce & P. B. Lyon 2–6 1–6 6–3 6–4 6–3
1889 final   E. W. Lewis & G. W. Hillyard
                        d. G. R. Mewburn & A. W. Gore
     challenge round   W. RENSHAW & E. RENSHAW
                        d. E. W. Lewis & G. W. Hillyard   6–4 6–4 3–6 0–6 6–1
1890 final   J. PIM & F. O. STOKER
                        d. E. W. Lewis & G. W. Hillyard   6–0 7–5 6–4
     challenge round   w.o.
1891 final   W. Baddeley & H. Baddeley
                        d. E. Renshaw & H. S. Barlow
     challenge round   W. BADDELEY & H. BADDELEY
                        d. J. Pim & F. O. Stoker   6–1 6–3 1–6 6–2
1892 final   E. W. Lewis & H. S. Barlow
                        d. J. Pim & H. S. Mahony
     challenge round   E. W. LEWIS & H. S. BARLOW
                        d. W. Baddeley & H. Baddeley   4–6 6–2 8–6 6–4
1893 final   J. Pim & F. O. Stoker
                        d. W. Baddeley & H. Baddeley
     challenge round   J. PIM & F. O. STOKER
                        d. E. W. Lewis & H. S. Barlow   4–6 6–3 6–1 2–6 6–0
1894 final   W. BADDELEY & H. BADDELEY
                        d. H. S. Barlow & C. H. Martin   5–7 7–5 4–6 6–3 8–6
     challenge round   w.o.
1895 final   E. W. Lewis & W. V. Eaves
                        d. C. F. Simond & W. G. Bailey
     challenge round   W. BADDELEY & H. BADDELEY
                        d. E. W. Lewis & W. V. Eaves   8–6 5–7 6–4 6–3
1896 final   R. F. Doherty & H. A. Nisbet
                        d. E. R. Allen & C. G. Allen
     challenge round   W. BADDELEY & H. BADDELEY
                        d. R. F. Doherty & H. A. Nisbet   1–6 3–6 6–4 6–2 6–1
1897 final   R. F. Doherty & H. L. Doherty
                        d. C. H. L. Cazalet & S. H. Smith
     challenge round   R. F. DOHERTY & H. L. DOHERTY
                        d. W. Baddeley & H. Baddeley   6–4 4–6 8–6 6–4
1898 final   C. Hobart & H. A. Nisbet
                        d. G. W. Hillyard & S. H. Smith
     challenge round   R. F. DOHERTY & H. L. DOHERTY
                        d. C. Hobart & H. A. Nisbet   6–4 6–4 6–2
1899 final   C. Hobart & H. A. Nisbet
                        d. A. W. Gore & H. Roper Barrett
     challenge round   R. F. DOHERTY & H. L. DOHERTY
                        d. C. Hobart & H. A. Nisbet   7–5 6–0 6–2

1900 final   H. Roper Barrett & H. A. Nisbet
                        d. S. H. Smith & F. L. Riseley
     challenge round   R. F. DOHERTY & H. L. DOHERTY
                        d. H. Roper Barrett & H. A. Nisbet   9–7 7–5 4–6 3–6 6–3
1901 final   Dwight F. Davis & Holcombe Ward
                        d. H. Roper Barrett & G. M. Simond
     challenge round   R. F. DOHERTY & H. L. DOHERTY
                        d. Dwight F. Davis & Holcombe Ward   4–6 6–2 6–3 9–7
1902 final   S. H. Smith & F. L. Riseley
                        d. C. H. L. Cazalet & G. W. Hillyard
     challenge round   S. H. SMITH & F. L. RISELEY
                        d. R. F. Doherty & H. L. Doherty   4–6 8–6 6–3 4–6 11–9
1903 final   R. F. Doherty & H. L. Doherty
                        d. H. S. Mahony & M. J. G. Ritchie
     challenge round   R. F. DOHERTY & H. L. DOHERTY
                        d. S. H. Smith & F. L. Riseley   6–4 6–4 6–4
1904 final   S. H. Smith & F. L. Riseley
                        d. A. W. Gore & G. A. Caridia
     challenge round   R. F. DOHERTY & H. L. DOHERTY
                        d. S. H. Smith & F. L. Riseley   6–1 6–2 6–4
1905 final   S. H. Smith & F. L. Riseley
                        d. N. E. Brookes & A. W. Dunlop
     challenge round   R. F. DOHERTY & H. L. DOHERTY
                        d. S. H. Smith & F. L. Riseley   6–2 6–4 6–8 6–3
1906 final   S. H. Smith & F. L. Riseley
                        d. C. H. L. Cazalet & G. M. Simond
     challenge round   S. H. SMITH & F. L. RISELEY
                        d. R. F. Doherty & H. L. Doherty   6–8 6–4 5–7 6–3 6–3
1907 final   N. E. BROOKES & A. F. WILDING
                        d. Beals C. Wright & K. Behr   6–4 6–4 6–2
     challenge round   w.o.
1908 final   A. F. WILDING & M. J. G. RITCHIE
                        d. A. W. Gore & H. Roper Barrett   6–1 6–2 1–6 1–6 9–7
     challenge round   w.o.
1909 final   A. W. GORE & H. ROPER BARRETT
                        d. S. N. Doust & H. A. Parker   6–2 6–1 6–4
     challenge round   w.o.
1910 final   A. F. Wilding & M. J. G. Ritchie
                        d. K. Powell & R. B. Powell
     challenge round   A. F. WILDING & M. J. G. RITCHIE
                        d. A. W. Gore & H. Roper Barrett   6–1 6–1 6–2
1911 final   M. Decugis & A. H. Gobert
                        d. S. Hardy & J. C. Parke
     challenge round   M. DECUGIS & A. H. GOBERT
                        d. A. F. Wilding & M. J. G. Ritchie   9–7 5–7 6–3 2–6 6–2
1912 final   H. Roper Barrett & C. P. Dixon
                        d. A. E. Beamish & J. C. Parke
     challenge round   H. ROPER BARRETT & C. P. DIXON
                        d. M. Decugis & A. H. Gobert   3–6 6–3 6–4 7–5
1913 final   H. Kleinschroth & F. W. Rahe
                        d. A. E. Beamish & J. C. Parke
     challenge round   H. ROPER BARRETT & C. P. DIXON
                        d. H. Kleinschroth & F. W. Rahe   6–2 6–4 4–6 6–2
1914 final   N. E. Brookes & A. F. Wilding
                        d. F. G. Lowe & A. H. Lowe
     challenge round   N. E. BROOKES & A. F. WILDING
                        d. H. Roper Barrett & C. P. Dixon   6–1 6–1 5–7 8–6
1915–1918 not held
1919 final   R. V. THOMAS & P. O'HARA WOOD
                        d. R. Lycett & R. W. Heath   6–4 6–2 4–6 6–2
     challenge round   w.o.
1920 final   R. N. WILLIAMS & C. S. GARLAND
                        d. A. R. F. Kingscote & J. C. Parke   4–6 6–4 7–5 6–2
     challenge round   w.o.
1921 final   R. LYCETT & M. WOOSNAM
                        d. F. G. Lowe & A. H. Lowe   6–3 6–0 7–5
     challenge round   w.o.
Challenge round abolished
1922   J. O. ANDERSON & R. LYCETT
                        d. G. L. Patterson & P. O'Hara Wood   3–6 7–9 6–4 6–3 11–9
1923   L. A. GODFREE & R. LYCETT
                        d. Count de Gomar & E. Flaquer   6–3 6–4 3–6 6–3
1924   F. T. HUNTER & V. RICHARDS
                        d. R. N. Williams & W. M. Washburn   6–3 3–6 8–10 8–6 6–3
1925   J. BOROTRA & R. LACOSTE
                        d. R. Casey & J. Hennessey   6–4 11–9 4–6 1–6 6–3

1926 J. BRUGNON & H. COCHET
d. H. Kinsey & V. Richards   7–5 4–6 6–3 6–2

1927 F. T. HUNTER & W. T. TILDEN
d. J. Brugnon & H. Cochet   1–6 4–6 8–6 6–3 6–4

1928 J. BRUGNON & H. COCHET
d. J. B. Hawkes & G. L. Patterson   13–11 6–4 6–4

1929 W. L. ALLISON & J. VAN RYN
d. I. G. Collins & J. C. Gregory   6–4 5–7 6–3 10–12 6–4

1930 W. L. ALLISON & J. VAN RYN
d. J. H. Doeg & G. M. Lott   6–3 6–3 6–2

1931 G. M. LOTT & J. VAN RYN
d. J. Brugnon & H. Cochet   6–2 10–8 9–11 3–6 6–3

1932 J. BOROTRA & J. BRUGNON
d. G. P. Hughes & F. J. Perry   6–0 4–6 3–6 7–5 7–5

1933 J. BOROTRA & J. BRUGNON
d. R. Nunoi & J. Satoh   4–6 6–3 6–3 7–5

1934 G. M. LOTT & L. R. STOEFEN
d. J. Borotra & J. Brugnon   6–2 6–3 6–4

1935 J. H. CRAWFORD & A. K. QUIST
d. W. L. Allison & J. Van Ryn   6–3 5–7 6–2 5–7 7–5

1936 G. P. HUGHES & C. R. D. TUCKEY
d. C. E. Hare & F. H. D. Wilde   6–4 3–6 7–9 6–1 6–4

1937 J. D. BUDGE & G. MAKO
d. G. P. Hughes & C. R. D. Tuckey   6–0 6–4 6–8 6–1

1938 J. D. BUDGE & G. MAKO
d. H. Henkel & G. von Metaxa   6–4 3–6 6–3 8–6

1939 E. T. COOKE & R. L. RIGGS
d. C. E. Hare & F. H. D. Wilde   6–3 3–6 6–3 9–7

1940–1945 not held

1946 T. BROWN & J. KRAMER
d. G. E. Brown & D. Pails   6–4 6–4 6–2

1947 R. FALKENBURG & J. KRAMER
d. A. J. Mottram & O. W. Sidwell   8–6 6–3 6–3

1948 J. E. BROMWICH & F. A. SEDGMAN
d. T. Brown & G. Mulloy   5–7 7–5 7–5 9–7

1949 R. GONZALES & F. PARKER
d. G. Mulloy & F. R. Schroeder   6–4 6–4 6–2

1950 J. E. BROMWICH & A. K. QUIST
d. G. E. Brown & O. W. Sidwell   7–5 3–6 6–3 3–6 6–2

1951 K. McGREGOR & F. A. SEDGMAN
d. J. Drobny & E. W. Sturgess   3–6 6–2 6–3 3–6 6–3

1952 K. McGREGOR & F. A. SEDGMAN
d. E. V. Seixas & E. W. Sturgess   6–3 7–5 6–4

1953 L. A. HOAD & K. R. ROSEWALL
d. R. Hartwig & M. G. Rose   6–4 7–5 4–6 7–5

1954 R. HARTWIG & M. G. ROSE
d. E. V. Seixas & M. A. Trabert   6–4 6–4 3–6 6–4

1955 R. HARTWIG & L. A. HOAD
d. N. A. Fraser & K. R. Rosewall   7–5 6–4 6–3

1956 L. A. HOAD & K. R. ROSEWALL
d. N. Pietrangeli & O. Sirola   7–5 6–2 6–1

1957 G. MULLOY & J. E. PATTY
d. N. A. Fraser & L. A. Hoad   8–10 6–4 6–4 6–4

1958 S. DAVIDSON & U. SCHMIDT
d. A. J. Cooper & N. A. Fraser   6–4 6–4 8–6

1959 R. S. EMERSON & N. A. FRASER
d. R. G. Laver & R. Mark   8–6 6–3 14–16 9–7

1960 R. H. OSUNA & R. D. RALSTON
d. M. G. Davies & R. K. Wilson   7–5 6–3 10–8

1961 R. S. EMERSON & N. A. FRASER
d. R. A. J. Hewitt & F. S. Stolle   6–4 6–8 6–4 6–8 8–6

1962 R. A. J. HEWITT & F. S. STOLLE
d. B. Jovanovic & N. Pilic   6–1 5–7 6–2 6–4

1963 R. H. OSUNA & A. PALAFOX
d. J. C. Barclay & P. Darmon   4–6 6–2 6–2 6–2

1964 R. A. J. HEWITT & F. S. STOLLE
d. R. S. Emerson & K. N. Fletcher   7–5 11–9 6–4

1965 J. D. NEWCOMBE & A. D. ROCHE
d. K. N. Fletcher & R. A. J. Hewitt   7–5 6–3 6–4

1966 K. N. FLETCHER & J. D. NEWCOMBE
d. W. W. Bowrey & O. K. Davidson   6–3 6–4 3–6 6–3

1967 R. A. J. HEWITT & F. D. McMILLAN
d. R. S. Emerson & K. N. Fletcher   6–2 6–3 6–4

1968 J. D. NEWCOMBE & A. D. ROCHE
d. K. R. Rosewall & F. S. Stolle   3–6 8–6 5–7 14–12 6–3

1969 J. D. NEWCOMBE & A. D. ROCHE
d. T. S. Okker & M. C. Riessen   7–5 11–9 6–3

1970 J. D. NEWCOMBE & A. D. ROCHE
d. K. R. Rosewall & F. S. Stolle   10–8 6–3 6–1

1971 R. S. EMERSON & R. G. LAVER
d. A. R. Ashe & R. D. Ralston   4–6 9–7 6–8 6–4 6–4

1972 R. A. J. HEWITT & F. D. McMILLAN
d. S. R. Smith & E. J. van Dillen   6–2 6–2 9–7

1973 J. S. CONNERS & I. NASTASE
d. J. R. Cooper & N. A. Fraser   3–6 6–3 6–4 8–9 6–1

1974 J. D. NEWCOMBE & A. D. ROCHE
d. R. C. Lutz & S. R. Smith   8–6 6–4 6–4

1975 V. GERULAITIS & A. MAYER
d. C. Dowdeswell & A. J. Stone   7–5 8–6 6–4

1976 B. E. GOTTFRIED & R. RAMIREZ
d. R. Case & G. Masters   3–6 6–3 8–6 3–6 7–5

WOMEN'S DOUBLES

A non-championship event was staged
at Wimbledon 1899 to 1907.

Winners:

1899 Mrs G. W. Hillyard & Miss B. Steedman
1900 Mrs W. H. Pickering & Miss M. E. Robb
1901 Mrs G. W. Hillyard & Mrs A. Sterry
1902 Miss A. M. Morton & Mrs A. Sterry
1903 Miss D. K. Douglass & Mrs W. H. Pickering
1904 Miss W. Longhurst & Miss E. W. Thomson
1905 Miss W. Longhurst & Miss E. W. Thomson
1906 Mrs G. W. Hillyard & Miss M. Sutton
1907 Mrs Lambert Chambers & Miss C. M. Wilson

Full championship event

1913 MISS D. BOOTHBY & MRS R. J. McNAIR
d. Mrs Lambert Chambers & Mrs A. Sterry   4–6 2–4 ret'd

1914 MISS A. M. MORTON & MISS E. RYAN
d. Mrs Hannam & Mrs D. R. Larcombe   6–1 6–3

1915–1918 not held

1919 MLLE S. LENGLEN & MISS E. RYAN
d. Mrs Lambert Chambers & Mrs D. R. Larcombe   4–6 7–5 6–3

1920 MLLE S. LENGLEN & MISS E. RYAN
d. Mrs Lambert Chambers & Mrs D. R. Larcombe   6–4 6–0

1921 MLLE S. LENGLEN & MISS E. RYAN
d. Mrs A. E. Beamish & Mrs G. Peacock   6–1 6–2

1922 MLLE S. LENGLEN & MISS E. RYAN
d. Miss K. McKane & Mrs A. D. Stocks   6–0 6–4

1923 MLLE S. LENGLEN & MISS E. RYAN
d. Miss J. Austin & Miss E. Colyer   6–3 6–1

1924 MRS G. WIGHTMAN & MISS H. WILLS
d. Mrs B. C. Covell & Miss K. McKane   6–4 6–4

1925 MLLE S. LENGLEN & MISS E. RYAN
d. Mrs A. V. Bridge & Mrs C. G. McIlquham   6–2 6–2

1926 MISS M. K. BROWNE & MISS E. RYAN
d. Miss E. L. Colyer & Mrs L. A. Godfree   6–1 6–1

1927 MISS H. WILLS & MISS E. RYAN
d. Miss E. L. Heine & Mrs G. Peacock   6–3 6–2

1928 MISS P. SAUNDERS & MRS M. WATSON
d. Miss E. Bennett & Miss E. H. Harvey   6–2 6–3

1929 MRS L. R. C. MICHELL & MRS M. WATSON
d. Mrs B. C. Covell & Mrs D. C. Shepherd-Barron   6–4 8–6

1930 MRS F. S. MOODY & MISS E. RYAN
d. Miss E. Cross & Miss S. Palfrey   6–2 9–7

1931 MRS D. SHEPHERD-BARRON & MISS P. MUDFORD
d. Mlle D. Metaxa & Mlle J. Sigart   3–6 6–3 6–4

1932 MLLE D. METAXA & MLLE J. SIGART
d. Miss H. H. Jacobs & Miss E. Ryan   6–4 6–3

1933 MME R. MATHIEU & MISS E. RYAN
d. Miss F. James & Miss A. M. Yorke   6–2 9–11 6–4

1934 MME R. MATHIEU & MISS E. RYAN
d. Mrs D. Andrus & Mme S. Henrotin   6–3 6–3

1935 MISS F. JAMES & MISS K. STAMMERS
d. Mme R. Mathieu & Fru S. Sperling   6–1 6–4

1936 MISS F. JAMES & MISS K. STAMMERS
d. Mrs S. P. Fabyan & Miss H. H. Jacobs   6–2 6–1

1937 MME R. MATHIEU & MISS A. M. YORKE
d. Mrs M. R. King & Mrs J. P. Pittman   6–3 6–3

1938 MRS S. P. FABYAN & MISS A. MARBLE
d. Mme R. Mathieu & Miss A. M. Yorke   6–2 6–3

1939 MRS S. P. FABYAN & MISS A. MARBLE
d. Miss H. H. Jacobs & Miss A. M. Yorke   6–1 6–0

1940-1945 not held

1946 MISS L. BROUGH & MISS M. OSBORNE
d. Miss P. Betz & Miss D. Hart   6–3 2–6 6–3

1947 MISS D. HART & MRS P. C. TODD
d. Miss L. Brough & Miss M. Osborne   3–6 6–4 7–5

1948 MISS L. BROUGH & MRS W. DU PONT
d. Miss D. Hart & Mrs P. C. Todd   6–3 3–6 6–3

1949 MISS L. BROUGH & MRS W. DU PONT
d. Miss G. Moran & Mrs P. C. Todd   8–6 7–5

1950 MISS L. BROUGH & MRS W. DU PONT
d. Miss S. Fry & Miss D. Hart   6–4 5–7 6–1

1951 MISS S. FRY & MISS D. HART
d. Miss L. Brough & Mrs W. du Pont   6–3 13–11

1952 MISS S. FRY & MISS D. HART
d. Miss L. Brough & Miss M. Connolly   8–6 6–3

1953 MISS S. FRY & MISS D. HART
d. Miss M. Connolly & Miss J. Sampson   6–0 6–0

1954 MISS L. BROUGH & MRS W. DU PONT
d. Miss S. Fry & Miss D. Hart   4–6 9–7 6–3

1955 MISS A. MORTIMER & MISS J. A. SHILCOCK
d. Miss S. J. Bloomer & Miss P. E. Ward   7–5 6–1

1956 MISS A. BUXTON & MISS A. GIBSON
d. Miss F. Muller & Miss D. G. Seeney   6–1 8–6

1957 MISS A. GIBSON & MISS D. R. HARD
d. Mrs K. Hawton & Mrs T. D. Long   6–1 6–2

1958 MISS M. E. BUENO & MISS A. GIBSON
d. Mrs W. du Pont & Miss M. Varner   6–3 7–5

1959 Miss J. ARTH & MISS D. R. HARD
d. Miss J. G. Fleitz & Miss C. C. Truman   2–6 6–2 6–3

1960 MISS M. E. BUENO & MISS D. R. HARD
d. Miss S. Reynolds & Miss R. Schuurman   6–4 6–0

1961 MISS K. HANTZE & MISS B. J. MOFFITT
d. Miss J. Lehane & Miss M. Smith   6–3 6–4

1962 MISS B. J. MOFFITT & MRS J. R. SUSMAN
d. Miss L. E. G. Price & Miss R. Schuurman   5–7 6–3 7–5

1963 MISS M. E. BUENO & MISS D. R. HARD
d. Miss R. A. Ebbern & Miss M. Smith   8–6 9–7

1964 MISS M. SMITH & MISS L. R. TURNER
d. Miss B. J. Moffitt & Mrs J. R. Susman   7–5 6–2

1965 MISS M. E. BUENO & MISS B. J. MOFFITT
d. Mlle F. Durr & Mlle J. Lieffrig   6–2 7–5

1966 MISS M. E. BUENO & MISS N. RICHEY
d. Miss M. Smith & Miss J. A. M. Tegart   6–3 4–6 6–4

1967 MISS R. CASALS & MRS L. W. KING
d. Miss M. E. Bueno & Miss N. Richey   9–11 6–4 6–2

1968 MISS R. CASALS & MRS L. W. KING
d. Mlle F. Durr & Mrs P. F. Jones   3–6 6–4 7–5

1969 MRS B. M. COURT & MISS J. A. M. TEGART
d. Miss P. S. A. Hogan & Miss M. Michel   9–7 6–2

1970 MISS R. CASALS & MRS L. W. KING
d. Mlle F. Durr & Miss S. V. Wade   6–2 6–3

1971 MISS R. CASALS & MRS L. W. KING
d. Mrs B. M. Court & Miss E. F. Goolagong   6–3 6–2

1972 MRS L. W. KING & MISS B. STOVE
d. Mrs D. E. Dalton & Mlle F. Durr   6–2 4–6 6–3

1973 MISS R. CASALS & MRS L. W. KING
d. Mlle F. Durr & Miss B. Stove   6–1 4–6 7–5

1974 MISS E. F. GOOLAGONG & MISS M. MICHEL
d. Miss H. F. Gourlay & Miss K. M. Krantzcke   2–6 6–4 6–3

1975 MISS A. K. KIYOMURA & MISS K. SAWAMATSU
d. Mlle F. Durr & Miss B. Stove   7–5 1–6 7–5

1976 MISS C. EVERT & MISS M. NAVRATILOVA
d. Mrs L. W. King & Miss B. Stove   6–1 3–6 7–5

MIXED DOUBLES

A non-championship event was staged
at Wimbledon 1900 to 1912.

Winners:

1900 H. A. Nisbet & Mrs W. H. Pickering
1901 H. L. Doherty & Mrs A. Sterry
1902 H. L. Doherty & Mrs A. Sterry
1903 S. H. Smith & Miss E. W. Thomson
1904 S. H. Smith & Miss E. W. Thomson
1905 A. W. Gore & Miss C. M. Wilson
1906 A. F. Wilding & Miss D. K. Douglass
1907 Beals C. Wright & Miss M. Sutton
1908 A. F. Wilding & Mrs Lambert Chambers
1909 H. Roper Barrett & Miss A. M. Morton
1910 S. N. Doust & Mrs Lambert Chambers
1911 T. M. Mavrogordato & Mrs E. G. Parton
1912 J. C. Parke & Mrs D. R. Larcombe

Full championship event

1913 HOPE CRISP & MRS C. O. TUCKEY
d. J. C. Parke & Mrs D. R. Larcombe   3–6 5–3 ret'd

1914 J. C. PARKE & MRS D. LARCOMBE
d. A. F. Wilding & Mlle M. Broquedis   4–6 6–4 6–2

1915–1918 not held

1919 R. LYCETT & MISS E. RYAN
d. A. D. Prebble & Mrs Lambert Chambers   6–0 6–0

1920 G. L. PATTERSON & MLLE S. LENGLEN
d. R. Lycett & Miss E. Ryan   7–5 6–3

1921 R. LYCETT & MISS E. RYAN
d. M. Woosnam & Miss P. L. Howkins   6–3 6–1

1922 P. O'HARA WOOD & MLLE S. LENGLEN
d. R. Lycett & Miss E. Ryan   6–4 6–3

1923 R. LYCETT & MISS E. RYAN
d. L. S. Deane & Mrs D. C. Shepherd-Barron   6–4 7–5

1924 J. B. GILBERT & MISS K. McKANE
d. L. A. Godfree & Mrs D. C. Shepherd-Barron   6–3 3–6 6–3

1925 J. BOROTRA & MLLE S. LENGLEN
d. H. L. de Morpurgo & Miss E. Ryan   6–3 6–3

1926 L. A. GODFREE & MRS L. A. GODFREE
d. H. Kinsey & Miss M. K. Browne   6–3 6–4

1927 F. T. HUNTER & MISS E. RYAN
d. L. A. Godfree & Mrs L. A. Godfree   8–6 0–0

1928 P. D. B. SPENCE & MISS E. RYAN
d. J. H. Crawford & Miss D. Akhurst   7–5 6–4

1929 F. T. HUNTER & MISS H. WILLS
d. I. G. Collins & Miss J. Fry   6–1 6–4

1930 J. H. CRAWFORD & MISS E. RYAN
d. D. Prenn & Frl H. Krahwinkel   6–1 6–3

1931 G. M. LOTT & MRS L. A. HARPER
d. I. G. Collins & Miss J. C. Ridley   6–3 1–6 6–1

1932 E. MAIER & MISS E. RYAN
d. H. C. Hopman & Mlle J. Sigart   7–5 6–2

1933 G. VON CRAMM & FRL H. KRAHWINKEL
d. N. G. Farquharson & Miss M. Heeley   7–5 8–6

1934 R. MIKI & MISS D. E. ROUND
d. H. W. Austin & Mrs D. C. Shepherd-Barron   3–6 6–4 6–0

1935 F. J. PERRY & MISS D. E. ROUND
d. H. C. Hopman & Mrs H. C. Hopman   7–5 4–6 6–2

1936 F. J. PERRY & MISS D. E. ROUND
d. J. D. Budge & Mrs S. P. Fabyan   7–9 7–5 6–4

1937 J. D. BUDGE & MISS A. MARBLE
d. Y. Petra & Mme R. Mathieu   6–4 6–1

1938   J. D. BUDGE & MISS A. MARBLE
        d. H. Henkel & Mrs S. P. Fabyan   6–1 6–4

1939   R. L. RIGGS & MISS A. MARBLE
        d. F. H. D. Wilde & Miss N. B. Brown   9–7 6–1

1940–1945 not held

1946   T. BROWN & MISS L. BROUGH
        d. G. E. Brown & Miss D. Bundy   6–4 6–4

1947   J. E. BROMWICH & MISS L. BROUGH
        d. C. F. Long & Mrs N. M. Bolton   1–6 6–4 6–2

1948   J. E. BROMWICH & MISS L. BROUGH
        d. F. A. Sedgman & Miss D. Hart   6–2 3–6 6–3

1949   E. W. STURGESS & MRS S. P. SUMMERS
        d. J. E. Bromwich & Miss L. Brough   9–7 9–11 7–5

1950   E. W. STURGESS & MISS L. BROUGH
        d. G. E. Brown & Mrs P. C. Todd   11–9 1–6 6–4

1951   F. A. SEDGMAN & MISS D. HART
        d. M. G. Rose & Mrs N. M. Bolton   7–5 6–2

1952   F. A. SEDGMAN & MISS D. HART
        d. E. Morea & Mrs T. D. Long   4–6 6–3 6–4

1953   E. V. SEIXAS & MISS D. HART
        d. E. Morea & Miss S. Fry   9–7 7–5

1954   E. V. SEIXAS & MISS D. HART
        d. K. R. Rosewall & Mrs W. du Pont   5–7 6–4 6–3

1955   E. V. SEIXAS & MISS D. HART
        d. E. Morea & Miss L. Brough   8–6 2–6 6–3

1956   E. V. SEIXAS & MISS S. FRY
        d. G. Mulloy & Miss A. Gibson   2–6 6–2 7–5

1957   M. G. ROSE & MISS D. R. HARD
        d. N. A. Fraser & Miss A. Gibson   6–4 7–5

1958   R. N. HOWE & MISS L. COGHLAN
        d. K. Nielsen & Miss A. Gibson   6–3 13–11

1959   R. G. LAVER & MISS D. R. HARD
        d. N. A. Fraser & Miss M. E. Bueno   6–4 6–3

1960   R. G. LAVER & MISS D. R. HARD
        d. R. N. Howe & Miss M. E. Bueno   13–11 3–6 8–6

1961   F. S. STOLLE & MISS L. R. TURNER
        d. R. N. Howe & Miss E. Buding   11–9 6–2

1962   N. A. FRASER & MRS W. DU PONT
        d. R. D. Ralston & Miss A. S. Haydon   2–6 6–3 13–11

1963   K. N. FLETCHER & MISS M. SMITH
        d. R. A. J. Hewitt & Miss D. R. Hard   11–9 6–4

1964   F. S. STOLLE & MISS L. R. TURNER
        d. K. N. Fletcher & Miss M. Smith   6–4 6–4

1965   K. N. FLETCHER & MISS M. SMITH
        d. A. D. Roche & Miss J. A. M. Tegart   12–10 6–3

1966   K. N. FLETCHER & MISS M. SMITH
        d. R. D. Ralston & Mrs L. W. King   4–6 6–3 6–3

1967   O. K. DAVIDSON & MRS L. W. KING
        d. K. N. Fletcher & Miss M. E. Bueno   7–5 6–2

1968   K. N. FLETCHER & MRS B. M. COURT
        d. A. Metreveli & Miss O. Morozova   6–1 14–12

1969   F. S. STOLLE & MRS P. F. JONES
        d. A. D. Roche & Miss J. A. M. Tegart   6–3 6–2

1970   I. NASTASE & MISS R. CASALS
        d. A. Metreveli & O. Morozova   6–3 4–6 9–7

1971   O. K. DAVIDSON & MRS L. W. KING
        d. M. C. Riessen & Mrs B. M. Court   3–6 6–2 15–13

1972   I. NASTASE & MISS R. CASALS
        d. K. G. Warwick & Miss E. F. Goolagong   6–4 6–4

1973   O. K. DAVIDSON & MRS L. W. KING
        d. R. Ramirez & Miss J. S. Newberry   6–3 6–2

1974   O. K. DAVIDSON & MRS L. W. KING
        d. M. J. Farrell & Miss L. J. Charles   6–3 9–7

1975   M. C. RIESSEN & MRS B. M. COURT
        d. A. J. Stone & Miss B. Stove   6–4 7–5

1976   A. D. ROCHE & MLLE F. DURR
        d. R. L. Stockton & Miss R. Casals   6–3 2–6 7–5

JUNIOR INTERNATIONAL TOURNAMENT

For juniors nominated by national lawn tennis associations

Boys' Singles

Winner		Runner-up
1949	S. Stockenberg (Sweden)	J. A. T. Horn (G.B.)
1950	J. A. T. Horn (G.B.)	K. Moubarek (Egypt)
1951	J. Kupferburger (S. Africa)	K. Moubarek (Egypt)
1952	R. K. Wilson (G.B.)	T. Fancutt (S. Africa)
1953	W. A. Knight (G.B.)	R. Krishnan (India)
1954	R. Krishnan (India)	A. J. Cooper (Australia)
1955	M. P. Hann (G.B.)	J. E. Lundquist (Sweden)
1956	R. Holmberg (U.S.A.)	R. G. Laver (Australia)
1957	J. I. Tattersall (G.B.)	I. Ribeiro (Brazil)
1958	E. Buchholz (U.S.A.)	P. Lall (India)
1959	T. Lejus (U.S.S.R.)	R. W. Barnes (Brazil)
1960	A. R. Mandelstam (S. Africa)	J. Mukerjea (India)
1961	C. E. Graebner (U.S.A.)	E. Blanke (Austria)
1962	S. J. Matthews (G.B.)	A. Metreveli (U.S.S.R.)
1963	N. Kalogeropoulos (Greece)	I. El Shafei (U.A.R.)
1964	I. El Shafei (U.A.R.)	V. Korotkov (U.S.S.R.)
1965	V. Korotkov (U.S.S.R.)	G. Goven (France)
1966	V. Korotkov (U.S.S.R.)	B. Fairlie (N.Z.)
1967	M. Orantes (Spain)	M. Estep (U.S.A.)
1968	J. Alexander (Australia)	J. Thamin (France)
1969	B. Bertram (S. Africa)	J. Alexander (Australia)
1970	B. Bertram (S. Africa)	F. Gebert (Germany)
1971	R. Kreiss (U.S.A.)	S. A. Warboys (G.B.)
1972	B. Borg (Sweden)	C. J. Mottram (G.B.)
1973	W. Martin (U.S.A.)	C. Dowdeswell (Rhod.)
1974	W. Martin (U.S.A.)	Ashok Amritraj (India)
1975	C. J. Lewis (N.Z.)	R. Ycaza (Ecuador)
1976	H. Guenthardt (Switz.)	P. Elter (Germany)

Girls' Singles

1949	Mlle C. Mercellis (Belgium)	Miss J. S. V. Partridge (G.B.)
1950	Miss L. Cornell (G.B.)	Miss A. Winther (Norway)
1951	Miss L. Cornell (G.B.)	Miss S. Lazzarino (Italy)
1952	Miss F. ten Bosch (Neth.)	Miss R. Davar (India)
1953	Miss D. Kilian (S. Africa)	Miss V. A. Pitt (G.B.)
1954	Miss V. A. Pitt (G.B.)	Mlle C. Monnot (France)
1955	Miss S. M. Armstrong (G.B.)	Mlle B. de Chambure (France)
1956	Miss A. S. Haydon (G.B.)	Miss I. Buding (Germany)
1957	Miss M. Arnold (U.S.A.)	Sta R. M. Reyes (Mexico)
1958	Miss S. M. Moore (U.S.A.)	Miss A. Dmitrieva (U.S.S.R.)
1959	Miss J. Cross (S. Africa)	Miss D. Schuster (Austria)
1960	Miss K. Hantze (U.S.A.)	Miss L. M. Hutchings (S. Africa)
1961	Miss G. Baksheeva (U.S.S.R.)	Miss K. D. Chabot (U.S.A.)
1962	Miss G. Baksheeva (U.S.S.R.)	Miss E. P. Terry (N.Z.)
1963	Mlle D. M. Salfati (France)	Miss K. Dening (Australia)
1964	Miss J. M. Bartkowicz (U.S.A.)	Sta E. Subirats (Mexico)
1965	Miss O. Morozova (U.S.S.R.)	Miss R. Giscafre (Arg.)
1966	Miss B. Lindstrom (Finland)	Miss J. Congdon (G.B.)
1967	Miss J. Salome (Neth.)	Miss M. Strandberg (Sweden)
1968	Miss K. Pigeon (U.S.A.)	Miss L. Hunt (Australia)
1969	Miss K. Sawamatsu (Japan)	Miss B. Kirk (S. Africa)
1970	Miss S. Walsh (U.S.A.)	Miss M. Kroshina (U.S.S.R.)
1971	Miss M. Kroshina (U.S.S.R.)	Miss S. Minford (Ireland)
1972	Miss I. Kloss (S. Africa)	Miss G. L. Coles (G.B.)
1973	Miss A. K. Kiyomura (U.S.A.)	Miss M. Navratilova (Czech.)
1974	Miss M. Jausovec (Yugo.)	Miss M. Simionescu (Rum.)
1975	Miss N. Y. Chmyreva (U.S.S.R.)	Miss R. Marsikova (Czech.)
1976	Miss N. Y. Chmyreva (U.S.S.R.)	Miss M. Kruger (S.A.)

ALL ENGLAND PLATE

For players beaten in
first or second round
of the singles

Men

1896	A. W. Gore
1897	H. Baddeley
1898	G. W. Hillyard
1899	W. V. Eaves
1900	G. Greville
1901	P. G. Pearsor
1902	B. Hillyard
1903	A. W. Gore
1904	G. Greville
1905	W. V. Eaves
1906	G. W. Hillyard
1907	A. F. Wilding
1908	O. Kreuzer
1909	R. B. Powell
1910	A. H. Gobert
1911	A. H. Lowe
1912	F. M. Pearson
1913	F. G. Lowe
1914	C. P. Dixon
1915–1918	not held
1919	F. R. L. Crawford
1920	F. G. Lowe
1921	J. B. Gilbert
1922	B. I. C. Norton
1923	J. Washer
1924	J. Condon
1925	B. von Kehrling
1926	J. B. Gilbert
1927	A. Gentien
1928	M. Sleem
1929	E. G. Chandler
1930	E. du Plaix
1931	V. G. Kirby
1932	H. Cochet
1933	F. H. D. Wilde
1934	H. W. Artens
1935	J. Yamagishi
1936	D. N. Jones
1937	W. Sabin
1938	D. W. Butler
1939	W. D. McNeill
1940–1945	not held
1946	R. Abdesselam
1947	E. W. Sturgess
1948	F. H. Ampon
1949	E. H. Cochell
1950	G. L. Paish
1951	N. M. Cockburn
1952	L. Ayala
1953	G. L. Paish
1954	H. W. Stewart
1955	N. A. Fraser
1956	H. W. Stewart
1957	G. L. Forbes
1958	P. Remy
1959	J. Javorsky
1960	T. Ulrich
1961	J. Ulrich
1962	J. A. Douglas
1963	E. L. Scott
1964	R. K. Wilson
1965	O. K. Davidson
1966	R. Taylor
1967	J. H. McManus
1968	G. Battrick
1969	T. Koch
1970	R. R. Maud
1971	R. D. Crealy
1972	K. G. Warwick
1973	J. G. Clifton
1974	T. I. Kakulia
1975	T. Koch
1976	B. E. Fairlie

Women

1933	Mlle C. Rosambert
1934	Miss L. Valerio
1935	Miss L. Valerio
1936	Miss F. S. Ford
1937	Miss F. James
1938	Miss D. Stevenson
1939	Mrs R. D. McKelvie
1940–1945	not held
1946	Panna J. Jedrzejowska
1947	Panna J. Jedrzejowska
1948	Señora H. Weiss
1949	Miss A. Bossi
1950	Miss K. L. A. Tuckey
1951	Mrs F. J. Bartlett
1952	Mrs B. Abbas
1953	Miss M. P. Harrison
1954	Miss R. Walsh
1955	Miss F. Muller
1956	Mrs T. D. Long
1957	Miss M. Hellyer
1958	Miss S. Reynolds
1959	Mrs C. W. Brasher
1960	Miss C. M. Catt
1961	Miss R. H. Bentley
1962	Miss M. L. Gerson
1963	Mlle F. Durr
1964	Mrs V. Sukova
1965	Miss A. Dmitrieva
1966	Miss P. M. Walkden
1967	Miss P. S. A. Hogan
1968	Miss S. V. Wade
1969	Miss B. A. Grubb
1970	Miss E. F. Goolagong
1971	Mrs M. R. Wainwright
1972	Miss K. M. Krantzcke
1973	Miss H. F. Gourlay
1974	Miss M. V. Kroschina
1975	Miss D. L. Fromholtz
1976	Miss M. Wikstedt

VETERANS' EVENT

A men's doubles for players 45 years or over
on 1st January was instituted in 1964.
It is not a championship event.

Winners:

1964	B. Destremau & W. F. Talbert
1965	G. Mulloy & W. F. Talbert
1966	G. Mulloy & W. F. Talbert
1967	J. Drobny & A. V. Martini
1968	J. Drobny & A. V. Martini
1969	J. Drobny & E. V. Seixas
1970	J. Drobny & R. L. Riggs
1971	G. Mulloy & A. Vincent
1972	L. S. Clark & E. V. Seixas
1973	J. D. Budge & F. A. Sedgman
1974	R. Dunas & G. Mulloy
1975	L. Bergelin & J. E. Patty
1976	L. Bergelin & J. E. Patty

MAJOR EVENTS AT WIMBLEDON

(other than the Championships)

1904	Davis Cup: Belgium d. France 3–2.
	Davis Cup, Challenge Round: British Isles d. Belgium 5–0.
1905	Davis Cup, Challenge Round: British Isles d. America 5–0.
1906	Davis Cup, Challenge Round: British Isles d. America 5–0.
1907	Davis Cup: Australasia d. America 3–2.
	Davis Cup, Challenge Round: Australasia d. British Isles 3–2.
1908	Olympic Games (Gold Medallists: M. J. G. Ritchie, Mrs Lambert Chambers, G. W. Hillyard and R. F. Doherty).
1913	Davis Cup: America d. Canada 3–0.
	Davis Cup, Challenge Round: America d. British Isles 3–2.
	Davis Cup: British Isles d. France 4–1.
1920	Davis Cup: U.S.A. d. British Isles 5–0.
1933	Davis Cup: Great Britain d. Australia 3–2.
1934	Davis Cup: U.S.A. d. Australia 3–2.
	Davis Cup, Challenge Round: Great Britain d. U.S.A. 4–1.
1935	Davis Cup: U.S.A. d. Germany 4–1
	Davis Cup, Challenge Round: Great Britain d. U.S.A. 5–0.
1936	Davis Cup: Australia d. Germany 4–1.
	Davis Cup, Challenge Round: Great Britain d. Australia 3–2.
1937	Davis Cup: U.S.A. d. Germany 3–2.
	Davis Cup, Challenge Round: U.S.A. d. Great Britain 4–1.
1939	Davis Cup: Great Britain d. France 3–2.
1949	Davis Cup: Czechoslovakia d. Great Britain 4–1.
1951	Davis Cup: Great Britain d. France 3–2.
1960	Davis Cup: Italy d. Great Britain 4–1.
1963	Davis Cup: Great Britain d. Sweden 3–2.
1967	World Professional Championship (Winner: R. G. Laver).
1969	Davis Cup: Great Britain d. Brazil 3–2.
	Davis Cup: Rumania d. Great Britain 3–2.

(Note: The Wightman Cup, Great Britain v U.S.A. (women), was staged at
Wimbledon in alternate years 1924–1938 and again in alternate years from
1946 to 1972.)

WIMBLEDON REFEREES

1877–1885	Henry Jones
1886–1889	Julian Marshall
1890–1904	B. C. Evelegh
1905–1914	H. S. Scrivener
1919–1936	F. R. Burrows
1937–1939	Hamilton Price
1946–1950	Capt. A. K. Trower
1951–1962	Col. W. J. Legg
1963–1975	Capt. M. B. Gibson
1976–	Fred Hoyles

WIMBLEDON SECRETARIES

1877–1879	J. W. Walsh
1880–1886	Julian Marshall
1887–1890	H. W. W. Wilberforce
1891–1898	Arthur Chitty
1899–1906	Archdale Palmer
1907–1924	Cdr G. W. Hillyard
1925–1939	D. R. Larcombe
1946–1963	Lt. Col. A. D. C. Macaulay
1964–	Major A. D. Mills

LONG MATCHES

(as by number of games played)

(1) Longest match: 1969. Men's singles, first round.
R. A. Gonzales d. C. Pasarell 22–24 1–6 16–14 6–3 11–9—112 games
(Played 24/25 June, match postponed overnight at one set all)
(Duration 5 hours 12 minutes)

(2) Longest men's singles—see (1) above

(3) Longest women's singles: 1948. Second round.
Miss A. Weiwers d. Mrs O. Anderson 8–10 14–12 6–4—54 games

(4) Longest men's doubles: 1966. First round.
N. Pilic & E. L. Scott d. C. Richey & T. Ulrich
19–21 12–10 6–4 4–6 9–7—98 games

(5) Longest women's doubles: 1933. First round.
Miss P. G. Brazier & Mrs I. H. Wheatcroft d.
Miss M. E. Nonweiler & Miss B. Soames 11–9 5–7 9–7—48 games

(6) Longest mixed doubles: 1967. Quarter-final.
K. Fletcher & Miss M. E. Bueno d.
A. Metreveli & Miss A. Dmitrieva 6–8 7–5 16–14—56 games

(7) Longest finals:
Men's singles: 1954. J. Drobny d. K. R. Rosewall—58 games
Women's singles: 1970. Mrs B. M. Court d. Mrs L. W. King—46 games
Men's doubles: 1968. J. D. Newcombe & A. D. Roche d.
K. R. Rosewall & F. S. Stolle—70 games
Women's doubles: 1933. Mme R. Mathieu & Miss E. Ryan d.
Miss F. James & Miss A. M. Yorke—38 games
and 1967. Miss R. Casals & Mrs L. W. King d.
Miss M. E. Bueno & Miss N. Richey—38 games
Mixed doubles: 1949. E. W. Sturgess & Mrs S. P. Summers d.
J. Bromwich & Miss L. Brough—48 games

(8) Longest set:
1968. Men's doubles, second round.
F. Segura & A. Olmedo d.
G. L. Forbes & A. Segal 32–30 5–7 6–4 6–4 32–30

CHAMPIONSHIPS WON FROM MATCH POINT DOWN

1889	Men's singles	W. RENSHAW in all-comers' final beat H. S. Barlow 3–6 5–7 8–6 10–8 8–6 after six match points in 4th set.
	Women's singles	MRS G. W. HILLYARD in all-comers' final for the title beat Miss L. Rice 4–6 8–6 6–4 after three match points in 2nd set.
1895	Men's singles	W. BADDELEY in all-comers' final for the title beat W. V. Eaves 4–6 2–6 8–6 6–2 6–3 after match point in 3rd set.
1901	Men's singles	A. W. GORE in quarter-final beat G. W. Hillyard 6–1 2–6 4–6 8–6 6–2 after match point in 4th set.
1908	Men's doubles	A. F. WILDING & M. J. G. RITCHIE in all-comers' final for the title beat A. W. Gore & H. Roper Barrett 6–1 6–2 1–6 1–6 9–7 after match point in 5th set.
1919	Women's singles	MLLE S. LENGLEN in challenge round beat Mrs Lambert Chambers 10–8 4–6 9–7 after two match points in 3rd set.
1921	Men's singles	W. T. TILDEN in challenge round beat B. I. C. Norton 4–6 2–6 6–1 6–0 7–5 after two match points in 5th set.
1926	Women's doubles	MISS E. RYAN & MISS M. K. BROWNE in second round beat Mlle S. Lenglen & Mlle D. Vlasto 3–6 9–7 6–2 after three match points in 2nd set.
1927	Men's singles	H. COCHET in final beat J. Borotra 4–6 4–6 6–3 6–4 7–5 after six match points in 5th set.
	Men's doubles	F. T. HUNTER & W. T. TILDEN in final beat J. Brugnon & H. Cochet 1–6 4–6 8–6 6–3 6–4 after two match points in 3rd set.
1932	Women's doubles	MLLE D. METAXA & MLLE J. SIGART in first round beat Miss F. James & Miss M. Heeley 2–6 6–4 7–5 after three match points in 3rd set.
1935	Women's singles	MRS F. S. MOODY in final beat Miss H. H. Jacobs 6–3 3–6 7–5 after match point in 3rd set.
	Men's doubles	J. H. CRAWFORD & A. K. QUIST in final beat W. L. Allison & J. Van Ryn 6–3 5–7 6–2 5–7 7–5 after match point in 5th set.

1947	Women's doubles	MISS D. HART & MRS P. C. TODD in final beat Miss L. Brough & Miss M. Osborne 3–6 6–4 7–5 after three match points in 3rd set.
1948	Men's singles	R. FALKENBURGH in final beat J. E. Bromwich 7–5 0–6 6–2 3–6 7–5 after three match points in 5th set.
1949	Men's singles	F. R. SCHROEDER in quarter-final beat F. A. Sedgman 3–6 6–8 6–3 6–2 9–7 after two match points in 5th set.
1954	Women's doubles	MISS L. BROUGH & MRS W. DU PONT in final beat Miss S. Fry & Miss D. Hart 4–6 9–7 6–3 after two match points in 2nd set.
1960	Men's singles	N. A. FRASER in quarter-final beat E. Buchholz 4–6 6–3 4–6 15–15 ret'd after six match points in 4th set.
	Mixed doubles	R. G. LAVER & MISS D. R. HARD in final beat R. N. Howe & Miss M. E. Bueno 13–11 3–6 8–6 after three match points in 3rd set.
1976	Mixed doubles	A. D. ROCHE & MLLE F. DURR in final beat R. L. Stockton & Miss R. Casals 6–3 2–6 7–5 after a match point at 4–5 in the final set.

TRIPLE WIMBLEDON CHAMPIONS

1920		Mlle S. Lenglen
1922		Mlle S. Lenglen
1925		Mlle S. Lenglen
1937	J. D. Budge	
1938	J. D. Budge	
1939	R. L. Riggs	Miss A. Marble
1948		Miss L. Brough
1950		Miss L. Brough
1951		Miss D. Hart
1952	F. A. Sedgman	
1967, 1973		Mrs L. W. King

(Women's doubles and mixed doubles were introduced as championship events at Wimbledon only in 1913. Prior to that year the comparable achievement of winning three events lay in taking the respective All England Championships. The men's singles, men's doubles and women's singles titles were those held at Wimbledon. The women's doubles was held at Buxton. The mixed doubles alternated between Liverpool and Manchester. The following were triple All England Champions:

1888	E. Renshaw	
1903		Miss D. K. Douglass
1907	N. E. Brookes	
1908		Mrs A. Sterry
1912		Mrs D. R. Larcombe

SINGLES WINNERS AT THEIR FIRST ATTEMPT

1877	Spencer W. Gore (inaugural year)	
1878	P. F. Hadow	
1879	J. T. Hartley	
1884		Miss M. Watson (inaugural year)
1887		Miss L. Dod
1905		Miss M. Sutton
1919	G. L. Patterson	Mlle S. Lenglen
1920	W. T. Tilden	
1932	H. E. Vines	
1939	R. L. Riggs	
1946		Miss P. Betz
1949	F. R. Schroeder	
1951	R. Savitt	
1952		Miss M. Connolly

(Note: not all details of the earlier meetings have survived)

U.S. championships

MEN'S SINGLES

Played at The Casino, Newport, Rhode Island.

1881 s. finals	R. D. Sears d. Gray W. E. Glyn d. Shaw	
final	R. D. SEARS d. W. E. Glyn 6–0 6–3 6–2	
1882 s. finals	R. D. Sears a bye C. M. Clark d. Gray	
final	R. D. SEARS d. C. M. Clark 6–1 6–4 6–0	
1883 s. finals	R. D. Sears d. F. Keene J. Dwight d. R. F. Conover	
final	R. D. SEARS d. J. Dwight 6–2 6–0 9–7	

Challenge Round instituted

1884 s. finals	H. A. Taylor d. W. P. Knapp W. V. S. Thorne d. C. M. Clark
final	Taylor d. Thorne
challenge round	R. D. SEARS d. H. A. Taylor 6–0 1–6 6–2 6–2
1885 s. finals	W. P. Knapp d. J. S. Clark G. M. Brinley d. W. V. R. Berry
final	Brinley d. Knapp
challenge round	R. D. SEARS d. G. M. Brinley 6–3 4–6 6–0 6–3
1886 s. finals	H. A. Taylor d. J. S. Clark R. L. Beeckman d. C. A. Chase
final	Beeckman d. Taylor
challenge round	R. D. SEARS d. R. L. Beeckman 4–6 6–1 6–3 6–4
1887 s. finals	H. W. Slocum d. J. S. Clark H. A. Taylor d. W. L. Thacher
final	Slocum d. Taylor
challenge round	R. D. SEARS d. H. W. Slocum 6–1 6–3 6–2
1888 s. finals	H. W. Slocum d. O. S. Campbell H. A. Taylor d. P. S. Sears
final	H. W. SLOCUM d. H. A. Taylor 6–4 6–1 6 0
challenge round	w.o.
1889 s. finals	O. A. Shaw d. W. P. Knapp O. S. Campbell d. E. G. Meers
final	Shaw d. Campbell
challenge round	H. W. SLOCUM d. O. A. Shaw 6–3 6–1 4–6 6–2
1890 s. finals	W. P. Knapp d. C. Hobart O. S. Campbell d. R. P. Huntington
final	Campbell d. Knapp
challenge round	O. S. CAMPBELL d. H. W. Slocum 6–2 4–6 6–3 6–1
1891 s. finals	C. Hobart d. V. G. Hall F. H. Hovey d. M. D. Smith
final	Hobart d. Hovey
challenge round	O. S. CAMPBELL d. C. Hobart 2–6 7–5 7–9 6–1 6–2
1892 s. finals	F. H. Hovey d. R. D. Wrenn W. A. Larned d. E. L. Hall
final	Hovey d. Larned
challenge round	O. S. CAMPBELL d. F. H. Hovey 7–5 3–6 6–3 7–5
1893 s. finals	R. D. Wrenn d. S. T. Chase F. H. Hovey d. C. Hobart
final	R. D. WRENN d. F. H. Hovey 6–4 3–6 6–4 6–4
challenge round	w.o.
1894 s. finals	M. F. Goodbody d. J. B. Read W. A. Larned d. M. G. Chace
final	Goodbody d. Larned
challenge round	R. D. WRENN d. M. F. Goodbody 6–8 6–1 6–4 6–4
1895 s. finals	F. H. Hovey d. C. B. Neel W. A. Larned d. R. S. Howland
final	Hovey d. Larned
challenge round	F. H. HOVEY d. R. D. Wrenn 6–3 6–2 6–4
1896 s. finals	R. D. Wrenn d. C. B. Neel W. A. Larned d. E. P. Fischer
final	Wrenn d. Larned
challenge round	R. D. WRENN d. F. H. Hovey 7–5 3–6 6–0 1–6 6–1
1897 s. finals	H. A. Nisbet d. W. A. Larned W. V. Eaves d. L. E. Ware
final	Eaves d. Nisbet
challenge round	R. D. WRENN d. W. V. Eaves 4–6 8–6 6–2 2–6 6–2
1898 s. finals	D. F. Davis d. W. S. Bond M. D. Whitman d. L. F. Ware
final	M. D. WHITMAN d. D. F. Davis 3–6 6–2 6–2 6–1
challenge round	w.o.

1899 s. finals	J. P. Paret d. L. E. Ware D. F. Davis d. K. Collins
final	Paret d. Davis
challenge round	M. D. WHITMAN d. J. P. Paret 6–1 6–2 3–6 7–5
1900 s. finals	W. A. Larned d. B. C. Wright R. D. Wrenn d. A. W. Gore
final	Larned d. Wrenn
challenge round	M. D. WHITMAN d. W. A. Larned 6–4 1–6 6–2 6–2
1901 s. finals	W. A. Larned d. L. E. Ware B. C. Wright d. R. D. Little
final	W. A. LARNED d. B. C. Wright 6–2 6–8 6–4 6–4
challenge round	w.o.
1902 s. finals	M. D. Whitman d. R. P. Huntington R. F. Doherty w.o. H. L. Doherty
final	R. F. Doherty d. Whitman
challenge round	W. A. LARNED d. R. F. Doherty 4–6 6–2 6–4 8–6
1903 s. finals	H. L. Doherty d. R. H. Carleton W. J. Clothier d. E. P. Larned
final	Doherty d. Clothier
challenge round	H. L. DOHERTY d. W. A. Larned 6–0 6–3 10–8
1904 s. finals	W. J. Clothier d. W. A. Larned H. Ward d. E. W. Leonard
final	H. WARD d. W. J. Clothier 10–8 6–4 9–7
challenge round	w.o.
1905 s. finals	C. Hobart d. K. Collins B. C. Wright d. W. A. Larned
final	Wright d. Hobart
challenge round	B. C. WRIGHT d. H. Ward 6–1 6–2 11–9
1906 s. finals	W. J. Clothier d. J. D. E. Jones K. H. Behr d. R. D. Little
final	Clothier d. Behr
challenge round	W. J. CLOTHIER d. B. C. Wright 6–3 6–0 6–4
1907 s. finals	W. A. Larned d. C. Hobart R. Leroy d. I. Mollenhauer
final	W. A. LARNED d. R. Leroy 6–2 6–2 6–4
challenge round	w.o.
1908 s. finals	F. B. Alexander d. W. J. Clothier B. C. Wright d. N. Emerson
final	Wright d. Alexander
challenge round	W. A. LARNED d. B. C. Wright 6–1 6–2 8–6
1909 s. finals	W. J. Clothier d. I. C. Bundy M. E. McLoughlin d. G. F. Touchard
final	Clothier d. McLoughlin
challenge round	W. A. LARNED d. W. J. Clothier 6–1 6–2 5–7 1–6 6–1
1910 s. finals	B. C. Wright d. E. H. Whitney T. C. Bundy d. F. C. Colston
final	Bundy d. Wright
challenge round	W. A. LARNED d. T. C. Bundy 6–1 5–7 6–0 6–8 6–4
1911 s. finals	M. E. McLoughlin d. G. F. Touchard B. C. Wright d. T. C. Bundy
final	McLoughlin d. Wright
challenge round	W. A. LARNED d. M. E. McLoughlin 6–4 6–4 6 2

Challenge Round abolished

1912 s. finals	M. E. McLoughlin d. W. J. Clothier W. F. Johnson d. K. H. Behr
final	M. E. McLOUGHLIN d. W. F. Johnson 3–6 2–6 6–2 6–4 6–2
1913 s. finals	R. N. Williams d. N. W. Niles M. E. McLoughlin d. W. F. Johnson
final	M. E. McLOUGHLIN d. R. N. WILLIAMS 6–4 5–7 6–3 6–1
1914 s. finals	R. N. Williams d. E. F. Fottrell M. E. McLoughlin d. W. J. Clothier
final	R. N. WILLIAMS d. M. E. McLoughlin 6–3 8–6 10–8

Played at the West Side Club, Forest Hills, New York.

1915 s. finals	W. M. Johnston d. R. N. Williams M. E. McLoughlin d. T. R. Pell
final	W. M. JOHNSTON d. M. E. McLoughlin 1–6 6–0 7–5 10–8
1916 s. finals	R. N. Williams d. C. J. Griffin W. M. Johnston d. R. L. Murray
final	R. N. WILLIAMS d. W. M. Johnston 4–6 6–4 0–6 6–2 6–4
1917 National Patriotic Tournament	
s. finals	R. L. Murray d. J. R. Strachan N. W. Niles d. R. N. Williams
final	R. L. MURRAY d. N. W. Niles 5–7 8–6 6–3 6–3

1918 s. finals   R. L. Murray d. S. H. Voshell
                 W. T. Tilden d. I. Kumagae
       final   R. L. MURRAY d. W. T. Tilden   6–3 6–1 7–5

1919 s. finals   W. M. Johnston d. W. F. Johnson
                 W. T. Tilden d. R. N. Williams
       final   W. M. JOHNSTON d. W. T. Tilden   6–4 6–4 6–3

1920 s. finals   W. M. Johnston d. G. C. Caner
                 W. T. Tilden d. W. F. Johnson
       final   W. T. TILDEN d. W. M. Johnston 6–1 1–6 7–5 5–7 6–3

Played at the Germantown Cricket Club, Philadelphia.

1921 s. finals   W. F. Johnson d. J. O. Anderson
                 W. T. Tilden d. W. E. Davis
       final   W. T. TILDEN d. W. F. Johnson   6–1 6–3 6–1

1922 s. finals   W. M. Johnston d. V. Richards
                 W. T. Tilden d. G. L. Patterson
       final   W. T. TILDEN d. W. M. Johnston   4–6 3–6 6–2 6–3 6–4

1923 s. finals   W. T. Tilden d. B. I. C. Norton
                 W. M. Johnston d. F. T. Hunter
       final   W. T. TILDEN d. W. M. Johnston   6–4 6–1 6–4

Played at the West Side Club, Forest Hills, New York.

1924 s. finals   W. T. Tilden d. V. Richards
                 W. M. Johnston d. G. L. Patterson
       final   W. T. TILDEN d. W. M. Johnston   6–1 9–7 6–2

1925 s. finals   W. M. Johnston d. R. N. Williams
                 W. T. Tilden d. V. Richards
       final   W. T. TILDEN d. W. M. Johnston   4–6 11–9 6–3 4–6 6–3

1926 s. finals   R. Lacoste d. H. Cochet
                 J. Borotra d. V. Richards
       final   R. LACOSTE d. J. Borotra   6–4 6–0 6–4

1927 s. finals   W. T. Tilden d. F. T. Hunter
                 R. Lacoste d. W. M. Johnston
       final   R. LACOSTE d. W. T. Tilden   11–9 6–3 11–9

1928 s. finals   F. T. Hunger d. G. M. Lott
                 H. Cochet d. F. X. Shields
       final   H. COCHET d. F. T. Hunter   4–6 6–4 3–6 7–5 6–3

1929 s. finals   W. T. Tilden d. J. Doeg
                 F. T. Hunter d. F. Mercur
       final   W. T. TILDEN d. F. T. Hunter   3–6 6–3 4–6 6–2 6–4

1930 s. finals   F. X. Shields d. S. B. Wood
                 J. Doeg d. W. T. Tilden
       final   J. DOEG d. F. X. Shields   10–8 1–6 6–4 16–14

1931 s. finals   H. E. Vines d. F. J. Perry
                 G. M. Lott d. J. Doeg
       final   H. E. VINES d. G. M. Lott   7–9 6–3 9–7 7–5

1932 s. finals   H. E. Vines d. C. Sutter
                 H. Cochet d. W. Allison
       final   H. E. VINES d. H. Cochet   6–4 6–4 6–4

1933 s. finals   F. J. Perry d. L. R. Stoefen
                 J. H. Crawford d. F. X. Shields
       final   F. J. PERRY d. J. H. Crawford   6–3 11–13 4–6 6–0 6–1

1934 s. finals   F. J. Perry d. V. G. Kirby
                 W. Allison d. S. B. Wood
       final   F. J. PERRY d. W. Allison   6–4 6–3 3–6 1–6 8–6

1935 s. finals   S. B. Wood d. B. M. Grant
                 W. Allison d. F. J. Perry
       final   W. ALLISON d. S. B. Wood   6–2 6–3 6–3

1936 s. finals   F. J. Perry d. B. M. Grant
                 J. D. Budge d. F. Parker
       final   F. J. PERRY d. J. D. Budge   2–6 6–2 8–6 1–6 10–8

1937 s. finals   J. D. Budge d. F. Parker
                 G. von Cramm d. R. L. Riggs
       final   J. D. BUDGE d. G. Von Cramm   6–1 7–9 6–1 3–6 6–1

1938 s. finals   J. D. Budge d. S. B. Wood
                 C. G. Mako d. J. E. Bromwich
       final   J. D. BUDGE d. C. G. Mako   6–3 6–8 6–2 6–1

1939 s. finals   R. L. Riggs d. J. R. Hunt
                 W. Van Horn d. J. E. Bromwich
       final   R. L. RIGGS d. W. Van Horn   6–4 6–2 6–4

1940 s. finals   W. D. McNeill d. J. A. Kramer
                 R. L. Riggs d. J. R. Hunt
       final   W. D. McNEILL d. R. L. Riggs   4–6 6–8 6–3 6–3 7–5

1941 s. finals   F. Kovacs d. W. D. McNeill
                 R. L. Riggs d. F. R. Schroeder
       final   R. L. RIGGS d. F. Kovacs   5–7 6–1 6–3 6–3

1942 s. finals   F. Parker d. F. Segura
                 F. R. Schroeder d. G. Mulloy
       final   F. R. SCHROEDER d. F. Parker   8–6 7–5 3–6 4–6 6–2

1943 s. finals   J. A. Kramer d. F. Segura
                 J. R. Hunt d. W. F. Talbert
       final   J. R. HUNT d. J. A. Kramer   6–3 6–8 10–8 6–0

1944 s. finals   W. F. Talbert d. F. Segura
                 F. Parker d. W. D. McNeill
       final   F. PARKER d. W. F. Talbert   6–4 3–6 6–3 6–3

1945 s. finals   F. Parker d. E. T. Cooke
                 W. F. Talbert d. F. Segura
       final   F. PARKER d. W. F. Talbert   14–12 6–1 6–2

1946 s. finals   J. A. Kramer d. R. Falkenburg
                 T. Brown d. G. Mulloy
       final   J. A. KRAMER d. T. Brown   9–7 6–3 6–0

1947 s. finals   J. A. Kramer d. J. Drobny
                 F. Parker d. J. E. Bromwich
       final   J. A. KRAMER d. F. Parker   4–6 2–6 6–1 6–0 6–3

1948 s. finals   R. A. Gonzales d. J. Drobny
                 E. W. Sturgess d. H. Flam
       final   R. A. GONZALES d. E. W. Sturgess   6–2 6–3 14–12

1949 s. finals   R. A. Gonzales d. F. Parker
                 F. R. Schroeder d. W. F. Talbert
       final   R. A. GONZALES d. F. R. Schroeder.   16–18 2–6 6–1 6–2 6–2

1950 s. finals   A. Larsen d. R. Savitt
                 H. Flam d. G. Mulloy
       final   A. LARSEN d. H. Flam   6–3 4–6 5–7 6–4 6–3

1951 s. finals   E. V. Seixas d. R. Savitt
                 F. A. Sedgman d. A. Larsen
       final   F. A. SEDGMAN d. E. V. Seixas   6–4 6–1 6–1

1952 s. finals   G. Mulloy d. H. Richardson
                 F. A. Sedgman d. M. G. Rose
       final   F. A. SEDGMAN d. G. Mulloy   6–1 6–2 6–3

1953 s. finals   M. A. Trabert d. K. R. Rosewall
                 E. V. Seixas d. L. A. Hoad
       final   M. A. TRABERT d. E. V. Seixas   6–3 6–2 6–3

1954 s. finals   R. Hartwig d. K. R. Rosewall
                 E. V. Seixas d. H. Richardson
       final   E. V. SEIXAS d. R. Hartwig   3–6 6–2 6–4 6–4

1955 s. finals   K. R. Rosewall d. E. V. Seixas
                 M. A. Trabert d. L. A. Hoad
       final   M. A. TRABERT d. K. R. Rosewall   9–7 6–3 6–3

1956 s. finals   K. R. Rosewall d. E. V. Seixas
                 L. A. Hoad d. N. A. Fraser
       final   K. R. ROSEWALL d. L. A. Hoad   4–6 6–2 6–3 6–3

1957 s. finals   A. J. Cooper d. H. Flam
                 M. J. Anderson d. S. Davidson
       final   M. J. ANDERSON d. A. J. Cooper   10–8 7–5 6–4

1958 s. finals   A. J. Cooper d. N. A. Fraser
                 M. J. Anderson d. U. Schmidt
       final   A. J. COOPER d. M. J. Anderson   6–2 3–6 4–6 10–8 8–6

1959 s. finals   N. A. Fraser d. B. Bartzen
                 A. Olmedo d. R. Holmberg
       final   N. A. FRASER d. A. Olmedo   6–3 5–7 6–2 6–4

1960 s. finals   R. G. Laver d. E. Buchholz
                 N. A. Fraser d. D. Ralston
       final   N. A. FRASER d. R. G. Laver   6–4 6–4 10–8

1961 s. finals   R. E. Emerson d. R. H. Osuna
                 R. G. Laver d. M. J. Sangster
       final   R. E. EMERSON d. R. G. Laver   7–5 6–3 6–2

1962 s. finals   R. G. Laver d. R. H. Osuna
                 R. E. Emerson d. C. McKinley
       final   R. G. LAVER d. R. E. Emerson   6–2 6–4 5–7 6–4

1963 s. finals   R. H. Osuna d. C. McKinley
                 F. Froehling d. R. Barnes
       final   R. H. OSUNA d. F. Froehling   7–5 6–4 6–2

1964 s. finals   R. E. Emerson d. C. McKinley
                 F. S. Stolle d. R. H. Osuna
       final   R. E. EMERSON d. F. S. Stolle   6–4 6–1 6–4

1965 s. finals   M. Santana d. A. R. Ashe
                 E. C. Drysdale d. R. H. Osuna
       final   M. SANTANA d. E. C. Drysdale   6–2 7–9 7–5 6–1

1966	s. finals	J. D. Newcombe d. M. Santana
		F. S. Stolle d. R. E. Emerson
	final	F. S. STOLLE d. J. D. Newcombe 4–6 12–10 6–3 6–4
1967	s. finals	J. D. Newcombe d. E. L. Scott
		C. Graebner d. J. Leschly
	final	J. D. NEWCOMBE d. C. Graebner 6–4 6–4 8–6

Played at Longwood Cricket Club, Chestnut Hill, Mass.

1968	s. finals	A. R. Ashe d. J. McManus
		R. C. Lutz d. C. Graebner
	final	A. R. ASHE d. R. C. Lutz 4–6 6–3 8–10 6–0 6–4
1969	s. finals	A. R. Ashe d. R. C. Lutz
		S. R. Smith d. C. Pasarell
	final	S. R. SMITH d. A. R. Ashe 9–7 6–3 6–1

MEN'S SINGLES
(U.S. OPEN CHAMPIONSHIPS)

Played at West Side Club, Forest Hills, New York.

1968	s. finals	A. R. Ashe d. C. Graebner
		T. S. Okker d. K. R. Rosewall
	final	A. R. ASHE d. T. S. Okker 14–12 5–7 6–3 3–6 6–3
1969	s. finals	R. G. Laver d. A. R. Ashe
		A. D. Roche d. J. D. Newcombe
	final	R. G. LAVER d. A. D. Roche 7–9 6–1 6–3 6–2
1970	s. finals	A. D. Roche d. C. Richey
		K. R. Rosewall d. J. D. Newcombe
	final	K.R. ROSEWALL d. A. D. Roche 2–6 6–4 7–6 6–3
1971	s. finals	J. Kodes d. A. R. Ashe
		S. R. Smith d. T. S. Okker
	finals	S. R. SMITH d. J. Kodes 3–6 6–3 6–2 7–6
1972	s. finals	A. R. Ashe d. C. Richey
		I. Nastase d. T. Gorman
	final	I. NASTASE d. A. R. Ashe 3–6 6–3 6–7 6–4 6–3
1973	s. finals	J. Kodes d. S. R. Smith
		J. D. Newcombe d. K. R. Rosewall
	final	J. D. NEWCOMBE d. J. Kodes 6–4 1–6 4–6 6–2 6–3
1974	s. finals	J. S. Connors d. R. Tanner
		K. R. Rosewall d. J. D. Newcombe
	final	J. S. CONNORS d. K. R. Rosewall 6–1 6–0 6–1
1975	s. finals	J. S. Connors d. B. Borg
		M. Orantes d. G. Vilas
	final	M. ORANTES d. J. S. Connors 6–4 6–3 6–3

WOMEN'S SINGLES

Played at the Philadelphia Cricket Club.

1887		MISS E. HANSELL
		d. Miss L. Knight 6–1 6–0
1888	challenge round	MISS B. TOWNSEND
		d. Miss E. Hansell
1889	challenge round	MISS B. TOWNSEND
		d. Miss L. D. Voorhees 7–5 6–2
1890	challenge round	MISS E. C. ROOSEVELT
		d. Miss B. Townsend
1891	challenge round	MISS M. E. CAHILL
		d. Miss E. C. Roosevelt
1892	challenge round	MISS M. E. CAHILL
		d. Miss E. H. Moore
1893	final*	MISS A. M. TERRY
		d. Miss A. Schultz
1894	challenge round	MISS H. R. HELWIG
		d. Miss A. M. Terry 7–5 3–6 6–0 3–6 6–3
1895	challenge round	MISS J. P. ATKINSON
		d. Miss H. R. Helwig 6–4 6–2 6 1
1896	challenge round	MISS E. H. MOORE
		d. Miss J. P. Atkinson 6–4 4–6 6–3 6–2

1897	challenge round	MISS J. P. ATKINSON
		d. Miss E. H. Moore 6–3 6–3 4–6 3–6 6–3
1898	challenge round	MISS J. P. ATKINSON
		d. Miss M. Jones 6–3 5–7 6–4 2–6 7–5
1899	final*	MISS M. JONES
		d. Miss M. Banks
1900	final*	MISS M. McATEER
		d. Miss E. Parker
1901	challenge round	MISS E. H. MOORE
		d. Miss M. McAteer 6–4 3–6 7–5 2–6 6–2
1902	challenge round	MISS M. JONES
		d. Miss E. H. Moore 6–1 1–0 ret'd
1903	challenge round	MISS E. H. MOORE
		d. Miss M. Jones 7–5 8–6
1904	challenge round	MISS M. SUTTON
		d. Miss E. H. Moore 6–1 6–2
1905	final*	MISS E. H. MOORE
		d. Miss H. Homans 6–4 5–7 6–1
1906	final*	MISS H. HOMANS
		d. Mrs M. Barger-Wallach
1907	final*	MISS E. SEARS
		d. Miss C. B. Neely 6–3 6–2
1908	challenge round	MRS M. BARGER-WALLACH
		d. Miss E. Sears 6–2 1–6 6–3
1909	challenge round	MISS H. HOTCHKISS
		d. Mrs M. Barger-Wallach 6–0 6–1
1910	challenge round	MISS H. HOTCHKISS
		d. Miss L. Hammond 6–4 6–2
1911	challenge round	MISS H. HOTCHKISS
		d. Miss F. Sutton 8–10 6–1 9–7
1912	final*	MISS M. K. BROWNE
		d. Miss E. Sears 6–4 6–2
1913	challenge round	MISS M. K. BROWNE
		d. Miss D. Green 6–2 7–5
1914	challenge round	MISS M. K. BROWNE
		d. Miss M. Wagner 6–2 1–6 6–1
1915	final*	MISS M. BJURDSTEDT
		d. Mrs H. Wightman 4–6 6–2 6–0
1916	challenge round	MISS M. BJURDSTEDT
		d. Mrs E. Raymond 6–0 6–1
1917	Patriotic Tournament	MISS M. BJURDSTEDT
		d. Miss M. Vanderhoef 4–6 6–0 6–2
1918	challenge round	MISS M. BJURDSTED
		d. Miss E. E. Goss 6–4 6–3

(*Championship decided on the outcome of the all-comers' final as the holder did not defend.)

Challenge Round abolished

1919		MRS G. W. WIGHTMAN
		d. Miss M. Zinderstein 6–1 6–2
1920		MRS F. MALLORY
		d. Miss M. Zinderstein 6–3 6–1

Played at the West Side Club, Forest Hills, New York.

1921		MRS F. MALLORY
		d. Miss M. K. Browne 4–6 6–4 6–2
1922		MRS F. MALLORY
		d. Miss H. Wills 6–3 6–1
1923		MISS H. WILLS
		d. Mrs F. Mallory 6–2 6–1
1924		MISS H. WILLS
		d. Mrs F. Mallory 6–1 6–2
1925		MISS H. WILLS
		d. Miss K. McKane 3–6 6–0 6–2
1926		MRS F. MALLORY
		d. Miss E. Ryan 4–6 6–4 9–7
1927		MISS H. WILLS
		d. Miss B. Nuthall 6–1 6–4
1928		MISS H. WILLS
		d. Miss H. H. Jacobs 6–2 6–1
1929		MISS H. WILLS
		d. Mrs P. H. Watson 6–4 6–2

1930	MISS B. NUTHALL d. Mrs L. A. Harper 6–4 6–1
1931	MRS F. S. MOODY d. Mrs E. F. Whittingstall 6–4 6–1
1932	MISS H. H. JACOBS d. Miss C. A. Babcock 6–2 6–2
1933	MISS H. H. JACOBS d. Mrs F. S. Moody 8–6 3–6 3–0 ret'd
1934	MISS H. H. JACOBS d. Miss S. H. Palfrey 6–1 6–4
1935	MISS H. H. JACOBS d. Mrs M. Fabyan 6–1 6–4
1936	MISS A. MARBLE d. Miss H. H. Jacobs 4–6 6–3 6–2
1937	Sta A. LIZANA d. Panna J. Jedrzejowska 6–4 6–2
1938	MISS A. MARBLE d. Miss N. Wynne 6–0 6–3
1939	MISS A. MARBLE d. Miss H. H. Jacobs 6–0 8–10 6–4
1940	MISS A. MARBLE d. Miss H. H. Jacobs 6–2 6–3
1941	MRS E. T. COOKE d. Miss P. M. Betz 6–1 6–4
1942	MISS P. M. BETZ d. Miss A. L. Brough 4–6 6–1 6–4
1943	MISS P. M. BETZ d. Miss A. L. Brough 6–3 5–7 6–3
1944	MISS P. M. BETZ d. Miss M. E. Osborne 6–3 8–6
1945	MRS E. T. COOKE d. Miss P. M. Betz 3–6 8–6 6–4
1946	MISS P. M. BETZ d. Miss D. J. Hart 11–9 6–3
1947	MISS A. L. BROUGH d. Miss M. E. Osborne 8–6 4–6 6–1
1948	MRS W. D. du PONT d. Miss A. L. Brough 4–6 6–4 15–13
1949	MRS W. D. du PONT d. Miss D. J. Hart 6–4 6–1
1950	MRS W. D. du PONT d. Miss D. J. Hart 6–3 6–3
1951	MISS M. CONNOLLY d. Miss S. J. Fry 6–3 1–6 6–4
1952	MISS M. CONNOLLY d. Miss D. J. Hart 6–3 7–5
1953	MISS M. CONNOLLY d. Miss D. J. Hart 6–2 6–4
1954	MISS D. J. HART d. Miss A. L. Brough 6–8 6–1 8–6
1955	MISS D. J. HART d. Miss P. E. Ward 6–4 6–2
1956	MISS S. J. FRY d. Miss A. Gibson 6–3 6–4
1957	MISS A. GIBSON d. Miss A. L. Brough 6–3 6–2
1958	MISS A. GIBSON d. Miss D. R. Hard 3–6 6–1 6–2
1959	MISS M. E. BUENO d. Miss C. C. Truman 6–1 6–4
1960	MISS D. R. HARD d. Miss M. E. Bueno 6–4 10–12 6–4
1961	MISS D. R. HARD d. Miss A. S. Haydon 6–3 6–4
1962	MISS M. SMITH d. Miss D. R. Hard 9–7 6–4
1963	MISS M. E. BUENO d. Miss M. Smith 7–5 6–4
1964	MISS M. E. BUENO d. Mrs C. Graebner 6–1 6–0

1965	MISS M. SMITH d. Miss B. J. Moffitt 8–6 7–5
1966	MISS M. E. BUENO d. Miss N. Richey 6–3 6–1
1967	MRS L. W. KING d. Mrs P. F. Jones 11–9 6–4

Played at the Longwood Cricket Club, Chestnut Hill, Mass.

| 1968 | MRS B. M. COURT
d. Miss M. E. Bueno   6–2 6–2 |
| 1969 | MRS B. M. COURT
d. Miss S. V. Wade   4–6 6–3 6–0 |

WOMEN'S SINGLES
(U.S. OPEN CHAMPIONSHIPS)

Played at West Side Club, Forest Hills, New York.

1968	MISS S. V. WADE Mrs L. W. King 6–4 6–2
1969	MRS B. M. COURT d. Miss N. Richey 6–2 6–2
1970	MRS B. M. COURT d. Miss R. Casals 6–2 2–6 6–1
1971	MRS L. W. KING d. Miss R. Casals 6–4 7–6
1972	MRS L. W. KING d. Miss K. Melville 6–3 7–5
1973	MRS B. M. COURT d. Miss E. F. Goolagong 7–6 5–7 6–2
1974	MRS L. W. KING d. Miss E. F. Goolagong 3–6 6–3 7–5
1975	MISS C. EVERT d. Mrs R. Cawley 5–7 6–4 6–2

MEN'S DOUBLES

Played at the Casino, Newport, Rhode Island.

1881	C. M. Clark & F. W. Taylor d. A. Van Rensselaer & A. E. Newbold
1882	R. D. Sears & J. Dwight d. W. Nightingale & G. M. Smith
1883	R. D. Sears and J. Dwight d. A. Van Rensselaer & A. E. Newbold
1884	R. D. Sears and J. Dwight d. A. Van Rensselaer & W. V. R. Berry
1885	R. D. Sears & J. S. Clark d. H. W. Slocum & W. P. Knapp
1886	R. D. Sears & J. Dwight d. H. A. Taylor & G. M. Brinley
1887	R. D. Sears & J. Dwight d. H. A. Taylor & H. W. Slocum
1888	O. S. Campbell & V. G. Hall d. C. Hobart & E. P. MacMullen
1889	H. A. Taylor & H. W. Slocum d. V. G. Hall & O. S. Campbell
1890	V. G. Hall & C. Hobart d. J. W. Carver & J. A. Ryerson
1891	O. S. Campbell & R. Huntington d. V. G. Hall & C. Hobart
1892	O. S. Campbell & R. Huntington d. V. G. Hall & E. L. Hall
1893	C. Hobart & F. H. Hovey d. O. S. Campbell & R. Huntington
1894	C. Hobart & F. H. Hovey d. C. B. Neel & S. R. Neel

1895	M. G. Chace & R. D. Wrenn d. C. Hobart & F. H. Hovey
1896	C. B. Neel & S. R. Neel d. M. G. Chace & R. D. Wrenn
1897	L. E. Ware & G. P. Sheldon d. H. S. Mahony & H. A. Nisbet
1898	L. E. Ware & G. P. Sheldon d. H. Ward & D. F. Davis
1899	H. Ward & D. F. Davis d. L. E. Ware & G. P. Sheldon
1900	H. Ward & D. F. Davis d. F. B. Alexander & R. D. Little
1901	H. Ward & D. F. Davis d. L. E. Ware & B. C. Wright
1902	R. F. Doherty & H. L. Doherty d. H. Ward & D. F. Davis
1903	R. F. Doherty & H. L. Doherty d. K. Collins & L. H. Waidner
1904	H. Ward & B. C. Wright d. K. Collins & R. D. Little
1905	H. Ward & B. C. Wright d. F. B. Alexander & H. H. Hackett
1906	H. Ward & B. C. Wright d. F. B. Alexander & H. H. Hackett
1907	F. B. Alexander & H. H. Hackett d. W. A. Larned & W. J. Clothier
1908	F. B. Alexander & H. H. Hackett d. R. D. Little & B. C. Wright
1909	F. B. Alexander & H. H. Hackett d. M. E. McLoughlin & G. J. Janes
1910	F. B. Alexander & H. H. Hackett d. T. C. Bundy & T. W. Hendrick
1911	R. D. Little & G. F. Touchard d. F. B. Alexander & H. H. Hackett
1912	M. E. McLoughlin & T. C. Bundy d. R. D. Little & G. F. Touchard
1913	M. E. McLoughlin & T. C. Bundy d. J. R. Strachan & C. J. Griffin
1914	M. E. McLoughlin & T. C. Bundy d. G. M. Church & D. Mathey
1915	W. M. Johnston & C. J. Griffin d. M. E. McLoughlin & T. C. Bundy
1916	W. M. Johnston & C. J. Griffin d. M. E. McLoughlin & W. Dawson
1917	Patroitic Tournament F. B. Alexander & H. A. Throckmorton d. H. C. Johnson & I. C. Wright
1918	W. T. Tilden & V. Richards d. F. B. Alexander & B. C. Wright
1919	N. E. Brookes & G. L. Patterson d. W. T. Tilden & V. Richards

Longwood Cricket Club, Chestnut Hill, Mass.

1920	W. M. Johnston & C. J. Griffin d. W. F. Davis & R. E. Roberts
1921	W. T. Tilden & V. Richards d. R. N. Williams & W. M. Washburn
1922	W. T. Tilden & V. Richards d. G. L. Patterson & P. O'Hara Wood
1923	W. T. Tilden & B. I. C. Norton d. R. N. Williams & W. M. Washburn
1924	H. Kinsey & R. Kinsey d. G. L. Patterson & P. O'Hara Wood
1925	R. N. Williams & V. Richards d. G. L. Patterson & J. B. Hawkes
1926	R. N. Williams & V. Richards d. W. T. Tilden & A. H. Chapin
1927	W. T. Tilden & F. T. Hunter d. W. M. Johnston & R. N. Williams
1928	G. M. Lott and J. Hennessey d. G. L. Patterson & J. B. Hawkes

1929	G. M. Lott & J. Doeg d. B. Bell & L. N. White
1930	G. M. Lott & J. Doeg d. J. Van Ryn & W. L. Allison
1931	J. Van Ryn & W. L. Allison d. B. Bell & G. Mangin
1932	H. E. Vines & K. Gledhill d. J. Van Ryn & W. L. Allison
1933	G. M. Lott & L. R. Stoefen d. F. X. Shields & F. Parker
1934	G. M. Lott & L. R. Stoefen d. J. Van Ryn & W. L. Allison
1935	J. Van Ryn & W. L. Allison d. J. D. Budge & C. G. Mako
1936	J. D. Budge & C. G. Mako d. J. Van Ryn & W. L. Allison
1937	G. Von Cramm & H. Henkel d. J. D. Budge & C. G. Mako
1938	J. D. Budge & C. G. Mako d. A. K. Quist & J. E. Bromwich
1939	A. K. Quist & J. E. Bromwich d. J. H. Crawford & H. C. Hopman
1940	J. A. Kramer & F. R. Schroeder d. G. Mulloy & H. J. Prussoff
1941	J. A. Kramer & F. R. Schroeder d. G. Mulloy & W. Sabin
1942	G. Mulloy & W. F. Talbert d. F. R. Schroeder & S. B. Wood
1943	J. A. Kramer & F. Parker d. D. Freeman & W. F. Talbert
1944	W. D. McNeill & R. Falkenburg d. F. Segura & W. F. Talbert
1945	G. Mulloy & W. F. Talbert d. R. Falkenburg & J. Tuero
1946	G. Mulloy & W. F. Talbert d. W. D. McNeill & F. Guernsey
1947	J. A. Kramer & F. R. Schroeder d. W. Sidwell & W. F. Talbert
1948	G. Mulloy & W. F. Talbert d. F. Parker & F. R. Schroeder
1949	J. E. Bromwich & W. Sidwell d. F. A. Sedgman & G. Worthington
1950	J. E. Bromwich & F. A. Sedgman d. G. Mulloy & W. F. Talbert
1951	K. McGregor & F. A. Sedgman d. D. Candy & M. G. Rose
1952	M. G. Rose & E. V. Seixas d. K. McGregor & F. A. Sedgman
1953	R. N. Hartwig & M. G. Rose d. G. Mulloy & W. F. Talbert
1954	E. V. Seixas & M. A. Trabert d. L. A. Hoad & K. R. Rosewall
1955	K. Kamo & A. Miyagi d. G. Moss & W. Quillan
1956	L. A. Hoard & K. R. Rosewall d. H. Richardson & E. V. Seixas
1957	A. J. Cooper & N. A. Fraser d. G. Mulloy & J. E. Patty
1958	H. Richardson & A. Olmedo d. S. Giammalva & B. MacKay
1959	R. E. Emerson & N. A. Fraser d. E. Buchholz & A. Olmedo
1960	R. E. Emerson & N. A. Fraser d. R. G. Laver & R. Mark
1961	C. McKinley & D. Ralston d. R. H. Osuna & A. Palafox
1962	R. H. Osuna & A. Palafox d. C. McKinley & D. Ralston
1963	C. McKinley & D. Ralston d. R. H. Osuna & A. Palafox

1964	C. McKinley & D. Ralston d. G. R. Stilwell & M. J. Sangster
1965	R. E. Emerson & F. S. Stolle d. F. Froehling & C. Pasarell
1966	R. E. Emerson & F. S. Stolle d. C. Graebner & D. Ralston
1967	J. D. Newcombe & A. D. Roche d. W. W. Bowrey & O. K. Davidson
1968	R. C. Lutz & S. R. Smith d. R. A. J. Hewitt & R. Moore
1969	R. D. Crealy & A. Stone d. W. W. Bowrey & C. Pasarell

MEN'S DOUBLES
(U.S. OPEN CHAMPIONSHIPS)

Played at West Side Club, Forest Hills, New York.

1968	R. C. Lutz & S. R. Smith d. A. R. Ashe & H. Gimeno
1969	K. R. Rosewall & F. S. Stolle d. C. Pasarell & D. Ralston
1970	P. Barthes & N. Pilic d. R. E. Emerson & R. G. Laver
1971	J. D. Newcombe & R. Taylor d. S. R. Smith & E. Van Dillen
1972	E. C. Drysdale & R. Taylor d. O. K. Davidson & J. D. Newcombe
1973	O. K. Davidson & J. D. Newcombe d. R. G. Laver & K. R. Rosewall
1974	R. C. Lutz & S. R. Smith d. P. Cornejo & J. Fillol
1975	J. S. Connors & I. Nastase d. T. S. Okker & M. C. Riessen

WOMEN'S DOUBLES

Played at the Philadelphia Cricket Club

1890	Miss E. C. Roosevelt & Miss G. W. Roosevelt
1891	Miss M. E. Cahill & Mrs F. Fellowes Morgan
1892	Miss M. E. Cahill & Miss A. M. McKinley
1893	Miss H. Butler & Miss A. M. Terry
1894	Miss J. P. Atkinson & Miss H. R. Helwig
1895	Miss J. P. Atkinson & Miss H. R. Helwig
1896	Miss J. P. Atkinson & Miss E. H. Moore
1897	Miss J. P. Atkinson & Miss K. Atkinson
1898	Miss J. P. Atkinson & Miss K. Atkinson
1899	Miss J. W. Craven & Miss M. McAteer
1900	Miss H. Caplin & Miss E. Parker
1901	Miss J. P. Atkinson & Miss M. McAteer
1902	Miss J. P. Atkinson & Miss M. Jones
1903	Miss E. H. Moore & Miss C. B. Neely
1904	Miss M. Hall & Miss M. Sutton
1905	Miss H. Homans & Miss C. B. Neely
1906	Mrs L. S. Coe & Mrs D. S. Platt
1907	Miss C. B. Neely & Miss M. Weimer
1908	Miss M. Curtis & Miss E. Sears
1909	Miss H. Hotchkiss & Miss E. E. Rotch
1910	Miss H. Hotchkiss & Miss E. E. Rotch
1911	Miss H. Hotchkiss & Miss E. Sears
1912	Miss M. K. Browne & Miss D. Green
1913	Miss M. K. Browne & Mrs R. H. Williams
1914	Miss M. K. Browne & Mrs R. H. Williams
1915	Miss E. Sears & Mrs G. W. Wightman
1916	Miss Bjurdstedt & Miss E. Sears
1917	Patriotic Tournament Miss M. Bjurdstedt & Miss E. Sears
1918	Miss E. Goss & Miss M. Zinderstein
1919	Miss E. Goss & Miss M. Zinderstein
1920	Miss E. Goss & Miss M. Zinderstein

Played at West Side Club, Forest Hills, New York

1921	Miss M. K. Browne & Mrs L. Williams
1922	Mrs J. B. Jessup & Miss H. Wills
1923	Mrs B. C. Covell & Miss K. McKane
1924	Mrs G. W. Wightman & Miss H. Wills
1925	Miss M. K. Browne & Miss H. Wills
1926	Miss E. Goss & Miss E. Ryan
1927	Mrs L. A. Godfree & Miss E. H. Harvey
1928	Mrs G. W. Wightman & Miss H. Wills
1929	Mrs L. R. C. Michell & Mrs P. H. Watson
1930	Miss B. Nuthall & Miss S. H. Palfrey
1931	Miss B. Nuthall & Mrs E. F. Whittingstall
1932	Miss H. H. Jacobs & Miss S. H. Palfrey
1933	Miss F. James & Miss B. Nuthall
1934	Miss H. H. Jacobs & Miss S. H. Palfrey

Played at Longwood Cricket Club, Chestnut Hill, Mass.

1935	Mrs M. Fabyan & Miss H. H. Jacobs
1936	Miss C. Babcock & Mrs J. Van Ryn
1937	Mrs M. Fabyan & Miss A. Marble
1938	Mrs M. Fabyan & Miss A. Marble
1939	Mrs M. Fabyan & Miss A. Marble
1940	Mrs M. Fabyan & Miss A. Marble
1941	Mrs E. T. Cooke & Miss M. E. Osborne
1942	Miss A. L. Brough & Miss M. E. Osborne
1943	Miss A. L. Brough & Miss M. E. Osborne
1944	Miss A. L. Brough & Miss M. E. Osborne
1945	Miss A. L. Brough & Miss M. E. Osborne
1946	Miss A. L. Brough & Miss M. E. Osborne
1947	Miss A. L. Brough & Miss M. E. Osborne
1948	Miss A. L. Brough & Mrs W. D. du Pont
1949	Miss A. L. Brough & Mrs W. D. du Pont
1950	Miss A. L. Brough & Mrs W. D. du Pont
1951	Miss S. J. Fry & Miss D. J. Hart
1952	Miss S. J. Fry & Miss D. J. Hart
1953	Miss S. J. Fry & Miss D. J. Hart
1954	Miss S. J. Fry & Miss D. J. Hart
1955	Miss A. L. Brough & Mrs W. D. du Pont
1956	Miss A. L. Brough & Mrs W. D. du Pont
1957	Miss A. L. Brough & Mrs W. D. du Pont
1958	Miss J. Arth & Miss D. R. Hard
1959	Miss J. Arth & Miss D. R. Hard
1960	Miss M. E. Bueno & Miss D. R. Hard
1961	Miss D. R. Hard & Miss L. Turner
1962	Miss M. E. Bueno & Miss D. R. Hard
1963	Miss R. Ebbern & Miss M. Smith
1964	Miss B. J. Moffitt & Mrs J. B. Sussman
1965	Mrs C. Graebner & Miss N. Richey
1966	Miss M. E. Bueno & Miss N. Richey
1967	Miss R. Casals & Mrs L. W. King
1968	Miss M. E. Bueno & Mrs B. M. Court
1969	Miss S. V. Wade & Mrs B. M. Court

WOMEN'S DOUBLES
(U.S. OPEN CHAMPIONSHIPS)

Played at West Side Club, Forest Hills, New York

1968	Miss M. E. Bueno & Mrs B. M. Court
1969	Mlle F. Durr & Miss D. R. Hard
1970	Mrs D. Dalton & Mrs B. M. Court
1971	Mrs D. Dalton & Miss R. Casals
1972	Mlle F. Durr & Miss B. Stove
1973	Miss S. V. Wade & Mrs B. M. Court
1974	Miss R. Casals & Mrs L. W. King
1975	Miss S. V. Wade & Mrs B. M. Court

MIXED DOUBLES

Played at the Philadelphia Cricket Club

1892	C. Hobart & Miss M. E. Cahill
1893	C. Hobart & Miss E. C. Roosevelt
1894	E. P. Fischer & Miss J. P. Atkinson
1895	E. P. Fischer & Miss J. P. Atkinson
1896	E. P. Fischer & Miss J. P. Atkinson
1897	D. L. Magruder & Miss L. Henson
1898	E. P. Fischer & Miss C. B. Neely
1899	A. L. Hoskins & Miss E. J. Rastall
1900	A. Codman & Miss M. J. Hunnewell
1901	R. D. Little & Miss M. Jones
1902	W. C. Grant & Miss E. H. Moore
1903	H. F. Allen & Miss H. Chapman
1904	W. C. Grant & Miss E. H. Moore
1905	C. Hobart & Mrs Hobart
1906	E. B. Dewhurst & Miss S. Coffin
1907	W. F. Johnson & Miss M. Sayres
1908	N. W. Niles & Miss E. E. Rotch
1909	W. F. Johnson & Miss H. Hotchkiss
1910	J. R. Carpenter & Miss H. Hotchkiss
1911	W. F. Johnson & Miss H. Hotchkiss
1912	R. N. Williams & Miss M. K. Browne
1913	W. T. Tilden & Miss M. K. Browne
1914	W. T. Tilden & Miss M. K. Browne
1915	H. C. Johnson & Mrs G. W. Wightman
1916	W. E. Davis & Miss E. Sears
1917	Patriotic Tournament
	I. C. Wright & Miss M. Bjurdstedt
1918	I. C. Wright & Mrs G. W. Wightman
1919	V. Richards & Miss M. Zinderstein
1920	W. F. Johnson & Mrs G. W. Wightman

Played at the Longwood Cricket Club
Chestnut Hill, Mass.

1921	W. M. Johnston & Miss M. K. Browne
1922	W. T. Tilden & Mrs F. Mallory
1923	W. T. Tilden & Mrs F. Mallory
1924	V. Richards & Miss H. Wills
1925	J. B. Hawkes & Miss M. McKane
1926	J. Borotra & Miss E. Ryan
1927	H. Cochet & Miss E. Bennett
1928	J. B. Hawkes & Miss H. Wills
1929	G. M. Lott & Miss B. Nuthall
1930	W. L. Allison & Miss E. Cross
1931	G. M. Lott & Miss B. Nuthall
1932	F. J. Perry & Miss S. H. Palfrey
1933	H. E. Vines & Miss E. Ryan
1934	G. M. Lott & Miss H. H. Jacobs
1935	E. Maier & Mrs M. Fabyan
1936	C. G. Mako & Miss A. Marble
1937	J. D. Budge & Mrs M. Fabyan
1938	J. D. Budge & Miss A. Marble
1939	H. C. Hopman & Miss A. Marble
1940	R. L. Riggs & Miss A. Marble
1941	J. A. Kramer & Mrs E. T. Cooke

Played at the West Side Club, Forest Hills, New York

1942	F. R. Schroeder & Miss A. L. Brough
1943	W. F. Talbert & Miss M. E. Osborne
1944	W. F. Talbert & Miss M. E. Osborne
1945	W. F. Talbert & Miss M. E. Osborne
1946	W. F. Talbert & Miss M. E. Osborne
1947	J. E. Bromwich & Miss A. L. Brough
1948	T. Brown & Miss A. L. Brough
1949	E. W. Sturgess & Miss A. L. Brough
1950	K. McGregor & Mrs W. D. du Pont
1951	F. A. Sedgman & Miss D. J. Hart
1952	F. A. Sedgman & Miss D. J. Hart
1953	E. V. Seixas & Miss D. J. Hart
1954	E. V. Seixas & Miss D. J. Hart
1955	E. V. Seixas & Miss D. J. Hart
1956	K. R. Rosewall & Mrs W. D. du Pont
1957	K. Neilsen & Miss A. Gibson
1958	N. A. Fraser & Mrs W. D. du Pont
1959	N. A. Fraser & Mrs W. D. du Pont
1960	N. A. Fraser & Mrs W. D. du Pont
1961	R. Mark & Miss M. Smith
1962	F. S. Stolle & Miss M. Smith
1963	K. Fletcher & Miss M. Smith
1964	J. D. Newcombe & Miss M. Smith
1965	F. S. Stolle & Miss M. Smith
1966	O. K. Davidson & Mrs H. G. Fales
1967	O. K. Davidson & Mrs L. W. King

Played at Longwood Cricket Club, Chestnut Hill, Mass.

1968	P. W. Curtis & Miss M. A. Eisel
1969	P. Sullivan & Miss P. S. A. Hogan

MIXED DOUBLES
(U.S. OPEN CHAMPIONSHIPS)

Played at West Side Club, Forest Hills, New York.

1969   M. C. Riessen & Mrs B. M. Court
1970   M. C. Riessen & Mrs B. M. Court
1971   O. K. Davidson & Mrs L. W. King
1972   M. C. Riessen & Mrs B. M. Court
1973   O. K. Davidson & Mrs L. W. King
1974   G. Masters & Miss P. Teeguarden
1975   R. L. Stockton & Miss R. Casals

U.S. CHAMPIONSHIPS WON FROM MATCH POINT

1901	Women's Singles	Miss E. H. MOORE in all-comers' final beat Miss M. Jones 4–6 1–6 9–7 9–7 6–3 after a match point in the third set.
1906	Men's Singles	W. J. CLOTHIER in the quarter-final beat F. D. Alexander 8–6 6–2 4–6 1–6 7–5 from 2–5, love-40, in the fifth set.
1923	Mixed Doubles	W. T. TILDEN & MRS F. MALLORY in final beat J. B. Hawkes & Miss K. McKane 6–3 2–6 10–8 after two match points in the third set.
1926	Women's Singles	MRS F. MALLORY in final beat Miss E. Ryan 4–6 6–4 9–7 after match point at 6–7 in the third set.
1932	Men's Singles	H. E. VINES in semi-final beat C. S. Sutter 4–6 8–10 12–10 10–8 6–1 after four match points in the fourth set.
1936	Men's Singles	F. J. PERRY in final beat J. D. Budge 2–6 6–2 8–6 1–6 10–8 after two match points at 4–5 in the fifth set.
1938	Women's Singles	MISS A. MARBLE in semi-final beat Mrs M. Fabyan 5–7 7–5 7–5 after two match points at 2–5 in the second set.
1946	Men's Doubles	G. MULLOY & W. F. TALBERT in 3rd round beat P. Washer & J. Van Den Eyne after two match points. In the final they beat F. D. Guernsey & W. D. McNeill 3–6 6–4 2–6 6–3 20–18 after seven match points in the fifth set.
1947	Women's Singles	MISS L. BROUGH in semi-final beat Mrs N. Bolton 4–6 6–4 7–5 after two match points in the third set.
1948	Women's Singles	MRS W. D. DU PONT in final beat Miss L. Brough 4–6 6–4 15–13 after match point at 5–6 in the third set.
	Mixed Doubles	T. BROWN & MISS L. BROUGH in semi-final beat F. A. Sedgman and Miss D. J. Hart 6–2 5–7 8–6 after match point in the third set.
1953	Women's Doubles	MISS S. J. FRY & MISS D. J. HART in final beat Miss L. Brough and Mrs W. D. du Pont 6–3 7–9 9–7 after two match points at 2–5 in the third set.
1954	Women's Singles	MISS D. J. HART in final beat Miss L. Brough 6–8 6–1 8–6 after three match points in the third set.
1963		C. R. McKINLEY & R. D. RALSTON in final beat R. H. Osuna & A. Palafox 9–7 4–6 5–7 6–3 11–9 after two match points at 5–6 in the third set.
1970	Men's Doubles	P. BARTHES & N. PILIC in semi-final beat P. Cornejo and J. Fillol 6–7 6–7 7–6 7–6 7–5 after match point in the fourth set.
1975	Men's Singles	M. ORANTES in semi-final beat G. Vilas 4–6 1–6 7–5 7–5 6–4 after being love-5 and having five match points against him at 1–5 and 2–5 in the fourth set.

Australian championships

MEN'S SINGLES

	Winner	Runner-up	Score
1905	R. W. Heath	A. H. Curtis	
1906	A. F. Wilding	H. A. Parker	
1907	H. M. Rice	H. A. Parker	
1908	F. B. Alexander	A. W. Dunlop	
1909	A. F. Wilding	E. F. Parker	
1910	R. W. Heath	H. M. Rice	
1911	N. E. Brookes	H. M. Rice	
1912	J. C. Parke	A. E. Beamish	3–6 6–2 1–6 6–1 7–5
1913	E. F. Parker	H. A. Parker	
1914	A. O'Hara Wood	G. L. Patterson	6–4 6–3 5–7 6–1
1915	F. G. Lowe	H. M. Rice	
1916–1918 not held			
1919	A. R. F. Kingscote	E. O. Pockley	6–4 6–0 6–3
1920	P. O'Hara Wood		
1921	R. H. Gemmell		
1922	J. O. Anderson	G. L. Patterson	6–0 3–6 3–6 6–3 6–2
1923	P. O'Hara Wood		
1924	J. O. Anderson	R. E. Schlesinger	6–3 6–4 3–6 5–7 6–3
1925	J. O. Anderson	G. L. Patterson	11–9 2–6 6–2 6–3
1926	J. B. Hawkes	J. Willard	6–1 6–3 6–1
1927	G. L. Patterson	J. B. Hawkes	3–6 6–4 3–6 18–16 6–3
1928	J. Borotra	R. O. Cummings	6–4 6–1 4–6 5–7 6–3
1929	J. C. Gregory	R. E. Schlesinger	6–2 6–2 5–7 7–5
1930	E. F. Moon	H. C. Hopman	6–3 6–1 6–3
1931	J. H. Crawford	H. C. Hopman	6–4 6–2 2–6 6–1
1932	J. H. Crawford	H. C. Hopman	4–6 6–3 3–6 6–3 6–1
1933	J. H. Crawford	K. Gledhill	2–6 7–5 6–3 6–2
1934	F. J. Perry	J. H. Crawford	6–3 7–5 6–1
1935	J. H. Crawford	F. J. Perry	2–6 4–6 6–4 6–4
1936	A. K. Quist	J. H. Crawford	6–2 6–3 4–6 3–6 9–7
1937	V. B. McGrath	J. E. Bromwich	6–3 1–6 6–0 2–6 6–1
1938	J. D. Budge	J. E. Bromwich	6–4 6–2 6–1
1939	J. E. Bromwich	A. K. Quist	6–4 6–1 6–3
1940	A. K. Quist		
1941–1945 not held			
1946	J. E. Bromwich	D. Pails	5–7 6–3 7–5 3–6 6–2
1947	D. Pails	J. E. Bromwich	4–6 6–4 3–6 7–5 8–6
1948	A. K. Quist	J. E. Bromwich	6–4 3–6 6–3 2–6 6–3
1949	F. A. Sedgman	J. E. Bromwich	6–3 6–3 6–2
1950	F. A. Sedgman	K. McGregor	6–3 6–4 4–6 6–1
1951	R. Savitt	K. McGregor	6–3 2–6 6–3 6–1
1952	K. McGregor	F. A. Sedgman	7–5 12–10 2–6 6–2
1953	K. R. Rosewall	M. G. Rose	6–0 6–3 6–4
1954	M. G. Rose	R. N. Hartwig	6–2 0–6 6–4 6–2
1955	K. R. Rosewall	L. A. Hoad	9–7 6–4 6–4
1956	L. A. Hoad	K. R. Rosewall	6–4 3–6 6–4 7–5
1957	A. J. Cooper	N. A. Fraser	6–3 9–11 6–4 6–4
1958	A. J. Cooper	M. J. Anderson	7–5 6–3 6–4
1959	A. Olmedo	N. A. Fraser	6–1 6–2 3–6 6–3
1960	R. Laver	N. A. Fraser	5–7 3–6 6–3 8–6 8–6
1961	R. Emerson	R. Laver	1–6 6–3 7–5 6–4
1962	R. Laver	R. Emerson	8–6 0–6 6–4 6–4
1963	R. Emerson	K. N. Fletcher	6–3 6–3 6–1
1964	R. Emerson	F. S. Stolle	6–3 6–4 6–2
1965	R. Emerson	F. S. Stolle	7–9 2–6 6–4 7–5 6–1
1966	R. Emerson	A. R. Ashe	6–4 6–8 6–2 6–3
1967	R. Emerson	A. R. Ashe	6–4 6–1 6–4
1968	W. W. Bowrey	J. M. Gisbert	7–5 2–6 9–7 6–4
1969	R. Laver	A. Gimeno	6–3 6–4 7–5
1970	A. R. Ashe	R. D. Crealy	6–4 9–7 6–2
1971	K. R. Rosewall	A. R. Ashe	6–1 7–5 6–3
1972	K. R. Rosewall	M. J. Anderson	7–6 6–3 7–5
1973	J. D. Newcombe	O. Parun	6–3 6–7 7–5 6–1
1974	J. S. Connors	P. Dent	7–6 6–4 4–6 6–3
1975	J. D. Newcombe	J. S. Connors	7–5 3–6 6–4 7–5
1976	M. Edmondson	J. D. Newcombe	6–7 6–3 7–6 6–1

WOMEN'S SINGLES

(Note: early records have not survived. Miss P. A. Stewart was champion in 1908 and again in 1914. Miss L. Addison was champion in 1910. A complete roll is available only from 1922.)

	Winner	Runner-up	Score
1922	Mrs B. H. Molesworth	Miss E. Boyd	6–3 10–8
1923	Mrs B. H. Molesworth		
1924	Miss S. Lance	Miss E. Boyd	6–3 3–6 6–4
1925	Miss D. Akhurst	Miss E. Boyd	1–6 8–6 6–4
1926	Miss D. Akhurst	Miss E. Boyd	6–1 6–3
1927	Miss E. Boyd	Mrs R. Harper	5–7 6–1 6–2
1928	Miss D. Akhurst	Miss E. Boyd	7–5 6–2
1929	Miss D. Akhurst	Miss L. Bickerton	6–1 5–7 6–2
1930	Miss D. Akhurst	Mrs R. Harper	10–8 2–6 7–5
1931	Mrs C. Buttsworth	Mrs J. H. Crawford	1–6 6–3 6–4
1932	Mrs C. Buttsworth	Miss K. le Messurier	9–7 6–4
1933	Miss J. Hartigan	Mrs C. Buttsworth	6–4 6–3
1934	Miss J. Hartigan	Mrs B. H. Molesworth	6–1 6–4
1935	Miss D. E. Round	Miss N. M. Lyle	1–6 6–1 6–3
1936	Miss J. Hartigan	Miss N. Wynne	6–4 6–4
1937	Miss N. Wynne	Mrs V. Westacott	6–3 5–7 6–4
1938	Miss D. M. Bundy	Miss D. Stevenson	6–3 6–2
1939	Mrs V. Westacott	Mrs H. C. Hopman	6–1 6–2
1940	Mrs N. Bolton		
1941–1945 not held			
1946	Mrs N. Bolton	Miss J. Fitch	6–4 6–4
1947	Mrs N. Bolton	Mrs H. C. Hopman	6–3 6–2
1948	Mrs N. Bolton	Miss M. Toomey	6–3 6–1
1949	Miss D. J. Hart	Mrs N. Bolton	6–3 6–4
1950	Miss A. L. Brough	Miss D. J. Hart	6–4 3–6 6–4
1951	Mrs N. Bolton	Mrs T. D. Long	6–1 7–5
1952	Mrs T. D. Long	Miss H. Angwin	6–2 6–3
1953	Miss M. Connolly	Miss J. Sampson	6–3 6–2
1954	Miss T. D. Long	Miss J. Staley	6–3 6–4
1955	Miss B. Penrose	Miss T. D. Long	6–4 6–3
1956	Miss M. Carter	Mrs T. D. Long	3–6 6–2 9–7
1957	Miss S. J. Fry	Miss A. Gibson	6–3 6–4
1958	Miss A. Mortimer	Miss L. Coghlan	6–3 6–4
1959	Mrs S. J. Reitano	Miss R. Schuurman	6–2 6–3
1960	Miss M. Smith	Miss J. Lehane	7–5 6–2
1961	Miss M. Smith	Miss J. Lehane	6–1 6–4
1962	Miss M. Smith	Miss J. Lehane	6–0 6–2
1963	Miss M. Smith	Miss J. Lehane	6–2 6–2
1964	Miss M. Smith	Miss L. R. Turner	6–3 6–2
1965	Miss M. Smith	Miss M. E. Bueno	5–7 6–4 5–2 rt'd
1966	Miss M. Smith	Miss N. Richey	w.o.
1967	Miss N. Richey	Miss L. R. Turner	6–1 6–4
1968	Mrs L. W. King	Mrs B. M. Court	6–1 6–2
1969	Mrs B. M. Court	Mrs L. W. King	6–4 6–1
1970	Mrs B. M. Court	Miss K. Melville	6–1 6–3
1971	Mrs B. M. Court	Miss E. Goolagong	2–6 7–6 7–5
1972	Miss S. V. Wade	Miss E. Goolagong	6–4 6–4
1973	Mrs B. M. Court	Miss E. Goolagong	6–4 7–5
1974	Miss E. Goolagong	Miss C. Evert	7–6 4–6 6–0
1975	Miss E. Goolagong	Miss M. Navratilova	6–3 6–2
1976	Mrs R. Cawley	Miss R. Tomanova	6–2 6–2

MEN'S DOUBLES

1905	T. Tachell & R. Lycett
1906	A. F. Wilding & R. W. Heath
1907	H. A. Parker & W. A. Begg
1908	F. B. Alexander & A. W. Dunlop
1909	E. F. Parker & J. P. Keane
1910	H. Rice & A. Campbell
1911	R. W. Heath & R. Lycett
1912	J. C. Parke & C. P. Dixon
1913	E. F. Parker & A. H. Hedemann
1914	A. Campbell & G. L. Patterson
1915	H. Rice & C. V. Todd
1916–1918 not held	
1919	P. O'Hara Wood & R. V. Thomas
1920	P. O'Hara Wood & R. V. Thomas
1921	R. H. Gemmell & S. H. Eaton
1922	G. L. Patterson & J. B. Hawkes
1923	P. O'Hara Wood & C. B. St. John
1924	N. E. Brookes & J. O. Anderson
1925	G. L. Patterson & P. O'Hara Wood
1926	G. L. Patterson & J. B. Hawkes
1927	G. L. Patterson & J. B. Hawkes
1928	J. Borotra & J. Brugnon
1929	J. H. Crawford & H. C. Hopman
1930	J. H. Crawford & H. C. Hopman
1931	C. Donohoe & R. Dunlop
1932	J. H. Crawford & E. F. Moon
1933	H. E. Vines & K. Gledhill
1934	F. J. Perry & G. P. Hughes
1935	J. H. Crawford & V. B. McGrath
1936	A. K. Quist & D. P. Turnbull
1937	A. K. Quist & D. P. Turnbull
1938	A. K. Quist & J. E. Bromwich

Australian championships

1939	A. K. Quist & J. E. Bromwich
1940	A. K. Quist & J. E. Bromwich
1941–1945 not held	
1946	A. K. Quist & J. E. Bromwich
1947	A. K. Quist & J. E. Bromwich
1948	A. K. Quist & J. E. Bromwich
1949	A. K. Quist & J. E. Bromwich
1950	A. K. Quist & J. E. Bromwich
1951	F. A. Sedgman & K. McGregor
1952	F. A. Sedgman & K. McGregor
1953	L. A. Hoad & K. R. Rosewall
1954	M. G. Rose & R. N. Hartwig
1955	E. V. Seixas & M. A. Trabert
1956	L. A. Hoad & K. R. Rosewall
1957	L. A. Hoad & N. A. Fraser
1958	A. J. Cooper & N. A. Fraser
1959	R. Laver & R. Mark
1960	R. Laver & R. Mark
1961	R. Laver & R. Mark
1962	R. Emerson & N. A. Fraser
1963	R. A. J. Hewitt & F. S. Stolle
1964	R. A. J. Hewitt & F. S. Stolle
1965	J. D. Newcombe & A. D. Roche
1966	R. Emerson & F. S. Stolle
1967	J. D. Newcombe & A. D. Roche
1968	R. D. Crealy & A. J. Stone
1969	R. Emerson & R. Laver
1970	R. C. Lutz & S. R. Smith
1971	J. D. Newcombe & A. D. Roche
1972	O. K. Davidson & K. R. Rosewall
1973	M. J. Anderson & J. D. Newcombe
1974	R. Case & G. Masters
1975	J. G. Alexander & O. Dent
1976	J. D. Newcombe & A. D. Roche

WOMEN'S DOUBLES

1922	Miss E. Boyd & Miss M. Mountain
1923	Miss E. Boyd & Miss S. Lance
1924	Miss D. Akhurst & Miss S. Lance
1925	Miss D. Akhurst & Mrs R. Harper
1926	Mrs P. O'Hara Wood & Miss E. Boyd
1927	Mrs P. O'Hara Wood & Miss L. Bickerton
1928	Miss D. Akhurst & Miss E. Boyd
1929	Miss D. Akhurst & Miss L. Bickerton
1930	Mrs B. H. Molesworth & Miss E. Hood
1931	Mrs R. Cozens & Miss L. Dickerton
1932	Mrs C. Buttsworth & Mrs J. H. Crawford
1933	Mrs B. H. Molesworth & Mrs V. Westacott
1934	Mrs B. H. Molesworth & Mrs V. Westacott
1935	Miss E. M. Dearman & Miss N. M. Lyle
1936	Miss T. Coyne & Miss N. Wynne
1937	Miss T. Coyne & Miss N. Wynne
1938	Miss I. Coyne & Miss N. Wynne
1939	Miss T. Coyne & Miss N. Wynne
1940	Miss T. Coyne & Miss N. Wynne
1941–1945 not held	
1946	Miss M. Bevis & Miss J. Fitch
1947	Mrs T. D. Long & Mrs N. Bolton
1948	Mrs T. D. Long & Mrs N. Bolton
1949	Mrs T. D. Long & Mrs N. Bolton
1950	Miss A. L. Brough & Miss D. J. Hart
1951	Mrs T. D. Long & Mrs N. Bolton
1952	Mrs T. D. Long & Mrs N. Bolton
1953	Miss M. Connolly & Miss J. Sampson
1954	Mrs K. Hawton & Miss B. Penrose
1955	Mrs K. Hawton & Miss B. Penrose
1956	Mrs K. Hawton & Mrs T. D. Long
1957	Miss S. J. Fry & Miss A. Gibson
1958	Mrs K. Hawton & Mrs T. D. Long
1959	Miss S. Reynolds & Miss R. Schuurman
1960	Miss M. E. Bueno & Miss C. C. Truman
1961	Mrs S. Reitano & Miss M. Smith
1962	Miss R. A. Ebbern & Miss M. Smith
1963	Miss R. A. Ebbern & Miss M. Smith
1964	Miss L. R. Turner & Miss J. A. M. Tegart
1965	Miss L. R. Turner & Miss M. Smith
1966	Mrs C. E. Graebner & Miss N. Richey
1967	Miss L. R. Turner & Miss J. A. M. Tegart
1968	Miss K. Krantzcke & Miss K. Melville
1969	Miss J. A. M. Tegart & Mrs B. M. Court
1970	Mrs D. Dalton & Mrs B. M. Court

1971	Miss E. Goolagong & Mrs B. M. Court
1972	Miss H. Gourlay & Miss K. Harris
1973	Mrs B. Court & Miss S. V. Wade
1974	Miss E. Goolagong & Miss M. Michel
1975	Miss E. Goolagong & Miss M. Michel
1976	Mrs R. Cawley & Miss H. F. Gourlay

MIXED DOUBLES

1922	J. B. Hawkes & Miss E. Boyd
1923	H. M. Rice & Miss S. Lance
1924	J. Willard & Miss D. Akhurst
1925	J. Willard & Miss D. Akhurst
1926	J. B. Hawkes & Miss E. Boyd
1927	J. B. Hawkes & Miss E. Boyd
1928	J. Borotra & Miss D. Akhurst
1929	E. F. Moon & Miss D. Akhurst
1930	H. C. Hopman & Miss N. Hall
1931	J. H. Crawford & Mrs J. H. Crawford
1932	J. H. Crawford & Mrs J. H. Crawford
1933	J. H. Crawford & Mrs J. H. Crawford
1934	E. F. Moon & Miss J. Hartigan
1935	C. Boussus & Miss L. Bickerton
1936	H. C. Hopman & Mrs H. C. Hopman
1937	H. C. Hopman & Mrs H. C. Hopman
1938	J. E. Bromwich & Miss M. Wilson
1939	H. C. Hopman & Mrs H. C. Hopman
1940	C. Long & Miss N. Wynne
1941–1945 not held	
1946	C. Long & Mrs N. Bolton
1947	C. Long & Mrs N. Bolton
1948	C. Long & Mrs N. Bolton
1949	F. A. Sedgman & Miss D. J. Hart
1950	F. A. Sedgman & Miss D. J. Hart
1951	G. A. Worthington & Mrs T. D. Long
1952	G. A. Worthington & Mrs T. D. Long
1953	R. N. Hartwig & Miss J. Sampson
1954	R. N. Hartwig & Mrs T. D. Long
1955	G. A. Worthington & Mrs T. D. Long
1956	N. A. Fraser & Miss B. Penrose
1957	M. J. Anderson & Miss F. Muller
1958	R. N. Howe & Mrs K. Hawton
1959	R. Mark & Miss S. Reynolds
1960	T. Fancutt & Miss J. Lehane
1961	R. A. J. Hewitt & Miss J. Lehane
1962	F. S. Stolle & Miss L. R. Turner
1963	K. N. Fletcher & Miss M. Smith
1964	K. N. Fletcher & Miss M. Smith
1965	J. D. Newcombe & Miss M. Smith
1966	A. D. Roche & Miss J. A. M. Tegart
1967	O. K. Davidson & Miss L. R. Turner
1968	R. D. Crealy & Mrs L. W. King
1969–1976 not held	

AUSTRALIAN CHAMPIONSHIPS WON FROM MATCH POINT

1927 Men's Singles	G. L. PATTERSON in final beat J. B. Hawkes 3–6 6–4 3–6 18–16 6–3 after three match points in the fourth set.
1947 Men's Singles	D. PAILS in final beat J. E. Bromwich 4–6 6–4 3–6 7–5 8–6 after match point at 5–6 in the fifth set.
1956 Women's Singles	MISS M. CARTER in final beat Mrs T. D. Long 3–6 6–2 9–7 after match point in the third set.
1960 Men's Singles	R. LAVER in final beat N. A. Fraser 5–7 3–6 6–3 8–6 8–6 after match point at 4–5 in the fourth set.
1975 Men's Singles	J. D. NEWCOMBE in semi-final beat A. D. Roche 6–4 4–6 6–4 2–6 11–9 after two match points at 2–5 in the fifth set and after a third match point at 7–8.

French championships

	Winner	Runner-up	Score
1925	R. Lacoste	J. Borotra	7–5 6–1 6–4
1926	H. Cochet	R. Lacoste	6–2 6–4 6–3
1927	R. Lacoste	W. T. Tilden	6–4 4–6 5–7 6–3 11–9
1928	H. Cochet	R. Lacoste	5–6 6–3 6–1 6–3
1929	R. Lacoste	J. Borotra	6–3 2–6 6–0 2–6 8–6
1930	H. Cochet	W. T. Tilden	3–6 8–6 6–3 6–1
1931	J. Borotra	C. Boussus	2–6 6–4 7–5 6–4
1932	H. Cochet	G. de Stefani	6–0 6–4 4–6 6–3
1933	J. H. Crawford	H. Cochet	8–6 6–1 6–3
1934	G. Von Cramm	J. H. Crawford	6–4 7–9 3–6 7–5 6–3
1935	F. J. Perry	G. Von Cramm	6–3 3–6 6–1 6–3
1936	G. Von Cramm	F. J. Perry	6–0 2–6 6–2 2–6 6–0
1937	H. Henkel	H. W. Austin	6–1 6–4 6–3
1938	J. D. Budge	R. Menzel	6–3 6–2 6–4
1939	W. D. McNeill	R. L. Riggs	7–5 6–0 6–3
1940–1945 not held			
1946	M. Bernard	J. Drobny	3–6 2–6 6–1 6–4 6–3
1947	J. Asboth	E. W. Sturgess	8–6 7–5 6–4
1948	F. Parker	J. Drobny	6–4 7–5 5–7 8–6
1949	F. Parker	J. E. Patty	6–3 1–6 6–1 6–4
1950	J. E. Patty	J. Drobny	6–1 6–2 3–6 5–7 7–5
1951	J. Drobny	E. W. Sturgess	6–3 6–3 6–3
1952	J. Drobny	F. A. Sedgman	6–2 6–0 3–6 6–4
1953	K. R. Rosewall	E. V. Seixas	6–3 6–4 1–6 6–2
1954	M. A. Trabert	A. Larsen	6–4 7–5 6–1
1955	M. A. Trabert	S. Davidson	2–6 6–1 6–4 6–2
1956	L. A. Hoad	S. Davidson	6–4 8–6 6–3
1957	S. Davidson	H. Flam	6–3 6–4 6–4
1958	M. G. Rose	L. Ayala	6–3 6–4 6–4
1959	N. Pietrangeli	I. C. Vermaak	3–6 6–3 6–4 6–1
1960	N. Pietrangeli	L. Ayala	3–6 6–3 6–4 4–6 6–3
1961	M. Santana	N. Pietrangeli	4–6 6–1 3–6 6–0 6–2
1962	R. Laver	R. Emerson	3–6 2–6 6–3 9–7 6–2
1963	R. Emerson	P. Darmon	3–6 6–1 6–4 6–4
1964	M. Santana	N. Pietrangeli	6–3 6–1 4–6 7–5
1965	F. S. Stolle	A. D. Roche	3–6 6–0 6–2 6–3
1966	A. D. Roche	I. Gulyas	6–1 6–4 7–5
1967	R. Emerson	A. D. Roche	6–1 6–4 2–6 6–2
1968	K. R. Rosewall	R. Laver	6–3 6–1 2–6 6–2
1969	R. Laver	K. R. Rosewall	6–4 6–3 6–4
1970	J. Kodes	Z. Franulovic	6–2 6–4 6–0
1971	J. Kodes	I. Nastase	8–6 6–2 2–6 7–5
1972	A. Gimeno	P. Proisy	4–6 6–3 6–1 6–1
1973	I. Nastase	N. Pilic	6–3 6–3 6–0
1974	B. Borg	M. Orantes	2–6 6–7 6–0 6–1 6–1
1975	B. Borg	G. Vilas	6–2 6–3 6–4
1976	A. Panatta	H. Solomon	6–1 6–4 4–6 7–6

	Winner	Runner-up	Score
1925	Mlle S. Lenglen	Miss K. McKane	6–1 6–2
1926	Mlle S. Lenglen	Miss M. K. Browne	6–1 6–0
1927	Mlle K. Bourman	Mrs G. Peacock	6–2 6–4
1928	Miss H. Wills	Miss E. Bennett	6–1 6–2
1929	Miss H. Wills	Mme R. Mathieu	6–3 6–4
1930	Mrs F. S. Moody	Miss H. Jacobs	6–2 6–1
1931	Frl C. Aussem	Miss B. Nuthall	8–6 6–1
1932	Mrs F. S. Moody	Mme R. Mathieu	7–5 6–1
1933	Miss M. C. Scriven	Mme R. Mathieu	6–2 4–6 6–4
1934	Miss M. C. Scriven	Miss H. Jacobs	7–5 4–6 6–1
1935	Fru S. Sperling	Mme R. Mathieu	6–2 6–1
1936	Fru S. Sperling	Mme R. Mathieu	6–3 6–4
1937	Fru S. Sperling	Mme R. Mathieu	6–2 6–4
1938	Mme R. Mathieu	Mme N. Landry	6–0 6–3
1939	Mme R. Mathieu	Panna J. Jedrzejowska	6–3 8–6
1940–1945 not held			
1946	Miss M. E. Osborne	Miss P. M. Betz	1–6 8–6 7–5
1947	Mrs P. C. Todd	Miss D. J. Hart	6–3 3–6 6–4
1948	Mme N. Landry	Miss S. J. Fry	6–2 0–6 6–0
1949	Mrs W. D. du Pont	Mme N. Adamson	7–5 6–2
1950	Miss D. J. Hart	Mrs P. C. Todd	6–4 4–6 6–2
1951	Miss S. J. Fry	Miss D. J. Hart	6–3 3–6 6–3
1952	Miss D. J. Hart	Miss S. J. Fry	6–4 6–4
1953	Miss M. Connolly	Miss D. J. Hart	6–2 6–4
1954	Miss M. Connolly	Mme G. Bucaille	6–4 6–1
1955	Miss A. Mortimer	Mrs D. P. Knode	2–6 7–5 10–8
1956	Miss A. Gibson	Miss A. Mortimer	6–0 12–10
1957	Miss S. J. Bloomer	Mrs D. P. Knode	6–1 6–3
1958	Mrs S. Kormoczy	Miss S. J. Bloomer	6–4 1–6 6–2
1959	Miss C. C. Truman	Mrs S. Kormoczy	6–4 7–5
1960	Miss D. R. Hard	Sen Y. Ramirez	6–3 6–4
1961	Miss A. S. Haydon	Sen Y. Ramirez	6–2 6–1
1962	Miss M. Smith	Miss L. R. Turner	6–3 3–6 7–5
1963	Miss L. R. Turner	Mrs P. F. Jones	2–6 6–3 7–5
1964	Miss M. Smith	Miss M. E. Bueno	5–7 6–1 6–2
1965	Miss L. R. Turner	Miss M. Smith	6–3 6–4
1966	Mrs P. F. Jones	Miss N. Richey	6–3 6–1
1967	Mlle F. Durr	Miss L. R. Turner	4–6 6–3 6–4
1968	Miss N. Richey	Mrs P. F. Jones	5–7 6–4 6–1
1969	Mrs B. M. Court	Mrs P. F. Jones	6–1 4–6 6–3
1970	Mrs B. M. Court	Frl H. Niessen	6–2 6–4
1971	Miss E. Goolagong	Miss H. Gourlay	6–3 7–5
1972	Mrs L. W. King	Miss E. Goolagong	6–3 6–3
1973	Mrs B. M. Court	Miss C. Evert	6–7 7–6 6–4
1974	Miss C. Evert	Mrs O. Morozova	6–1 6–2
1975	Miss C. Evert	Miss M. Navratilova	2–6 6–2 6–1
1976	Miss S. Barker	Miss R. Tomanova	6–2 0–6 6–2

MEN'S DOUBLES

1925	J. Borotra & R. Lacoste
1926	V. Richards & H. Kinsey
1927	H. Cochet & J. Brugnon
1928	J. Borotra & J. Brugnon
1929	J. Borotra & R. Lacoste
1930	H. Cochet & J. Brugnon
1931	G. M. Lott & J. Van Ryn
1932	H. Cochet & J. Brugnon
1933	F. J. Perry & G. P. Hughes
1934	J. Borotra & J. Brugnon
1935	J. H. Crawford & A. K. Quist
1936	J. Borotra & M. Bernard
1937	G. Von Cramm & H. Henkel
1938	B. Destremau & Y. Petra
1939	W. D. McNeill & C. Harris
1940–1945	not held
1946	M. Bernard & Y. Petra
1947	E. Fannin & E. W. Sturgess
1948	L. Bergelin & J. Drobny
1949	R. A. Gonzales & F. Parker
1950	W. F. Talbert & M. A. Trabert
1951	K. McGregor & F. A. Sedgman
1952	K. McGregor & F. A. Sedgman
1953	L. A. Hoad & K. R. Rosewall
1954	E. V. Seixas & M. A. Trabert
1955	E. V. Seixas & M. A. Trabert
1956	D. W. Candy & R. M. Perry
1957	M. J. Anderson & A. J. Cooper
1958	A. J. Cooper & N. A. Fraser
1959	O. Sirola & N. Pietrangeli
1960	R. Emerson & N. A. Fraser
1961	R. Emerson & R. Laver
1962	R. Emerson & N. A. Fraser
1963	R. Emerson & M. Santana
1964	R. Emerson & K. N. Fletcher
1965	R. Emerson & F. S. Stolle
1966	C. E. Graebner & R. D. Ralston
1967	J. D. Newcombe & A. D. Roche
1968	K. R. Rosewall & F. S. Stolle
1969	J. D. Newcombe & A. D. Roche
1970	I. Nastase & I. Tiriac
1971	A. R. Ashe & M. C. Riessen
1972	R. A. J. Hewitt & F. D. McMillan
1973	J. D. Newcombe & T. S. Okker
1974	R. D. Crealy & O. Parun
1975	B. E. Gottfried & R. Ramirez
1976	F. McNair & S. Stewart

WOMEN'S DOUBLES

1925	Mlle S. Lenglen & Mlle D. Vlasto
1926	Mlle S. Lenglen & Mlle D. Vlasto
1927	Miss E. L. Heine & Mrs G. Peacock
1928	Miss E. Bennett & Mrs B. C. Watson
1929	Sen L. de Alvarez & Mlle K. Bouman
1930	Mrs F. S. Moody & Miss E. Ryan
1931	Miss B. Nuthall & Mrs E. F. Whittingstall
1932	Mrs F. S. Moody & Miss E. Ryan
1933	Mme R. Mathieu & Miss E. Ryan
1934	Mme R. Mathieu & Miss E. Ryan
1935	Miss M. C. Scriven & Miss K. E. Stammers
1936	Mme R. Mathieu & Miss A. M. Yorke
1937	Mme R. Mathieu & Miss A. M. Yorke
1938	Mme R. Mathieu & Miss A. M. Yorke
1939	Mme R. Mathieu & Panna J. Jedrzejowska
1940–1945	not held
1946	Miss A. L. Brough & Miss M. E. Osborne
1947	Miss A. L. Brough & Miss M. E. Osborne
1948	Miss D. J. Hart & Mrs P. C. Todd
1949	Miss A. L. Brough & Mrs W. D. du Pont
1950	Miss D. J. Hart & Miss S. J. Fry
1951	Miss D. J. Hart & Miss S. J. Fry
1952	Miss D. J. Hart & Miss S. J. Fry
1953	Miss D. J. Hart & Miss S. J. Fry
1954	Miss M. C. Connolly & Mrs H. C. Hopman
1955	Miss J. Fleitz & Miss D. R. Hard
1956	Miss A. Gibson & Miss A. Buxton
1957	Miss S. J. Bloomer & Miss D. R. Hard
1958	Sen Y. Ramirez & Sen R. M. Reyes
1959	Miss S. Reynolds & Miss R. Schuurman
1960	Miss M. E. Bueno & Miss D. R. Hard
1961	Miss S. Reynolds & Miss R. Schuurman
1962	Mrs L. E. G. Price & Miss R. Schuurman
1963	Mrs P. F. Jones & Miss R. Schuurman
1964	Miss M. Smith & Miss L. R. Turner
1965	Miss M. Smith & Miss L. R. Turner
1966	Miss M. Smith & Miss J. A. M. Tegart
1967	Mlle F. Durr & Miss G. V. Sheriff
1968	Mlle F. Durr & Mrs P. F. Jones
1969	Mlle F. Durr & Mrs P. F. Jones
1970	Mlle F. Durr & Mme G. Chanfreau
1971	Mlle F. Durr & Mme G. Chanfreau
1972	Mrs L. W. King & Miss B. Stove
1973	Miss S. V. Wade & Mrs B. M. Court
1974	Miss C. Evert & Mrs O. Morozova
1975	Miss C. Evert & Miss M. Navratilova
1976	Miss F. Bonicelli & Mrs G. Lovera

MIXED DOUBLES

1925	J. Brugnon & Mlle S. Lenglen
1926	J. Brugnon & Mlle S. Lenglen
1927	J. Borotra & Mme M. Bordes
1928	H. Cochet & Miss E. Bennett
1929	H. Cochet & Miss E. Bennett
1930	W. T. Tilden & Frl C. Aussem
1931	P. D. B. Spence & Miss B. Nuthall
1932	F. J. Perry & Miss B. Nuthall
1933	J. H. Crawford & Miss M. C. Scriven
1934	J. Borotra & Mlle C. Rosambert
1935	M. Bernard & Mlle L. Payot
1936	M. Bernard & Miss A. M. Yorke
1937	Y. Petra & Mme R. Mathieu
1938	D. Mitic & Mme R. Mathieu
1939	E. T. Cooke & Mrs S. P. Fabyan
1940–1945	not held
1946	J. E. Patty & Miss P. M. Betz
1947	E. W. Sturgess & Mrs S. P. Summers
1948	J. Drobny & Mrs P. C. Todd
1949	E. W. Sturgess & Mrs S. P. Summers
1950	E. Morea & Miss B. Scofield
1951	F. A. Sedgman & Miss D. J. Hart
1952	F. A. Sedgman & Miss D. J. Hart
1953	E. V. Seixas & Miss D. J. Hart
1954	L. A. Hoad & Miss M. Connolly
1955	G. L. Forbes & Miss D. R. Hard
1956	L. Ayala & Mrs T. D. Long
1957	J. Javorsky & Mme V. Puzejova
1958	N. Pietrangeli & Miss S. J. Bloomer
1959	W. A. Knight & Sen Y. Ramirez
1960	R. N. Howe & Miss M. E. Bueno
1961	R. Laver & Miss D. R. Hard
1962	R. N. Howe & Miss R. Schuurman
1963	K. N. Fletcher & Miss M. Smith
1964	K. N. Fletcher & Miss M. Smith
1965	K. N. Fletcher & Miss M. Smith
1966	F. D. McMillan & Miss A. M. van Zyl
1967	O. K. Davidson & Mrs L. W. King
1968	J. C. Barclay & Mlle F. Durr
1969	M. C. Riessen & Mrs B. M. Court
1970	R. A. J. Hewitt & Mrs L. W. King
1971	J. C. Barclay & Mlle F. Durr
1972	K. Warwick & Miss E. Goolagong
1973	J. C. Barclay & Mlle F. Durr
1974	I. Molina & Miss M. Navratilova
1975	T. Koch & Miss F. Bonicelli
1976	K. Warwick & Miss I. Kloss

FRENCH CHAMPIONSHIPS WON FROM MATCH POINT

1927	Men's Singles	R. LACOSTE in final beat W. T. Tilden 6–4 4–6 5–7 6–3 11–9 after two match points at 8–9 in the fifth set.
1034	Men's Singles	G VON CRAMM in final beat J. H. Crawford 6–4 7–9 3–6 7–5 6–3 after match point at 4–5 in the fourth set.
	Men's Doubles	J. BOROTRA & J. BRUGNON in final beat J. H. Crawford & V. McGrath 11–9 6–3 2–6 4–6 9–7 after match point at 5–6 in the fifth set.
1939	Men's Doubles	W. D. McNEILL & C. HARRIS in final beat J. Borotra and J. Brugnon 4–6 6–4 6–0 2–6 10–8 after three match points in the fifth set.
1946	Women's Singles	MISS M. E. OSBORNE in final beat Miss P. Betz 1–6 8–6 7–5 after two match points at 5–6 in the second set.
1950	Women's Doubles	MISS S. J. FRY & MISS D. J. HART in final beat Miss L. Brough and Mrs W. D. du Pont 1–6 7–5 6–2 after match point in the second set.
1957	Women's Doubles	MISS S. J. BLOOMER & MISS D. R. HARD in final beat Sen Y. Ramirez and Sen R. M. Reyes 7–5 4–6 7–5 after three match points in the third set.
1962	Men's Singles	R. LAVER in quarter-final beat M. F. Mulligan 6–4 3–6 2–6 10–8 6–2 after match point in the fourth set.
	Women's Singles	MISS M. SMITH in final beat Miss L. R. Turner 3–6 6–3 7–5 after match point at 3–5 in the third set.
1976	Men's Singles	A. PANATTA in first round beat P. Hutka 2–6 6–2 6–2 0–6 12–10 after match point at 9–10 in the fifth set.

Italian championships

MEN'S SINGLES

(Held in Milan until 1935, subsequently in Rome except for 1961 when the venue was Turin.)

	Winner	Runner-up	Score
1930	W. T. Tilden	H. L. de Morpurgo	6–1 6–1 6–2
1931	G. P. Hughes	H. Cochet	6–4 6–3 6–2
1932	A. Merlin	G. P. Hughes	0–1 5–7 6–0 0–6
1933	E. Sertorio	A. Martin Legeay	6–3 6–1 6–3
1934	G. Palmieri	G. de Stefani	6–3 6–0 7–5
1935	W. Hines	G. Palmieri	6–3 10–8 9–7
1936–1949 not held			
1950	J. Drobny	W. F. Talbert	6–4 6–3 7–9 6–2
1951	J. Drobny	G. Cucelli	6–1 10–8 6–0
1952	F. A. Sedgman	J. Drobny	7–5 6–3 1–6 6–4
1953	J. Drobny	L. A. Hoad	6–2 6–1 6–2
1954	J. E. Patty	E. Morea	11–9 6–4 6–4
1955	F. Gardini	G. Merlo	1–6 6–1 3–6 6–6 ret'd
1956	L. A. Hoad	S. Davidson	7–5 6–2 6–0
1957	N. Pietrangeli	G. Merlo	8–6 6–2 6–0
1958	M. G. Rose	N. Pietrangeli	5–7 8–6 6–4 1–6 6–2
1959	L. Ayala	N. A. Fraser	6–3 3–6 6–3 6–3
1960	B. McKay	L. Ayala	7–5 7–5 0–6 0–6 6–1
1961	N. Pietrangeli	R. G. Laver	6–8 6–1 6–1 6–2
1962	R. G. Laver	R. Emerson	6–2 3–6 6–3 6–1
1963	M. F. Mulligan	B. Jovanovic	6–2 4–6 6–3 8–6
1964	J. E. Lundquist	F. S. Stolle	1–6 7–5 6–3 6–1
1965	M. F. Mulligan	M. Santana	1–6 6–4 6–3 6–1
1966	A. D. Roche	N. Pietrangeli	11–9 6–1 6–3
1967	M. F. Mulligan	A. D. Roche	6–3 0–6 6–4 6–1
1968	T. S. Okker	R. A. J. Hewitt	10–8 6–8 6–1 1–6 6–0
1969	J. D. Newcombe	A. D. Roche	6–3 4–6 6–2 5–7 6–3
1970	I. Nastase	J. Kodes	6–3 1–6 6–3 8–6
1971	R. G. Laver	J. Kodes	7–5 6–3 6–3
1972	M. Orantes	J. Kodes	4–6 6–1 7–5 6–2
1973	I. Nastase	M. Orantes	6–1 6–1 6–1
1974	B. Borg	I. Nastase	6–3 6–4 6–2
1975	R. Ramirez	M. Orantes	7–6 7–5 7–5
1976	A. Panatta	G. Vilas	2–6 7–6 6–2 7–6

WOMEN'S SINGLES

	Winner	Runner-up	Score
1930	Sta. E. de Alvarez	Sign. L. Valerio	3–6 8–6 6–0
1931	Sign. L. Valerio	Miss D. Andrus	2–6 6–2 6–2
1932	Mlle I. Adamoff	Sign. L. Valerio	6–4 7–5
1933	Miss E. Ryan	Mlle I. Adamoff	6–1 6–1
1934	Miss H. H. Jacobs	Sign. L. Valerio	6–3 6–0
1935	Fru H. Sperling	Sign. L. Valerio	6–4 6–1
1936–1949 not held			
1950	Sign. L. Bossi	Miss J. Curry	6–4 6–4
1951	Miss D. J. Hart	Miss S. J. Fry	6–3 8–6
1952	Miss S. Partridge	Miss P. Harrison	6–3 7–5
1953	Miss D. J. Hart	Miss M. Connolly	4–6 9–7 6–3
1954	Miss M. Connolly	Miss P. E. Ward	6–3 6–0
1955	Miss P. E. Ward	Frau E. Vollmer	6–4 6–3
1956	Miss A. Gibson	Miss S. Kormoczy	6–3 7–5
1957	Miss S. J. Bloomer	Mrs D. Knode	1–6 9–7 6–2
1958	Miss M. E. Bueno	Miss L. Coghlan	3–6 6–3 6–3
1959	Miss C. C. Truman	Miss S. Reynolds	6–0 6–1
1960	Miss S. Kormoczy	Miss A. S. Haydon	6–4 4–6 6–1
1961	Miss M. E. Bueno	Miss L. Turner	6–4 6–4
1962	Miss M. Smith	Miss M. E. Bueno	8–6 5–7 6–4
1963	Miss M. Smith	Miss L. Turner	6–3 6–4
1964	Miss M. Smith	Miss L. Turner	6–1 6–1
1965	Miss M. E. Bueno	Miss N. Richey	6–1 1–6 6–3
1966	Mrs P. F. Jones	Miss A. Van Zyl	8–6 6–1
1967	Miss L. Turner	Miss M. E. Bueno	6–3 6–3
1968	Miss L. Turner	Mrs B. M. Court	2–6 6–2 6–3
1969	Miss J. Heldman	Miss K. Melville	7–5 6–4
1970	Mrs L. W. King	Miss J. Heldman	6–1 6–3
1971	Miss S. V. Wade	Frau H. Masthoff	6–4 6–4
1972	Miss L. Tuero	Mrs O. Morozova	6–4 6–3
1973	Miss E. Goolagong	Miss C. Evert	7–6 6–0
1974	Miss C. Evert	Miss M. Navratilova	6–3 6–3
1975	Miss C. Evert	Miss M. Navratilova	6–1 6–0
1976	Miss M. Jausovec	Miss L. Hunt	6–1 6–3

MEN'S DOUBLES

1930	W. T. Tilden & W. F. Coen
1931	G. P. Hughes & A. del Bono
1932	G. de Stefani & G. P. Hughes
1933	J. Lesueur & A. Martin Legeay
1934	G. Palmieri & G. L. Rogers
1935	J. H. Crawford & V. B. McGrath
1936–1949 not held	
1950	W. F. Talbert & M. A. Trabert
1951	J. Drobny & R. Savitt
1952	F. A. Sedgman & J. Drobny
1953	L. A. Hoad & K. R. Rosewall
1954	J. Drobny & E. Morea
1955	A. Larsen & E. Morea
1956	J. Drobny & L. A. Hoad
1957	N. A. Fraser & L. A. Hoad
1958	K. Nielsen & A. Jancso
1959	R. Emerson & N. A. Fraser
1960	N. Pietrangeli & O. Sirola, R. Emerson & N. A. Fraser div'd
1961	R. Emerson & N. A. Fraser
1962	R. G. Laver & N. A. Fraser
1963	R. A. J. Hewitt & F. S. Stolle
1964	R. A. J. Hewitt & F. S. Stolle
1965	A. D. Roche & J. D. Newcombe, R. W. Barnes & T. Koch div'd
1966	R. Emerson & F. S. Stolle
1967	R. A. J. Hewitt & F. D. McMillan
1968	T. S. Okker & M. C. Riessen
1969	A. D. Roche & J. D. Newcombe, T. S. Okker & M. C. Riessen div'd
1970	I. Nastase & I. Tiriac
1971	A. D. Roche & J. D. Newcombe
1972	I. Nastase & I. Tiriac
1973	J. D. Newcombe & T. S. Okker
1974	B. E. Gottfried & R. Ramirez
1975	B. E. Gottfried & R. Ramirez
1976	B. E. Gottfried & R. Ramirez, G. Masters & J. D. Newcombe div'd

WOMEN'S DOUBLES

1930	St. E. de Alvarez & Sign. L. Valerio
1931	Sign. Prouse & Sign Luzatti
1932	Mlle C. Rosambert & Mlle L. Payot
1933	Mrs A. Burke & Mlle I. Adamoff
1934	Miss H. H. Jacobs & Miss E. Ryan
1935	Miss E. M. Dearman & Miss N. M. Lyle
1936–1949 not held	
1950	Miss J. Quertier & Mrs. J. Walker-Smith
1951	Miss S. J. Fry & Miss D. J. Hart
1952	Mrs T. D. Long & Mrs H. C. Hopman
1953	Miss M. Connolly & Miss J. Sampson
1954	Miss P. E. Ward & Miss E. M. Watson
1955	Mlle C. Mercelis & Miss P. E. Ward
1956	Mrs T. D. Long & Mrs M. Hawton
1957	Mrs T. D. Long & Mrs M. Hawton
1958	Miss S. J. Bloomer & Miss C. C. Truman
1959	Sta R. Reyes & Sta Y. Ramirez
1960	Sta Y. Ramirez & Miss M. Hellyer
1961	Miss J. Lehane & Miss L. Turner
1962	Miss M. E. Bueno & Miss D. R. Hard
1963	Miss R. Ebbern & Miss M. Smith
1964	Miss M. Smith & Miss L. Turner
1965	Miss M. Schacht & Miss A. Van Zyl
1966	Miss N. Baylon & Miss A. Van Zyl
1967	Miss R. Casals & Miss L. Turner
1968	Mrs B. M. Court & Miss S. V. Wade
1969	Mlle F. Durr & Mrs P. F. Jones
1970	Miss R. Casals & Mrs L. W. King
1971	Frau H. Masthoff & Miss S. V. Wade
1972	Miss L. Hunt & Mrs O. Morozova
1973	Miss S. V. Wade & Mrs O. Morozova
1974	Miss C. Evert & Mrs O. Morozova
1975	Miss C. Evert & Miss M. Navratilova
1976	Miss L. Boshoff & Miss I. Kloss

MIXED DOUBLES

1930	H. L. de Morpurgo & Sta E. de Alvarez
1931	G. P. Hughes & Sign. L. Valerio
1932	J. Bonte & Mlle L. Payot
1933	A. Martin Legeay & Mrs A. Burke
1934	H. M. Culley & Miss E. Ryan
1935	H. C. Hopman & Panna J. Jedrzejowska
1936–1949 not held	
1950	A. K. Quist and Miss G. Moran, G. Cucelli & Sign. L. Bossi div'd
1951	F. Ampon & Miss S. J. Fry
1952	K. Nielsen & Miss A. McGuire
1953	E. V. Seixas & Miss D. J. Hart
1954	M. A. Trabert & Miss B. M. Kimbrell, E. V. Seixas & Miss M. Connolly div'd
1955	E. Morea & Miss P. E. Ward
1956	L. Ayala & Mrs T. D. Long
1957	L. Ayala & Mrs T. D. Long
1958	G. Fachini & Miss S. J. Bloomer
1959	F. Contreras & Sta A. M. Reyes
1960	not held
1961	R. Emerson & Miss M. Smith
1962	F. S. Stolle & Miss L. Turner
1963	not held
1964	J. D. Newcombe & Miss M. Smith
1965	J. E. Mandarino & Sta C. Coronado
1966	not held
1967	W. W. Bowrey & Miss L. Turner
1968	M. C. Riessen & Mrs B. M. Court
1969–1976 not held	

Other championships

DAVIS CUP

International Men's Team Championship

Challenge Rounds

	Venue	Winner	Loser	Score
1900	Boston	U.S.A.	British Isles	3–0
1901	not held			
1902	New York	U.S.A.	British Isles	3–2
1903	Boston	British Isles	U.S.A.	4–1
1904	Wimbledon	British Isles	Belgium	5–0
1905	Wimbledon	British Isles	U.S.A.	5–0
1906	Wimbledon	British Isles	U.S.A.	5–0
1907	Wimbledon	Australasia	British Isles	3–2
1908	Melbourne	Australasia	U.S.A.	3–2
1909	Sydney	Australasia	U.S.A.	5–0
1910	not held			
1911	Christchurch, N.Z.	Australasia	U.S.A.	5–0
1912	Melbourne	British Isles	Australasia	3–2
1913	Wimbledon	U.S.A.	British Isles	3–2
1914	New York	Australasia	U.S.A.	3–2
1915–1918 not held				
1919	Sydney	Australasia	British Isles	4–1
1920	Auckland, N.Z.	U.S.A.	Australasia	5–0
1921	New York	U.S.A.	Japan	5–0
1922	New York	U.S.A.	Australasia	4–1
1923	New York	U.S.A.	Australasia	4–1
1924	Philadelphia	U.S.A.	Australia	5–0
1925	Philadelphia	U.S.A.	France	5–0
1926	Philadelphia	U.S.A.	France	4–1
1927	Philadelphia	France	U.S.A.	3–2
1928	Paris	France	U.S.A.	4–1
1929	Paris	France	U.S.A.	3–2
1930	Paris	France	U.S.A.	4–1
1931	Paris	France	Great Britain	3–2
1932	Paris	France	U.S.A.	3–2
1933	Paris	Great Britain	France	3–2
1934	Wimbledon	Great Britain	U.S.A.	4–1
1935	Wimbledon	Great Britain	U.S.A.	5–0
1936	Wimbledon	Great Britain	Australia	3–2
1937	Wimbledon	U.S.A.	Great Britain	4–1
1938	Philadelphia	U.S.A.	Australia	3–2
1939	Philadelphia	Australia	U.S.A.	3–2
1940–1945 not held				
1946	Melbourne	U.S.A.	Australia	5–0
1947	New York	U.S.A.	Australia	4–1
1948	New York	U.S.A.	Australia	5–0
1949	New York	U.S.A.	Australia	4–1
1950	New York	Australia	U.S.A.	4–1
1951	Sydney	Australia	U.S.A.	3–2
1952	Adelaide	Australia	U.S.A.	4–1
1953	Melbourne	Australia	U.S.A.	3–2
1954	Sydney	U.S.A.	Australia	3–2
1955	New York	Australia	U.S.A.	5–0
1956	Adelaide	Australia	U.S.A.	5–0
1957	Melbourne	Australia	U.S.A.	3–2
1958	Brisbane	U.S.A.	Australia	3–2
1959	New York	Australia	U.S.A.	3–2
1960	Sydney	Australia	Italy	4–1
1961	Melbourne	Australia	Italy	5–0
1962	Brisbane	Australia	Mexico	5–0
1963	Adelaide	U.S.A.	Australia	3–2
1964	Cleveland, Ohio	Australia	U.S.A.	3–2
1965	Sydney	Australia	Spain	4–1
1966	Melbourne	Australia	India	4–1
1967	Brisbane	Australia	Spain	4–1
1968	Adelaide	U.S.A.	Australia	4–1
1969	Cleveland, Ohio	U.S.A.	Rumania	5–0
1970	Cleveland, Ohio	U.S.A.	West Germany	3–2
1971	Charlotte, N.C.	U.S.A.	Rumania	3–2

Challenge Round abolished
Final Round

	Venue	Winner	Loser	Score
1972	Bucharest	U.S.A.	Rumania	3–2
1973	Cleveland, Ohio (indoors)	Australia	U.S.A.	5–0
1974	—	S. Africa	India	w.o.
1975	Stockholm (indoors)	Sweden	Czechoslovakia	3–2

FEDERATION CUP

International Women's Team Championship

Final Round

	Venue	Winner	Runner-up	Score
1963	Queen's Club	U.S.A.	Australia	2–1
1964	Philadelphia	Australia	U.S.A.	2–1
1965	Melbourne	Australia	U.S.A.	2–1
1966	Turin	U.S.A.	West Germany	3–0
1967	Berlin	U.S.A.	Great Britain	2–0
1968	Paris	Australia	Netherlands	3–0
1969	Athens	U.S.A.	Australia	2–1
1970	Freiburg	Australia	West Germany	3–0
1971	Perth, W. Aust.	Australia	Great Britain	3–0
1972	Johannesburg	South Africa	Great Britain	2–1
1973	Bad Homburg	Australia	S. Africa	3–0
1974	Naples	Australia	U.S.A.	2–1
1975	Aix-en-Provence	Czechoslovakia	Australia	3–0

GALEA CUP

International Under 21 Team Championship

1950	Italy
1951	France
1952	Italy
1953	France
1954	Italy
1955	Italy
1956	Spain
1957	Spain
1958	Spain
1959	Germany
1960	France
1961	France
1962	France
1963	Czechoslovakia
1964	U.S.S.R.
1965	Czechoslovakia
1966	Czechoslovakia
1967	France
1968	Spain
1969	Spain
1970	Czechoslovakia
1971	Sweden
1972	Great Britain
1973	Spain
1974	Czechoslovakia
1975	Czechoslovakia

ANNIE SOISBAULT CUP

International Under 21 Women's Team Championship

1965	Netherlands
1966	France
1967	Netherlands
1968	U.S.S.R.
1969	U.S.S.R.
1970	U.S.S.R.
1971	France
1972	U.S.S.R.
1973	Great Britain
1974	Czechoslovakia
1975	Great Britain

KING OF SWEDEN'S CUP

International Team Championship on Indoor Courts

1936	France
1937	France
1938	Germany
1939–1951	not held
1952	Denmark
1953	Denmark
1954	Denmark
1955	Sweden
1956	Sweden
1957	Sweden
1958	Sweden
1959	Denmark
1960	Denmark
1961	Sweden
1962	Denmark
1963	Yugoslavia
1964	Great Britain
1965	Great Britain
1966	Great Britain
1967	Great Britain
1968	Sweden
1969	Czechoslovakia
1970	France
1971	Italy
1972	Spain
1973	Sweden
1974	Italy
1975	not held
1976	Hungary

VIRGINIA SLIMS CHAMPIONS

	Venue	Winner
1971	Houston	Mrs L. W. King
1972	Boca Raton	Miss C. Evert
1973	Boca Raton	Miss C. Evert
1974	Los Angeles	Miss E. F. Goolagong
1975	Los Angeles	Miss C. Evert
1976	Los Angeles	Mrs R. Cawley

WIGHTMAN CUP

Great Britain v U.S.A. (Women)

1923	U.S.A.
1924 1925	Great Britain
1926 1927	U.S.A.
1928	Great Britain
1929	U.S.A.
1930	Great Britain
1931–1939	U.S.A.
1940–1945	not held
1946–1957	U.S.A.
1958	Great Britain
1959	U.S.A.
1960	Great Britain
1961–1967	U.S.A.
1968	Great Britain
1969–1973	U.S.A.
1974 1975	Great Britain

W.C.T. CHAMPIONS

	Singles	Doubles
1971	K. R. Rosewall	—
1972	K. R. Rosewall	—
1973	S. R. Smith	R. C. Lutz & S. R. Smith
1974	J. D. Newcombe	R. A. J. Hewitt & F. D. McMillan
1975	A. R. Ashe	B. E. Gottfried & R. Ramirez
1976	B. Borg	W. Fibak & K. Meiler

INTERNATIONAL LAWN TENNIS FEDERATION GRAND PRIX WINNERS

	Men	Women
1970	C. Richey	not held
1971	S. R. Smith	Mrs L. W. King
1972	I. Nastase	Mrs L. W. King
1973	I. Nastase	Miss C. Evert
1974	G. Vilas	not held
1975	G. Vilas	not held

GRAND PRIX MASTER'S TOURNAMENT

	Winner	Venue
1970	S. R. Smith	Tokyo
1971	I. Nastase	Paris
1972	I. Nastase	Barcelona
1973	I. Nastase	Boston
1974	G. Vilas	Melbourne
1975	I. Nastase	Stockholm

MARRIED NAMES

The following are recorded under different names

Mme N. Adamson—Mme N. Landry
Mrs N. Bolton—Miss N. Wynne
Mrs R. Cawley—Miss E. Goolagong
Mrs E. T. Cooke—Mrs M. Fabyan—Miss S. Palfrey
Mrs B. M. Court—Miss M. Smith
Mrs R. Cozens—Miss D. Akhurst
Mrs D. Dalton—Miss J. A. M. Tegart
Mrs W. du Pont—Miss M. E. Osborne
Mrs M. Fabyan—Miss S. Palfrey
Mrs J. G. Fleitz—Miss B. Baker
Mrs L. A. Godfree—Miss K. McKane
Mrs G. Greville—Miss L. Austin
Mrs R. Harper—Miss S. Lance
Mrs G. W. Hillyard—Miss B. Bingley
Mrs H. C. Hopman—Miss N. Hall
Mrs P. F. Jones—Miss A. S. Haydon
Mrs L. W. King—Miss B. J. Moffitt
Mrs Lambert Chambers—Miss D. K. Douglass
Mrs D. R. Larcombe—Miss E. W. Thomson
Mrs T. D. Long—Miss T. Coyne
Mrs F. Mallory—Miss M. Bjurstedt
Mrs L. R. C. Michel—Miss P. Saunders
Mrs F. S. Moody—Miss H. Wills
Mrs J. B. Pittman—Miss E. Goldsack
Mrs L. E. G. Price—Miss S. Reynolds
Mrs E. Raymond—Miss L. Hammond
Mrs G. E. Reid—Miss K. Melville
Mrs S. Reitano—Miss M. Carter
Fru S. Sperling—Frl. H. Krahwinkel
Mrs A. Sterry—Miss C. Cooper
Mrs J. R. Susman—Miss K. Hantze
Mrs E. F. Whittingstall—Miss E. Bennett
Mrs G. W. Wightman—Miss H. Hotchkiss